W9-BGP-635

How
I Got To
Harvard

Dear Victor —
great working
across from you
at Small Press Book
Fair. Good luck —
Laurie James

How
I Got To
Harvard

Off and On Stage with Margaret Fuller

by Laurie James

Volume 4
in a series on the life and work of
Margaret Fuller Ossoli (1810-1850)

Golden Heritage Press, Inc.
New York
1998

Designer and Compositor: Diane Genender, *Pro•To•Type*, Middletown, New York.

Body text set in 10/12 Garamond with Macintosh™ computers and Apple LaserWriter® IINT. Cover pages output on a Linotronic® L300.

Printed in the United States of America
First Printing: 1998

Publisher's Cataloging-in-Publication

James, Laurie.
    How I got to Harvard : off and on stage with Margaret Fuller /
by Laurie James. -- 1st ed.
    p. cm. -- (Life and work of Margaret Fuller Ossoli ; v. 4)
    Includes bibliographical references.
    Preassigned LCCN: 97-72195
    ISBN: 0-944382-03-07
    1. James, Laurie. 2. Fuller, Margaret, 1810-1850--In literature.
3. Feminist theater. 4. Feminism and theater. I. Title.

PN2287.J36A3 1998   792'.082'092
                      QB197-959

ISBN 0-944382-00-2 (Volume 1)
ISBN 0-944382-01-0 (Volume 2)
ISBN 0-944382-02-9 (Volume 3)
ISBN 0-944382-03-7 (Volume 4)
ISBN 0-944382-04-5 (4 Volume Set)

This book is dedicated to the people in these pages

and

to all those I haven't been able to mention

who helped me forward the name of

Margaret Fuller.

HOW I GOT TO HARVARD

1843
Margaret Fuller took a giant step for womankind
by being the first woman to set foot inside
Harvard Library.

1979
I first stepped inside Harvard when I performed my Margaret
Fuller solo drama at Longfellow Hall.

1995
A Margaret Fuller scholar said to me:
"Your books are in Harvard Library!"

CONTENTS

Acknowledgements

A one-woman show is never a one-woman show.

Several people must be involved in order to stage even one simple performance.

You will read about many of these behind-the-scenes enthusiasts in the pages of this book, and I hope that — if you don't already understand their significant role — you will develop a better awareness of their vital contributions.

Nothing would please me more than to name everyone who has helped in almost five hundred performances — and I would like to name the many audience members which have played a vital part in the development of my drama — but this is virtually impossible. You who have offered your diverse kindnesses, I thank you. The following is a partial list of hard-workers, most of whom I haven't been able to mention in the text of my story.

Supporters of Wantagh CAP: Betty Blake; Ron Dilg; Doris Esposito; Grace Flynn; Dave Garvin; Don and Nancy Gephardt; Lee Gouthreau; Roz Italiano; Albert Monheit; Bernard Perlman, Esq.; Karen Rosenblatt; Myra and Nat Schwartz; Norma Siran; Hale Smith; Joe Sugar; Marilyn Sussman; Annette Schwartz; Al Strauss; and Mitch Weiss, and others.

North Shore Unitarian Universalist Society, Inc.*: Richard Bock; Susan Dermon; Toni Hoak; Pat Luciano; Dottie Prunhuber; Ruth Reeves; Sherry Smith; Marie Stark; Lois Teta; and many others.

Unitarians: The Reverend Barry Andrews; The Reverend Kim Beach; Barbara Beach; Sandy Brooks; Freda Carnes; Sandra Mitchell Caron; Billie Drew; The Reverend Dana Greeley; Helen Grosman; Gail Hamaker; The Reverend Maren Hansen; Mary Ann Lash, editor at Beacon Press; Ed Lawrence, VEATCH Committee; Diane Miller; Ruby Sills Miller; The Reverends Carolyn S. and Tom Owen-Towle, co-ministers, The First Unitarian

---

*Now known as Unitarian Universalist Congregation at Shelter Rock.

vii

Church, San Diego, CA; David B. Parke, editor, UU World; Alice Patterson; Diana Peters; Christine Rouse; The Reverend Bruce Southworth, Community Church, NY, NY; The Reverend Douglas Morgan Strong, Santa Monica Unitarian-Universalist Fellowship; Eleanor Vendig, VEATCH Committee; Leslie Westbrook; Dr. Conrad Wright, UU historian; and many, many others.

Mexico City: Jessie Reinburg, director, Benjamin Franklin Library; Carolyn Sammet; Diane Stanley, cultural representative, Embassy of the United States, and Katie Walsh.

Maine Humanities grant: Caroline Gentile; Elly Haney; Carol Taylor; Marie Olesen Urbanski; Barbara Warner

Massachusetts Humanities grant: David Kronberg and ArtiCulture staff; Eugenia Kalendin; Ethel Klein.

New York Humanities grant: Margaret Allen; Bell Gale Chevigny; Jay Estep; Naomi Kaapcki; Anne Forman; Gloria Glaser, publicity director, Nassau County Library System; Mike James

Pennsylvania Humanities grant: Frank Allen; Margaret Allen; Virginia Babb; Ed McAndrew; Christy Roysdon; Douglas Roysdon; Peggy Schneck; Carol V. Richards, scholar; Ann Yourga; Lorraine Zeller.

Wisconsin Humanities grant: Jerry Bower; Rachel Caldwell; Judith Green; Dion Kempthorne; Carl Krug; Audrey Roberts; Marion Thompson; Connie Fuller Threinen; Katherine White; Shirley Wile.

Women's International League for Peace and Freedom (WILPF): Pat Lauthian, Elizabeth Morin, and Margaret Washington.

Dedication of the Margaret Fuller Ossoli Plaque: Ronald Lee Fleming; Saundra Graham; Charles M. Sullivan, Executive Director, Cambridge Historical Commission; Mayor Walter J. Sullivan; Vice-Mayor Alfred Vellucci; and the mayor's office staff.

Dedication of the Margaret Fuller Ossoli Room at Marriott Hotel: Bill Munck, general manager; and committee.

The Burbage Theater: Walter Barnes, for cooking a delicious dinner at the opening-theatre party; Doug Dutton, Dutton's Books; Anne Dunn, Asst. to the executive director, Commission on the Status of Women; Andy Griggs, artistic director, Burbage Theater; Yoon Hee Kim, special advisor to the Mayor; Ellen Marano, Siegal Marano Productions; Sandra Siegel, Siegal Marano Productions; The Reverend Douglas Morgan Strong, Santa Monica Unitarian-Universalist Fellowship.

Other Supporters: Francine Berger, communications consultant; Joan Burton; Joan Daly of Paul Weiss, Rifkind, Wharton, Garrison; Marydythe DiPirro, East End Arts and Humanities Council; Karen Lindsay; Dale Spender; Susan Storey Lyman; Mary K. O'Mara, Old Bethpage Village Restoration; Laura X; and many others.

Audience members who, in letters, wrote "rave reviews" about performances: Bell Chevigny, author, *The Woman and The Myth*; Sylvia B. Davidson, NY; Thomas G. Devine, professor of education, 71st Annual Convention, National Council of Teachers of English, University of Lowell, MA; Ronald Lee Fleming, founding chairman, Cambridge Arts Council, MA; Helen Grossman, Pacific Unitarian Church, Rancho Palos Verdes, CA; The Reverend Maren T. Hansen, Santa Barbara UU church, CA; Thomas F. Johnson, United States International Communication Agency, Embassy of the United States of America, Mexico; Bob and Claire Kerrigan, NY; Patricia King, director, The Arthur and Elizabeth Schlesinger Library on the History of Women in America, Radcliffe College; David Kronberg, executive director, ArtiCulture, Cambridge, MA; Roger and Helen Maher; Eleanor J. McCormick, president, W.I.L.L., Suffolk County Community College, Brentwood, NY; Ann E. McLaughlin, Thomas Crane Public Library, Quincy, MA; The Reverend Diane Miller, First Unitarian Church of San Francisco, CA; Inabeth Miller, librarian, Monroe C. Gutman Library, Harvard University; The Reverends Carolyn S. and Tom Owen-Towle, co-ministers, The First Unitarian Church, San Diego, CA; Alexa de Payan, Mexico City; Nancy S. Prichard, executive director, Unitarian Universalist Women's Federation, Boston, MA; Henry J. Schumacher, Major General, U. S. Army Commander, Augusta, GA; John J. Shordone, director of theatre, University of Maine at Presque Isle; Ruth Splitter, Ph.D.; Robert A. Storer, D. D., Director of Winchester Players, MA; Pricilla Swain; Constance Fuller Threinen, great-grand niece of Margaret Fuller, Middleton, Wisconsin; Leslie Westbrook, minister for Women and Religion, Department of Ministerial and Congregational Services, Unitarian Universalist Association. And thanks to the many anonymous persons who filled out complimentary evaluations for the Humanities councils.

My husband: Clifton G. James, who has given professional advice as well as financial support.

My children: Waldron Welles Schultz has been a highly diligent behind-the-scenes worker on my books. Mike, Hardy, Lynn, and Mary (all of whom I've mentioned in the text) have helped in numerous capacities over the years. My sons-in-law have given of their expertise in their fields: Andy Gross; Andy McWhirter; Robert Schultz.

Editing and Reading: Joseph Carbonara, Anne Forman, Diane Genender, Gwen Harper, Kathy Kikkert, Jennifer Langdon, Rosemary Matson, Eloise Niederkirchner, Billie Snow, Constance Fuller Threinen, Tom Tolnay, Katheryn White.

Picture Layout: Lynn James Gross.

Picture Permissions: Belinda Amermary, *Times-Herald*, (Alliance, Nebraska); Jessica Backhaus, *Bangor Daily News* (Maine); Gail Bryan, *Boston Herald American*; Betsy Cole; Ronald Lee Fleming; Hardy James; Irene Kleopfer, *Lincoln County News* (Damariscotta, Maine); Rosemary Matson; Jane Reed, *Harvard Gazette*; Chris Samp; Martha Stewart; Anne Vendig.

WHO WAS MARGARET FULLER?

Woman of the 19th Century...
Margaret Fuller...forgotten genius...buried in history...
Your spirit moves me.
Your words sent shock waves throughout the world...
They called you scandalous...
They called you immoral...
They called you hysterical...
Yet you were labeled genius by some...
But in the end you agreed you were an exotic
Unfit for industrial, Puritan America.
   Proud, ambitious, with a fiery will
   An intellect and a wit
   Some adored you; some threatened by you.
   You dared to tell the truth as you saw it.
   Your name resounded throughout the 1840s...
   A woman of brains and of heart
   A revolutionist who revolted without violence...
   Who envisioned the best for woman and man...
     Truth
       Beauty
         Equality
           The harmony of nature and
           The divinity of humankind.
By birth a child of New England
By adoption a citizen of Rome
By genius belonging to the world,
Margaret Fuller
Woman of the 19th Century
Your spirit moves me.

Do not feel guilty if you've never heard of Margaret Fuller. Her writings are forgotten and she has not been given much space in texts. Yet she was world famous in the 1840s. She was controversial because she dared to speak and write truthfully about the literary, human, and social scene.

Intelligencia throughout the English-speaking world snapped up her book, *Woman in the Nineteenth Century*, which was the first in the United States to advocate equal rights for women. Fuller laid the groundwork for the women's rights movement in the U.S.A.

Every American who kept up with what was most current read her words for they appeared regularly on the front pages of Horace Greeley's *New York Daily Tribune* from 1845-50. She was one of our first female journalists.

She was first editor of the *Dial*, one of America's first literary journals, the voice of the Transcendentalists. She accepted, rejected, and edited the submitted work of Ralph Waldo Emerson, Henry David Thoreau, Bronson Alcott, Theodore Parker, Henry Hedge, George Ripley, and other intellectuals of the era.

As one of our first female literary critics, Margaret Fuller critiqued the work of such writers as Goethe, Emerson, Melville, Hawthorne, Lowell, Irving, Longfellow, Poe, and many others.

She was first woman foreign correspondent and first woman war correspondent to serve under combat conditions in Italy during the Revolution of 1848-49.

She was first woman to start "Conversations" (for payment) or "rap sessions" as they would be called today, for women in the Boston area. Her aim was to expose women to the great ideas and to encourage them to utilize their potentials.

And she was first female to step foot inside Harvard library, a giant step for humankind since women in the early nineteenth century were excluded from all institutions of higher education.

*   *   *

After a precocious childhood during which she was tutored by her father as if she were a boy being prepped for Harvard, she was launched into the literary arena by Ralph Waldo Emerson who appointed her editor of the *Dial*, the journal for the radical new wave of thinkers called Transcendentalists. As editor, she wrote many literary criticisms herself.

In New York she continued her terse reviewing on *The Tribune*, but Greeley soon had her doing exposes on the city's downtrodden. Finally, she convinced him to sign her on as foreign correspondent and she traveled throughout Europe sending *The Tribune* accounts of her observations.

She landed in Rome when Italy was in revolutionary ferment, and soon fell in love with a nobleman, the Marchese Giovanni Angelo Ossoli, who became a captain in the people's militia. As Americans abandoned the warzone, she wrote eye-witness descriptions of the combat. While Ossoli fought on the walls of Rome, she accepted the assignment of directing a hospital for the war wounded.

She left the city briefly to give birth to her son — secretly, for Ossoli would be disinherited if his family realized he was allied with a revolutionary American Protestant. Whether or not they were married is a matter for conjecture today because marital records have not been located, though Fuller's personal letters do indicate the legality of the liasion.

After the failure of the Italian Revolution, Ossoli, Fuller, and Angelino, their baby son, fled to Florence where they subsisted for better than a year while Fuller wrote a history of the revolution, which she felt Emerson would help her publish in the United States.

Word of Fuller's actions spread to America, and Horace Greeley discontinued printing her articles.

Friends wrote her that rumors indicated she had given birth out-of-wedlock and that many Americans were not about to welcome her return.

The sun shown in Liverpool as they embarked on the three-masted American merchant ship, the *Elizabeth*. Off the shores of Fire Island, New York, a sudden summer hurricane swept in with rain and winds of gale force. The ship cracked in half and went down. The three Ossolis drowned. It was July 19, 1850. Fuller was forty years old. Emerson sent Henry David Thoreau to investigate. A trunk was found, some love letters, a piece of Ossoli's clothing.

•   •   •

When Horace Greeley wanted to publish a memoir of Fuller, Emerson countered in his journal: "Margaret Fuller & Her Friends" must be written, but not post haste.

In 1852 Fuller's *Memoirs* was published, written by Emerson, William Henry Channing and James Freeman Clark. The authors had unabashedly tampered with and destroyed her letters and papers. They pictured Fuller as a personality rather than as a woman of notable achievement.

Scholars down through the century have accordingly discounted Margaret Fuller's significance, so that today she is still buried in history.

INTRODUCTION

This book is about dreams and visions and making them come true.

Specifically, it is about my vision to bring, through the spoken and the written word, the life and work of a forgotten American into the hearts and minds of every living person.

Beyond that, it is about the many people who helped along the way; it is about their dreams and visions and how they made them happen.

It is a book about beginnings and realizations. It presents the joys of commitment to a belief, the satisfactions of forging a work of one's choice, the rewards of learning and growth that result through the process of taking up a challenge.

I cannot think of a better way to explain why Margaret Fuller became my abiding interest for so many years than to reprint my keynote speech at the Delta Kappa Gamma New York State Convention at the Marriott Hotel, Uniondale, Long Island, on May 14, 1988.

Costumed as Margaret Fuller, I spoke as though Margaret Fuller were talking across the century about myself. The Convention theme was illiteracy. I hope you enjoy reading this as much as I enjoyed delivering it.

Laurie James

I, Margaret Fuller, one of America's most brilliant, accomplished and influential women, was known in my lifetime as arrogant, pedantic, aggressive, ugly, manly.

My writing was called absurd, immoral, scandalous.

Edgar Allen Poe called me "an ill-tempered old maid."

Ralph Waldo Emerson said my pen was a non-conductor.

Elizabeth Barret Browning said, "Margaret Fuller is a great woman writing, but never read what she has written."

People in the twentieth century don't remember who I was.

But there is one person in the twentieth century who I have inspired. That's Laurie James.

Laurie James copied my dress, my hairstyle, my lorgnette — even my shoes — by the way, she couldn't find the type of high-button shoes I wore in the stores until 1988.

Laurie James tried to walk like she thought I walked.

She collected adjectives and descriptions of me — many of the things my friends said and wrote about me.

And she studied and copied my gestures and mannerisms.

She kept a list of the flowers I liked; she listened to the music I liked.

She tried to use a voice and diction like she thought I must have spoken.

She memorized many of the things I said and wrote.

She not only read all of the books about me and all of the books I had written, but she also read most of the books written about my friends.

I've led Laurie James down a long path.

Over the years she has followed my footsteps throughout the world.

She found my birthhouse in Cambridge, Massachusetts...in fact, she found all of the locations of the houses I occupied and visited...the houses of my friends, Ralph Waldo Emerson, being one of them, Nathaniel Hawthorne, another one.

She found the Margaret Fuller Cottage at Brook Farm in Roxbury, a bit delapidated — and then it burned down.

She found Elizabeth Peabody's West Street bookstore where I gave my famous Conversations in Boston, now a restaurant.

She found the spot where Gore Hall stood in Harvard Yard, now Widener Library — Gore Hall was the newly built, most spectacular library in the entire USA, and I was the first woman to cross its threshold, to do research for one of my books.

Laurie James found the Fuller family plot at Mt. Auburn cemetery in Cambridge — a plot Susan B. Anthony could not find — a plot the Mt. Auburn administrators do not commemorate on their list of celebrated Cantabrigians.*

In Boston Laurie James walked on all the streets I walked on.

In New York she walked on all the streets I walked on.

And in Rome she walked on all the streets I walked on.

Laurie James went to Houghton Library — that's the rare book library at Harvard. She'd never known such libraries even existed — and she ordered up all the letters I'd written, personal and otherwise, including some of my school girl exercises.

She treasured reading my diaires and journals, all in my original handwriting, the pages a bit brown at the edges now.

She even found a lock of my hair at Houghton Library — this was a real thrill to her, because it was the same color as her own hair, and for some strange reason she thought this verified a close connection between me and her.

Not that Laurie James could ever, in anybody's most wildest imagination, emulate me.

After all, there is a great gap between Laurie James' mind and mine.

But then that could be truely said of almost anybody.

Laurie James took my value system, my ideas, my thoughts and made them her own.

Laurie James lifted my words from my writings and put them into a drama about me, and began presenting it to small groups. She tried to introduce me to the twentieth century.

She made a lot of mistakes. She had a lot to learn.

She had to learn how to shape a dramatic script out of the mass of material she had on me.

She had to learn how to cut and write sparingly, to leave some things to the audience's imagination.

She had to learn how to use a stage with props consisting of a couple of tables and chairs, which had to represent nineteenth-century Boston, New York and Rome.

She had to learn how to adapt her playing area to different spaces in different places.

---

*Visiting Mt. Auburn cemetary in 1996, I found Margaret Fuller had finally been included on the list.

And she just had to learn the craft of acting a one-person show, which is an art in itself.

But all this was only the beginning.

She had to learn to sell herself and her drama on the telephone.

She had to generate lists of people who might be interested.

She had to figure schedules and fees.

She had to work up news releases and flyers and brochures.

She had to deal with printers, talk with media people, with artistic directors of arts organizations and other potential presenters.

She found herself talking to a mayor and had a street named after me.

She, and a friend, were influential in having a hotel room named after me.

She found herself talking to people who awarded grants in state Humanties Councils and she found herself learning how to write grant proposals.

She talked to Buckminster Fuller, my great-grandnephew, and found out he was a great advocate of mine and she, along with a friend, got him to agree to introduce her drama at Harvard and in the state of Maine.

She found other living relatives of mine, one who was an artist who had copied my pictures.

She wrote to American embassies all around the world and staged her drama in Hong Kong.

The list of things she had to do to stage those performances went on and on.

All during this process, the people who saw the drama kept asking a lot of intelligent questions about me.

Laurie James just didn't know the answers. She would have to run to the library the next day.

That's how she realized she didn't know anything about Transcendentalism.

What had my religion been anyway?

How did it correspond to what was happening in religion in my day?

She had never thought to find out; most biographers underplayed the religious question, which was a major factor in my life.

Finding out drove her to the kinds of books she'd never been concerned with before.

What was my mother like?

That was difficult to find because biographers always gave the majority of print space to my father who died when I was twenty-three, but wrote very little about my mother who outlived me.

What about my real relationship to Ralph Waldo Emerson?

She had to dig for it because it's not in the books and because my excellent friend Waldo destroyed many of my letters to him, because biographers have skirted this relationship, or have distorted the reality.

The truth could only be found by a very careful and knowledgeable reading of our letters that do still exist.

What was the living reality for nineteenth-century women — a time when illiteracy in women was as common as apple pie?

What were the barriers that self-educated women like me had to overcome?

When exactly did higher education become an option for women? — I, of course, couldn't go to college since no colleges were open to women.

Could I manage my father's estate after he died? No. That was given unto Uncle Abraham, who wanted my young sister to become a governness instead of acquiring what little education she could, who wanted my brothers to work on other people's farms, rather than going to Harvard. In order for my brothers and sister to avoid all this, I went to work.

What kind of work could a woman like me do for money?

Teaching was about the only acceptable occupation.

Could I earn the same money as a male teacher? No.

Could women own property? No.

That women were more constrained in the early nineteenth century than at any other period in history was something Laurie James had to learn. This reality is not included in your classroom textbooks.

Laurie James also had to absorb the fact that I, a self-educated person, stood against the norm of purity, piety, submissiveness, and domesticity, against the standard of womanhood of my day.

In growing up, it was not at all disgraceful or unusual for women to be illiterate.

Illiteracy was almost an advantage because men would find you nonthreatening, and would marry you.

But as I was growing up, times were changing.

I began to hear comments that illiteracy in a woman was actually not in the best interests of the husband. She should have a bit of schooling, in order to be a better partner for him — not, you see, to develop her own potential because she had a God-given gift that needed to grow.

As Laurie James kept dramatizing me, she became more and more obsessed with her project — to some people's great concern.

Wasn't she almost sick or slow to stay with Margaret Fuller for such a stretch of years?

Why didn't she move on to some other woman, some other material?

"Because," Laurie James would say, "Margaret Fuller is worth it!" — for by now it had became obvious through her vast reading just how I, and all that I stood for, had been forgotten in history — and still was forgotten.

Clearly, Laurie James was connecting with a foremother.

She was building her sense of her own individuality through personal roots.

She identified with parts of my struggle as a woman.

She aspired to my intellectual acumen.

She wanted to absorb and make as her own some of my qualities, those of fearless aggressiveness, achievement against odds, and an understanding and humanity broader than any she had achieved.

And she wanted to share all this.

But there was even more to what she liked to call her "mission" — to bring my name back into the hearts and minds of every living person. The truth is that my cause has served as a great learning process for Laurie James.

Her mission has given her a sense of self-esteem.

First, you have to understand that Laurie James had a stereotypical upbringing and education, with all the mixed and damaging sexist messages given to educated twentieth-century girls.

It was permissable to get D in history and science and math, and to be inferior in sports, because all of these subjects were beyond the ken of women.

Though she was led to believe she could achieve in some areas of endeavor, there were other areas best left to the men who were the logical and rational creatures who intrinsically knew how to handle and deal.

Women were happier when they attached themselves to men.

What men were doing was important, and mattered.

Though she looked at herself as a worthy individual, she internalized her skills and talent as second class.

The parallels with illiteracy are obvious.

Illiteracy, like gender sterotyping, can only limit and diminish self-esteem.

A limited and diminished self-esteem is one of the greatest blocks to learning and achievement.

So from across a century, I had the pleasure of educating Laurie James — just as I educated the women in my Conversations, and with my book, *Woman in the Nineteenth Century.*

From me Laurie James took a sense of power and competency.

When I came to New York and wrote front page articles on Horace Greeley's *Tribune*, I said: "Now I know all the people in America worth knowing, and I can find no intellect comparable to my own."

People scorned me for making such arrogant statements, made in good humor, but in an environment like mine, what may have seemed too lofty and ambitious in my character, was absolutely needed to keep the heart from breaking and enthusiasm from extinction.

In Laurie James' commitment to me, she found that it is permissible to give yourself credit.

It's permissible to expand your opportunities.

It's permissible to take pride in your own acomplishment.

It's permissible to promote yourself, promotion which is necessary to success.

Women don't have to be modest, to sit passively, as "nice girls" throughout the ages have been taught to do.

We don't have to wait for someone else to hand us what we want — to wait for someone else to give us recognition.

We can and we should celebrate our successes.

We must counter the biases of traditional history.

We must take power, our self-esteem, wherever we may find it.

If there is one gift I would give people, especially women, in the latter half of the twentieth century, it would be the rightful heritage of self-affirmation.

Aspiration teaches; God leads by inches.

Very early in life I saw that the only object in life was to grow.

Whatever the soul knows how to seek, it cannot fail to attain.

Nothing, not even perfection, is unattainable.

ME AND MARGARET FULLER:
A LOVE STORY

Margaret Fuller is my mentor, my role model, my passion, my alter-ego, my strength, my frustration, my truth, my divinity, my commitment.

Now, after having taken her identity in nearly five hundred performances, traveling a long road that ended at two Off-Broadway theaters in repertory, I know she is adored as much by some others.

Yet despite my efforts to spread the word, Margaret Fuller remains unknown today, and those who don't know about her don't know there's somebody out there who might be able to give them something of what they are looking for.

Was it her heart which spoke to me first? Or her words which always attract? Her intellect? Her courage and fight? Her conflicts? Her daring to stand alone, and then her aloneness? Her wrenched soul as she sought to blend the life of brain with a life of love?

Having trained in acting and writing, I started out by wanting to perform in my own original solo drama and to write a book that captured Fuller's spirit and significance. Broadway offered no opportunities because of the prevailing star system and my inexperience, and my idea for a book was vetoed by publishers because, first, Fuller hadn't achieved concretely, her views were too aesthetic, too difficult to describe and interest and, secondly, readers would not respond to her flowery words, too erudite for today's standards, though her story was dramatic and intriguing.

Totally without confidence in my own opinions, I accepted these views as authoritative. Deep down inside me, I thought: They say *this* about someone whose name was known throughout the English-speaking world by 1846, whose book jolted the nation, was so popular that the first edition sold out within a week, was even pirated in Europe. They say *this* about one of America's earliest advocates of equal rights, who was as giant as Ralph Waldo Emerson, Henry David Thoreau, Nathaniel Hawthorne? About the first editor of America's earliest literary journal, the *Dial*? About a critic who, along with Edgar Allen Poe, set standards for literary criticism in our country? About our first female foreign correspondent who served under combat conditions in Italy during 1848-9? Whose words appeared regularly in Horace Greeley's *New York Daily Tribune*?

Women like me have rarely been asked their opinions, have learned to remain quiet, to defer to the gods, whoever they may be. Margaret Fuller was not like that. She instantly spoke her truths no matter who might disagree, and that was in the early nineteenth century when women were not allowed schooling beyond the age of fourteen, were supposed to think of nothing beyond purity, piety, and domesticity.

During my research (and even to this day) I asked: Who was I — who'd never done much in the way of theater and writing, and nothing in scholarship — to think I could achieve success in such a dream? Why would anyone want to spend years on one woman? What a freak I was to identify with a woman who'd been dead for one hundred and fifty years. How amazingly foolish I was to jump with joy at the unearthing of every tiny detail. Why would anyone want to know anything about Margaret Fuller anyway, genius though she may have been in the 1840s — but who cared today? Even if I got my drama on, who would come to see <u>me</u>? The word "nobody" has reverberated.

Hitting my head against a wall.

I relate to Fuller when she wrote out of her heartache in 1843: "I have tried to work from an earnest faith...if I cannot make this plot of ground yield corn and roses, famine must be my lot forever and forever, surely."*

I have laid many things aside to bring Margaret Fuller forward, to try to give her her just place in history. If I do nothing else with my life, I will be satisfied.

If I fail, I fail.

This is my personal judgment, and today this is a judgment I value.

Margaret Fuller would have approved of that statement. After her words had appeared regularly on the front page of *The New York Daily Tribune*, she said, "Now I know all the people in America worth knowing, and I can find no intellect comparable to my own...God forbid that anyone should conceive more highly of me than I myself."

How she has led to the making of me.

Long before Julie Harris ever thought of doing her solo Emily Dickinson in *The Belle of Amherst,*** I discovered Fuller one day while reviewing my knowledge of American literature. I had heard of all the women writers listed in the text except this one. I found about two lines on Margaret Fuller. In the library I found a biography.

What I could not yet put into words was that I needed an image, a model, an inspiration — someone from whom I could derive strength and renewal. It took a host of refreshing thinkers like Gerda Lerner, Betty Friedan, Gloria Steinem, to articulate the needs we women have for role models.

Writing and presenting a solo drama was work I could do at home and still take care of the children. Using Fuller's own words seemed not only truer to the truth, but better than anything I could construct. I began taking notes as a writer, as an actress...her personal characteristics...what people said about her.

---

*From *Memoirs*, edited by James Freeman Clarke, Ralph Waldo Emerson, and William H. Channing, 2 vols. Boston: Phillips Sampson, 1852.

**Solo drama has long been popular. Ruth Draper (1884-1956), who wrote her own monologues, won applause throughout the world. Hal Holbrook launched the contemporary form with his *Mark Twain Tonight!* Other well-known actors who have involved themselves in the one-person process are Cornelia Otis Skinner, Emlyn Williams, Roy Dotrice, John Gielgud, Pat Carroll, Fionnula Flanagan, Zoe Caldwell, Lily Tomlin, Whoopie Goldberg, James Whitmore, Irene Worth, Celeste Holm, and Spalding Gray.

After consuming books from nearby libraries, I ordered out-of-print books through inter-library loan, waiting up to three months for some. Notes and manuscript piled up until I thought I'd finished the job. Much later I discovered I had barely taken first steps.

All was sandwiched between countless domestic responsibilites and the temporary office work I often took to help pay bills. Great gaps of time would pass with no work done on the project while daily concerns took precedence. Every once in a while I would look over my piles of paper, re-read the notes, strike out parts, re-type pages, and then pack everything away again, forgetting...not knowing what to do with so much paper...really having little knowledge of how to shape it...how to breathe life into it. Then I took a full-time job for three years — and Margaret Fuller was buried again.

Eventually, my sources led me to the discovery of Houghton Library, that rare-book haven at Harvard University, but how does one get to Cambridge when one has no money and anyway how does one get into those hallowed halls? Occasion developed on my job that I must give a workshop in Boston so, all-expenses-paid, I scheduled an extra day in Cambridge.

What a marvellous morning as I checked my coat in the outside foyer, placed purse in a locked locker, and was buzzed through a locked door into a hushed room where no one was allowed to bring a pen — only pencils could be used. A few people sat at the tables, heads buried in large, thick books, all of which seemed to have black leather bindings. I filled out a form stating I was a writer and then was handed an odd slim index book on Fuller. Never having done research of this depth, I was confused.

And then the excitement of seeing Fuller's handwriting, turning the pages of her diary, gazing at her childhood's practice scriptwriting page in large, neat, circular, lines, "Love Thy Enemy Love Thy Enemy," touching a broken seal on a letter to Ralph Waldo Emerson, seeing for the first time her habit of saving letter paper and postage by turning a page sideways and writing across words already written — "crossing," as it was called.

And Fuller's words...so vital, full of the life of the era...I was immediately drawn into her world, her friends, her concerns. Then...

Then I opened a small, white, tissue-like envelope...and pulled out a soft, blond/brown curl, a lock of hair. I was stunned. I sat, quivering. It was the same color as mine.

Margaret Fuller had claimed me.

You have to understand that in college I'd gotten "D" in history. And that was a gift. I'd never connected with the history professor's lectures, nor the texts which rarely included the contributions of women. I could never remember a date.

Now I converse in detail about the Italian Revolution of 1848. I have sat with one of the most eminent scholars in the country and for over an hour discussed the Harvard class of 1829. I can name the men, for they were Fuller's friends. I have answered ministers who have asked, "What is Transcendentalism?" And I can talk at length about Brook Farm and the heady philosophy of Bronson Alcott.

Research has taken me on a rewarding road.

"If you don't get it, don't worry your pretty little head." My generation of young women was told that our purpose in going to college was to find a husband who would support us in a fashion to which we were accustomed.

There were terrible gaps in my script. Among other things, I failed to take into account the impact of historical and cultural forces.

What happened after I finally began performing, was that people asked me questions. I wouldn't know the answers — and so off I'd go on a library hunt to ferret out the information and make script changes. It was the audience that forced me to open those rusty doors of our heritage.

People have asked, don't I feel alone standing in front of an audience, being Margaret Fuller? No, I am not alone. The audience is a breathing, vital entity. I am communicating, we become a team. I give to them, but they give back more. They may applaud, but my instinct is to applaud them for giving me and Margaret their minds for a piece of time.

Many actors, when the performance is over, like to make a quick getaway, prefer not to be bored or bothered by the compliments and comments they have heard many times before. But for me, this is the growth period. The things people say after a performance are my guiding light. It is the audience who has directed, who has taught, shown me how to improve.

After my three-year job phased out, I took stock of where I was in life: "If I'm ever to do Margaret Fuller, I'd better do her now." So I began the process of trying to wipe out the extraneous and to make Margaret Fuller my priority. If you're a woman with husband and large family, you know how nearly impossible this is.

I began by reading passages of my script to a women's studies class at Dowling College in Oakdale, New York, near my home. The students responded well, were quite amazed that they had never heard of the woman.

More readings to small groups: same reactions. I went to my hometown, Portland, Oregon, for a visit, and gave a reading for friends of my mother-in-law at a tiny library. My aunt, Mamie Harper, who had long chaired programming for organizations, arranged another reading at the retirement home in which she was living. Since this was to have a larger audience, I found a long skirt and promised to return a marvelous, circular, dark purple, knitted shawl belonging to Beverly Anslow, my sister-in-law. (I am still "borrowing" this shawl.) When I arrived, an audience of over a hundred and fifty were gathering. What a wonderful warm encouraging audience they were. I came home, and Margaret Fuller was dropped for months. Without audiences, actors stagnate.

Then I asked a programmer at a nearby library if she would like to present my drama as a try-out.

Next afternoon I was in the bathroom with a picture of Margaret Fuller, devising a makeup and hairdo. I remember my feelings when I saw myself looking like Fuller: How foolish I am to attempt this. I scurried around to find a quill pen and inkwell at a historical-restoration gift shop. I rehearsed for hours in the living room. I made cuts, additions. I re-read the books: Everything had to be historically accurate. Every detail had to be told in an hour and a half. I memorized. I decided on the staging and gathered props. I looked over the small rectangular room in the library and wondered how anyone could do anything dramatic there; there were no lights for effects. Talked to the librarian about the publicity.

I thought I would forget all my lines. I set up all the small props, put on makeup, and combed my hair in a bathroom hardly large enough to turn around in, and then the hour came.

The librarian pattered in with great liveliness and anticipation. "I think we'll just hold for another five to eight minutes — give everyone a bit more time to get here...is that all right with you?"

"Oh, of course. Whatever you think," I whispered.

As she turned, I heard her mumble, "I think it's started to rain."

Ten minutes later she returned and smiled broadly, "I think they're all here now, so if you're ready...."

Obediently, I followed her and was soon peeking through the doorway to see my library audience.

There were two gray-haired women and about ten teen-agers who were enjoying throwing wads of paper at each other.

They shuffled to a semblance of attention when the librarian made her introduction, but when I made my entrance it was impossible not to hear them stifling bursts of laughter. They darted their secret sign language to each other: "Isn't-she-a-riot?-Can-you-believe-we-have-to-sit-through-this?"

Words like *Art* and *Culture* and *Exposure* ran through my mind: *It is of utmost importance to expose young people to cultural arts programming...If they never see operas, they'll never know what operas are....*

I should have thrown my script out the window, should have sat down in front of them, and started to tell them about Margaret Fuller. I should have gotten on their level by relating to them, by bringing out their ideas.

But I'd been theater trained. Were all those dramatic lessons during high school for naught? Hadn't I attended, at the age of seventeen, the American Academy of Dramatic Arts, a professional acting school in New York? What about all those college and community and summer theater productions where I'd landed leading roles? Hadn't I studied with Herbert Berghof at the HB Studio for two years and for another two years with Lee Strasberg at the Actor's Studio? — the best acting teachers in the country. Actors plan and rehearse. You don't suddenly do whatever comes to mind when on stage.

Old adages flashed across my mind: *The show must go on. There are no small parts, only small actors*...which I mentally paraphrased: *There are no small audiences....*

The two gray-haired women listened intently, politely. The teen-agers cocked their heads and opened their mouths in mock pretense of rapturous listening, followed by winking to their friends and pantomiming horrendous stomach pains accompanied by vomiting.

The two gray-haired women did not come backstage and congratulate me. (There was no backstage.)

The librarian said, "What a pity we had so many young people. You know, those young people attend all our Wednesday night programs. I've tried to discourage them, but I suppose they came tonight because in the publicity I compared Margaret Fuller with Simon and Garfunkel."

Then she added, "You know, rain always keeps everyone at home."

I've found that to be true. Rain, thunderstorms, windstorms, snow, ice, and cold keeps people away. Also, I've learned that beautiful sunny days, lovely moonlit nights, warm luscious spring evenings, and crisp autumn weather keeps people away. Also, there's usually some event over at the high school that everyone is attending, they're putting on *Kiss Me Kate* or they're having a student/faculty volley-ball-on-donkeys game and no one can miss that. Or the next city is miles away and no one will drive distances at night, what with the crime rate and all. Sometimes the President is making a speech on TV. Or there's a championship fight. When I go to colleges, everyone is studying for mid-terms tomorrow. It is unfortunate, but that's the way it is in this community (or college)...just so much going on all the time. Those who did come, enjoyed it, of course. It's quality, not quantity that counts.

Why am I doing this?

Fanatic that I am, I fight hard to contain myself when I'm told: "You may be all wrapped up in what you're doing and think it's the greatest thing going, but how in hell can you expect other people to feel the same way?"

And that's why groups like Wantagh Community Arts Programs are so important. CAP was the dream of a woman who became in many ways my mentor, staunch support, and dear friend.

Anne Forman is a red-haired visual artist who proved that your suburban home can serve your art. She had turned the walls of her home into an art gallery with track lights and her dining room into studio with easels and paints.

Anne's idea was born because as a girl she'd seen WPA* artists, hired by the government during the Great Depression of the 1930s, painting a mural on a proscenium arch. Her concept was the first in New York State and, as far as she knows, the first in the entire country. Her vision has since been picked up by many arts councils throughout the U.S.A.

The premise is that professional artists of all disciplines living in the community are hired as nonteaching personnel to "do their thing" within the schools and local institutions. Thus, community residents, both children and adults, learn to understand and appreciate the creative processes through firsthand experiences with the artist and the medium.

Her plan encompassed painters, sculptors, composers, muscians, playwrights, directors, poets, choreographers, dancers, actors. Artists were to maintain studios open to residents and to establish visible set-ups in public places such as the library or schools. There would also be exhibits, performances, workshops, as well as exchanges of work with neighboring communities which would broaden cultural consciousness. The school/community would eventually own a large collection of original art, and benefit financially and culturally.

Growing up, I never met a painter or poet, nor saw one at work — other than my mother, a novelist who never had her books published. I went to zoos and ice-skating rinks, but not museums. While in high school I did see community theater and some road shows because my best girl friend's family owned the movie theater in which touring companies performed and I was invited to sit with her in a secret viewing room behind the highest row in the balcony. In high school we never studied poetry. I heard opera because my mother often played recordings while she worked around the house. When I did become aware of the major painters, I, like most people, developed a romantic idea about them; I had no conception of their struggles nor of their dedication to their artform.

Anne had formulated her idea in her master's thesis while painting, teaching art, and doing graduate work at Columbia during the 1960s.

---

*Works Progress Administration, part of President Franlin D. Roosevelt's New Deal.

Here's what Anne wrote:

It is a time for the community and schools to become the new patron of the arts so that the arts of the nation will belong to the people...not stored away in basement museums...not held for profit by the wealthy. Works of art must be used to enrich human life everywhere...in public buildings, schools, libraries, homes.

The place of the creative fine artist in contemporary society is unique in that he has almost no place in community life today.

In the suburbs, people tend to grow complacent, drifting into conformity.

There is a tremendous need for the spirit of creative beings in the suburbs...to initiate search into the unknown and to arouse interest in the enjoyment of natural and aesthetic beauty....

The reawakening of men to higher intellectual and emotional forms of entertainment through intense cultural experiences is needed to contribute to the development of man's intellect.

Leisure hours must not be filled in emptiness and boredom, but rather in the unleashing of stored, creative energies through cultural interests, creative labor, and intense search through knowledge.

It is now of tremendous importance that Education, Art, and Society work together to stimulate and fulfill that which urbanization has almost destroyed.

Art must become part of life...not separated from it. People surrounded by and involved in the arts cannot remain apathetic.

Every suburban community and every small town in the United States could have its own collection of Fine Art and varied cultural activities. These advantages are the rights of the people. Cultural advantages should not be solely the province of city dwellers and the rich.

State aid plays a major role within certain states...Wisconsin, Illinois, Colorado, Texas, Virginia and California. Within the last few years an Arts Council has been sustained in New York.

Many foreign countries have well-organized art assistance programs. The United States remains without a plan for the present. It is essential that the small community now take the lead.

Anne looked for funding, but found none. An advisor suggested she become politically active, but politicizing would leave little time for painting. Her idea was buried in a drawer for about ten years while she, a single mother, went to Europe with her children, studied art, and rejected the art world wherein art dealers got rich. Remarrying and settling in a small community on the south shore of Long Island, she became the kind of teacher people remember as "always standing up on chairs hanging things up." In 1969 a teacher/artist friend, Viggo Holm Madsen, thought the New York State Council on the Arts could help fund Anne's project.

Because she needed the umbrella of an organization in order to apply, she submitted a proposal to The Preservation Society. They turned the project down because a male board member claimed she'd never get the grant.

Later a sparky woman who'd danced professionally, Jay Estep, approached Anne to do posters for the community-school, Seven-Twelve Association. Anne told her about her artists-in-communities project and Jay responded, "That's fantastic!" Jay convinced her president, Al Strauss — a person who made things happen — to call an emergency meeting of the board.

At the New York State Council on the Arts committee meeting, Jay emotionally described Wantagh as "a community where life began and ended for so many." She burst into tears.

They won a grant of $14,000 for visual arts in 1970, and a half year later $10,000 was added for performing arts programs — all of which increased the budget of the Seven-Twelve Association by about $24,000. At first the project covered only the visual arts, and Anne made all arrangements with the school administrators, Dr. Charles St. Claire and Wally Seuss, to set up her easel in hallways and classrooms. Whatever she saw she painted in pastels and oils: children studying at desks and playing in the schoolyard. This was positively revolutionary.

As the weeks went by, she rotated her easel from one school to another, and charming portraits of children were soon hanging in halls and classrooms. The response that came from mothers and children, who recognized themselves in Anne's paintings, was overwhelming. The attitude of the principals was, oh my goodness, we have all this valuable work and suppose someone defaces it.

Anne said, don't worry about the paintings, worry about the person who vandalized — do something for that one.

Before long, Anne recognized the value of sharing the opportunity with Bronka Stern, a highly gifted sculptor who worked in wood. The school administrator so questioned her presence that he assigned her to a back room where garbage was temporarily stored. Nevertheless, Stern set up and one day, after she'd heard Apollo 13 had landed on the moon, there were suddenly four bright-eyed youngsters surrounding her. She sculpted four children's faces in a rocketlike structure. The children added stairs, exits, and entrances. Later a black and an oriental child appeared, so Bronka changed two sets of eyes. Her sculpture was entitled *Four Faces of the Moon.*

Many thought Anne's ideas far fetched. How do you explain your vision to people whose backgrounds and worlds are so foreign to the artistic insight? Reaction from some teachers was tinged with resentment, even hostility; they felt threatened by artists entering their territory. The pioneers had to convince them that artists enhanced and were supportive. Anne never pushed. She'd just say she had some different intentions.

She went to each principal for approval, pinpointing precisely what was going to happen, and convincing each to allow the artists freedom to do the thing they did best.

She scurried about and recruited artists, such as dancer Yurek Lazowski and sculptor Clemente Spanpinato, to work for $10 an hour. Naomi Kaapcke, who'd formerly trained as a dancer, brought in Dorothy Villard who'd danced with Martha Graham, and what a thrill parents had when they peeked around corners and watched Villard creating dances with youngsters with scarves. Then Dorothy convinced Naomi, a mother of two, that she was perfectly capable of conducting weekly dance classes.

The kids had never seen anyone like avant-guard filmmaker Ed Emswiller, who came into the schools bearded like a shaggy dog. Emswiller was nationally known for his films shown at the Museum of Modern Art in New York.

Playwright Bill Parchman was another oddity who worked out of the library, getting kids on their feet reading and acting out stories and plays.

There was Vivian Herman. Everyone seemed thrown by this aggressive surviver of Nazi concentration camps. In her garage she built magnificent, grotesque wire sculptures, reproductions of the horrors she'd lived through. Jay protested against sending her work into schools, but Anne felt the youngsters' exposure to diversity would broaden.

Some parents who came to observe were so intrigued that several of them became a vital arm of volunteers. And Anne was not above recruiting her own family for specialized services: her son, David Goldin, a lawyer, and her husband, Jules Goldin, a dentist who hung exhibits, sold raffle tickets to patients, and cooperated in every way. There were others supporters: Pat Hinricks who eventually became administrative director and claimed, "I was Anne's 'No' man. Anne would get all these great ideas and I would have to say 'No.'"

As to administration, Jay oversaw the performing arts while Anne nurtured the visual arts in her office, a desk in her bedroom. They made more arrangements with the Wantagh Public Library director, and the Senior Center coordinator to put on artist exhibits, concerts, performances, lectures, demonstrations, workshops, trips, parades, and fairs. Anne, who is quiet and unaggressive, found appointments difficult. But no one could explain the program as well as she.

Opening up a tightly sealed town was like opening up a tin can. Groups of women got together and stayed together. When they lacked money, Jay cleaned out a sweater factory and got material for needed costumes.

Anne was first to get the kids to do street performances. The kids were uptight. Perform on the *street?* Now it doesn't seem so strange.

There were films made about Wantagh and CAP. The kids had never had an opportunity to participate in making a film.

Anne's attitude always was: Never mind if you don't know anything about art; it's better sometimes if you know nothing. Just look and the work will say something to you.

She said, "This is where I'm at. This is where I want to give whatever I've got to give right now. I live here, this is my town, I don't have to go somewhere else, I can do it right here, because Wantagh has a tremendous need."

When black and oriental families started moving in, it was Anne who made them feel welcome by inviting them into the art program.

With her unassuming attitude, she could reach people on a one-to-one basis like nobody else could. She could figure things out, anticipate the needs, such as a fund-raising drive. When the Seven-Twelve Association wanted a report to decide whether or not CAP was worth sponsorship, Anne and Pat Hinrichs walked out of the room. They were not interested in long-winded reports. That's when CAP decided to avoid bureaucracy, to go on their own.

Then came the day when the New York State Council on the Arts declared Wantagh CAP the pilot project in New York. They sent a consultant to the tune of $200 a day, and Anne and the CAP people figured that, with a professional consultant, they'd be able to bridge the gaps in their own knowledge. When the consultant arrived with four others, he said, "We want you, Anne, to tell us all about your program and what you're doing." The New York Council on the Arts had come to pick Anne's brains.

In 1971 CAP planned a massive free outdoor Expo on high school grounds wherein every artist worked in an individual space while the community observed and interacted. Anne got dancers, muscians, singers, craftspeople, etc. I was asked to be a poetry troubadour.

While many in the community loved engaging in the activities, others remained nonparticipants. Some complained that the event and the artists weren't professional enough, offering unfair comparisons with first-rate talent in New York City. But Anne saw people getting together, loosening up, trying something new.

When Expo '73 rolled around, CAP realized that the community must be totally involved and committed to keeping the program going, and people must lend financial help, however small. So, near the high school entrance, Anne placed a bin the size of a card table with a big sign made by Jules reading: "Contributions!" About 3000 people passed by, but at the end of the day the bin contained about $3.00 in change.

When the inevitable discouragement occurred — Why knock yourself out? Why should I do this? — Anne said, "We must increase the community's awareness of what artists are trying to do. The arts belong to all people, not just the wealthy, not stored in some museum, or basement."

One day Anne called me on the phone and we set a date to present my Margaret Fuller drama at the library. I was ecstatic. For the first time I felt like a true member of the artistic world. I would be paid $100.

While I began to work earnestly on my drama, I began to hear that some Wantagh residents thought the paintings the artists created in school and library should be sold and the proceeds should pay for school supplies, such as for athletics. This kind of suggestion is insulting to artists.

I worked for about two months on my Margaret Fuller performance, fitting my work around family routines. I kept changing the script. I had no idea how to incorporate Fuller's entire life story in so succinct a time period as an hour, so I limited my monologue to her American years — I would do the European years later.

I decided, instead of a set with backdrop (which I couldn't afford), I would project slides of the houses Margaret Fuller lived in and the people she knew on the wall. This required a great deal of research in many biographies, for it was a day and age before cameras. In many cases, prints of Fuller's houses just didn't exist, so I had to take dramatic license and substitute with something typical, as described in the books. I could find pictures of Hawthorne or Thoreau or Emerson easily enough, but when it came to her less-known female friends, there was often nothing available — so I was forced to leave the images of the women to the imaginations of the audience. Then Anne connected me with one of her CAP film makers, Ron Dilg, who processed what I had into slides, at a fraction of what a commercial photographer would charge.

I needed a costume that was more authentic than the modern version of the old-fashioned blouse and skirt I'd been wearing. I dug into costume books at the library and, because Margaret Fuller had been a teacher and had struggled economically during so many of those years, I chose a modest, homespun, schoolmarm-type dress with long sleeves and cuffs, and a simple, round collar. I took a picture to a seamstress, and she sent me on a buying trip. Searching about in 5-10 cent stores (and rightfully feeling inadequate for this task), I did find some light-weight cotton which I hoped would not wrinkle easily. But what color? Back in the library, I dug into the books again. Dyes in the early nineteenth century were nothing like what we have today — I chose a dull steel-blue and plain white for collar and cuffs. The purple knit shawl would be set off attractively.

And I picked up extra large underarm pads — I could anticipate perspiring heavily. As for shoes — high boots with buttons — there was no way I could find them, so I would just slip into some black flats I had — no one would notice them under that long skirt.

Since I understood the emotions of the woman, I now strove for some of the physical aspects: a Margaret Fuller walk, a Margaret Fuller voice, a Margaret Fuller diction. I learned how to hold a lorgnette, and how to say some words with a New England accent. I had to color the scenes for interest, give myself Margaret Fuller tasks such as pouring water from a pitcher into a washbowl in order to dampen a cloth to ease my headache. Every gesture had to offer information. I wanted to think like Margaret Fuller.

In every scene I built, I had to ask myself as an actress portraying Fuller: What is my relationship to the people I'm talking about? What do I want from this particular section? What do I do as an actor to touch off a "tingling" in the audience?

False starts. Repetition. Uncertainties.

Acting is called the "bastard art" because your body is your instrument. In other art forms the artist starts with an object, i. e., a violinist with a violin. In acting, it is you, yourself, that makes the material come alive.

You start by ignoring the script and words, by putting yourself in a circumstance and improvising the scene, trusting your instincts and impulses, opening the door, allowing yourself the freedom to go with what happens.

You must have the courage to "fall on your face," to make preposterous mistakes. You don't know if your choices are conveying what is needed. You can't see yourself.

The secret is not to "act." You need to try to find the truth of feelings. If you go for the words of the manuscript and the performance straight off, you deprive yourself of discovery, the fullness of what there is lying beyond those words. Later, the blending of actor, material and words can take place. If you do this work, you have a possibility of capturing a richness all your own. That's what makes one actor different than another.

The process changes as you proceed. You set up objects to evoke your own emotion. You might be pleased you said and did one thing realistically or casually, but then nothing happened. So you search further. Can what you capture in one rehearsal be captured on stage in front of an audience, with diverse distractions all around you?

Perhaps my greatest challenge was setting aside my naturally compliant nature — the dreamy little girl in me who wanted to please and idealize others — and to get inside me the confident, even arrogant, towering intellectual who had dared to criticize the male literati. I had to be the bold, self-assured individualist who stood against traditional attitudes, who foresaw new possibilities and envisioned a better world. In once sense, taking on Margaret Fuller was a liberation for me.

Naomi Kaapcke volunteered to run lights. Because she'd formerly held the position of lighting technician with a dance company, she'd "inherited" two theatrical lights which she set up on stands and then she had cables to which somebody attached a wooden box with a simple dimmer system. There's quite a problem when you project slides. The theatrical lights must be placed so they won't wash out the slides, and you can't act in the light from the slide projector. Thank goodness for Naomi who worked patiently with me and always kept her sense of humor and graciousness.

The community room in the Wantagh Library was packed.

Was I nervous?

Yes. I hardly knew what I was doing.

Yet this was my dream.

Everyone listened intently.

They clapped.

I at least said all the lines and got through the entire thing.

Thinking back, it was barely a beginning.

Though after my performance Anne Forman said, "We want you to continue to work with us!", I felt, pulling out of the Wantagh Library parking lot in my car, a great well of emptiness. It was over. I had given my all. And though the experience had seemed successful, I still had that gnawing feeling that my best wasn't totally satisfying. I must try again. What were next steps? The answer to that question was a blank.

Margaret Fuller was dropped for what seemed a couple of years. Finally, somebody asked me to do twenty minutes at a New York State Education Department Conference for Women in Albany, for which I pared down the script, and all went well.

Next, I decided NOW groups were a way to go and I talked my way into doing teeny tiny presentations at meetings in Queens and on the South Shore of Long Island, and at a State Conference in Plainview, Long Island. There, I performed in a hotel on a strange set of shaky platforms about the height of tables — and in that poor light, nearly fell off — and went on without a technical rehearsal or training anyone to run slides because the volunteer showed up two minutes before we were to start. Conditions like these have enabled me to improve at ad libbing.

Then, I wrote a letter to the East End Arts Center, Riverhead, Long Island, and achieved a date to perform in a charming Victorian house; almost no one showed up and the event faded away. A few days later, I covered a Setauket Unitarian Universalist Fellowship worship service at which the large crowd cheered with a standing ovation.

Now, I've forgotten to tell you about C. W. Post College. I know why; I've blocked it out of my mind.

I'd made contact with the woman who ran the Women's Center. At that time I was not aware that colleges readily lend space to the public for special events, nor did I have the least conception of how such events were organized.

The Women's Center director enthusiastically showed me a wonderfully intimate theater. She'd put a notice in the campus newspaper and would even do a small mailing under the campus mailing privileges if I would give her my publicity in addressed envelopes. She'd even see that two students ran lights and slides. And she would help me scrounge furniture from the theater department. We set a date and time, decided we would sell tickets, a percentage going to the Center. The entire idea seemed marvellous. I rehearsed for weeks at home for my most important performance to date. I wrote my news releases, addressed the envelopes, and gave them to her.

I unloaded the small props from my car for a technical rehearsal prior to the performance, and when I found the director she informed me the organizers of another event had taken over my intimate theater space. I would have to move to a lecture hall but it did seat 500 people so it was okay. This piece of news threw me a bit, but if the technical people showed maybe I would survive. They did.

The lecture hall was weird, with an extremely high corner area for a stage, but I adapted and we spent about two hours on tech. I managed to find a space to hurriedly do makeup and change into costume. The director was handling front of door; she'd made a big sign and had a box in which to collect the money. From a curtain peekhole I discerned six people in the 500-seat lecture area, and four of these were members of my family.

Never mind, this is a test. I am in a Broadway Theater rehearsing for opening night tomorrow and the famous director Elia Kazan is sitting out front.

After the performance one person who was not a family member found me and told me I was excellent. She introduced herself as an agent on Long Island and I should call her.

My ego boosted, I phoned and went to her office. She emoted; she'd like to be my agent. I agreed and went home feeling I had been discovered.

To this day that agent has never called me.

Later I found out that my friends had received the C. W. Post mailing *after* my performance was over. I do not blame the director. As she saw it, she had done her job as administrator (except for the late mailout), and she had been gracious as well. The rest was up to me, and if I was stupid enough not to be organized, then that was my problem.

Yes, in my marvellous naivety, I thought actors *acted.* Certainly that is what I had trained for and what other actors did. I was soon to find out, grassroots that I am: Actor is expected to find locations; set dates; tell coordinator every detail; get picture taken; pay for it; write publicity releases; find contacts; find out newspaper, TV, radio deadlines; mail publicity; pay for paper and postage; make innumerable phone calls; organize a team of volunteers; decide on how best to set up the facility; work out lights in the facility; mark a script with lighting cues; pay for light rental; transport lights; set lights up and train a volunteer to run them; decide on props; find and pay for props; transport props; set props up in theater; find furniture; transport furniture; set up, research and decide on the slides I wanted; take pictures to photographer; tell him how to photograph; pick slides up and pay the bill; fill the slide trays; mark a script for slide cues; train volunteer who has never run a slide projector; decide on makeup and hairdo; buy makeup and hair paraphernalia; research costume; find tailor to make costume; buy the material; have several fittings; pay for costume; find and pay for shoes; find and pay for antique lorgnette; find shawl; bring all makeup and costume to performance; direct technical rehearsal with volunteer technicians; find volunteer narrator; mark narrator's script; work with narrator (who can usually stay at technical performance for five minutes); make phone calls ensuring an audience; yes, get into costume and put on makeup and comb hair; act and, more often than not, lead a follow-up discussion and question-and-answer session with the audience; be charming during a reception given in my honor and answer more questions; and then strike all props and equipment; thank all the volunteer help; and transport all the stuff home again and unload the car.

That's what grassroots acting is all about.

One time I was asked by the coordinator if I would bring home-baked hors d'oeuvres to the reception. When I said, "I'll let you attend to that," she remarked scornfully, "Thanks a lot!"

Only stars exclusively act, and also those lucky professional actors who sit around waiting for the jobs to come to them.

Did people want to pay me for my work? Of course not. No one had any money. These groups and organizations struggle along. As for selling tickets, they couldn't. No one would come. But would it be all right if they asked for donations — for their organizational expenses? I did wish I could get enough to pay my expenses. Of course, money was not my object. But I could hardly feel competent or valued without a paycheck.

Meanwhile, my favorite arts council, Wantagh CAP, was expanding, managing to pay salary and expenses for an artist residency for a week, and they were able to present several programs: Composers, Edward Smaldone of Wantagh and Leo Kraft, as well as the second company of Alvin Ailey, and the American Ballet. This was followed by a premiere ABT New York performance with Fernando Bujones, a dancer from Latin America who later developed into an internationally-known performer.

CAP was learning that when a performance was free, the high school auditorium was packed, but when they charged $1.00 per ticket, the room would be two-thirds empty. The general attitude was that, because people paid school taxes, they thought programs should be free.* The third year the New York State Council on the Arts cut back on funding.

Nevertheless, Anne's dream continued because PTAs and CAP raised money through bake sales, craft fairs, etcetera, and from time to time enough legislative funds would come through to pay for some artists.

"Nothing anyone does that is different is without problems," Anne says. "In trying to work within the structure of society you have to find how to balance the various people and elements involved. It's worth doing. Once you break through, it will continue. There'll be cutbacks and drawbacks, but it will continue because someone, somehow, will take it further. When I decided I had to withdraw from administering the program, new people came in. It was important that these new people conduct in their own way. They'd consult with me, yes, but if I had tried to dominate, I think the program would have died. It's like a child — you have to give direction, give rope. The present director, Roz Italiano, is really committed and effective, and now she's formed a whole new group of people around her. CAP is cut back to $2,500 per year, but I really feel that at some point somebody is going to determine that this program has got to be a part of the total school or library budget, and somebody is going to make it happen."**

I learned from Anne Forman.

Now I will tell you about Farmingdale.

Farmingdale is a Long Island college where a women's educational group was having a conference for arts leaders associated with

---

*Anne Forman's idea to put the community arts program on the ballot, to include it as part of the library budget or as part of the school budget so performances could be offered without charge, has not yet been realized.

**CAP still functions today, though funding has been greatly cut. People have come to observe, including an international group, and Ted Berger who eventually formed the New York Foundation on the Arts with a strong artists-in-schools programs. Many of the paintings and sculptures Anne arranged for still remain in the schools — generations will enjoy them. The New York State Council on the Arts would have given funds for a full-time administrator, but Anne envisioned a *part-time* administrator and *more* artists.

colleges and programming throughout New York state. It sounded like the perfect opportunity. I was given a stage in a large theater deficient in acoustics, intimacy, and charisma. I was also given technical support and assured an audience of conference participants.

I chose to perform on the apron of the stage, in front of closed curtains, figuring that this would offer greater intimacy than by using the vast stage area.

By this time I had recruited a director who was giving me notes:

"You hold the tea cup too long."

"You insist on getting too loud and you lose strength."

"Longer pause after 'dream.'"

"Shouldn't you say migraine headaches."

"Take glasses down when you say 'heaven help you.'"

"You're too angry in father speech."

"Say 'suffocates minds in our country,' instead of 'paralizes.'"

"Bow to Goethe — straight out front."

"I could not understand the word 'citadel.' Watch your pronunciation."

"'Pain has no effect...Steal some of my time'...too poetic."

He hammered, "Hide the emotion! Hide the emotion!" This was excellent advice, but in my inexperience I had a hard time understanding how to apply it.

This director had said he would not come to the performance. So you can imagine my utter undoing when I ran into him in a tiny curtained side hall during intermission. With a worried expression on his face, he told me everything was wrong and I needed to come down off the stage and stand directly in front of the audience. Of course, the furniture was all set on the stage and I had no stagehands to suddenly move it. During the last half of that performance about half the audience walked out. Though I did follow-up mailings and phone calls, not one of those program planners ever invited me to their college.

The feeling of failure from that performance was almost unbearable.

I don't know what has made me tenaciously cling to this work.

If I had looked at it realistically, I would never have done it. The frustrations would breed discontent. As indeed they have.

Perhaps the thought keeps running through my mind: *It's okay to pour energy with every ounce of soul on what I consider to be my work and aim to satisfy only one person, myself.*

It was at about this point that people began gently to suggest that I give my script to a star who might be interested in playing Margaret Fuller. An interested star could bring the script to a top-notch producer, who in turn could raise the money on the strength of the star's name, and the piece could get produced in a slick and professional way, and have every chance of being highly successful.

I admire stars — they have gone through their own struggles, and if they can swing a deal easily and command high salaries, I am the first to cheer them on to even higher fame and privilege, for they have earned every piece of pie they get.

But stars are offered scripts every day.

Even people close to me didn't understand.

The seeds of ambition had been sewn early in me and, at the same time, I was acculturized to pattern myself in the role of wife and mother. A mover and a shaker, friend Ramona Barth calls me a victim of the compassion trap, as so many women are.

It took a long time for me to become aware of the host of forces that keep women from achieving.

To be sure there are worse fates than mine, but why does a woman feel obliged to sublimate her desires into home and family while a man feels obliged to pursue his ambitions?

Why are older women ridiculed or condemned when they wish to pick up and pursue youthful ambitions?

Why does a woman who is finally surrounded by material comforts, and even children, feel she has so little?

Why does a woman devalue her work and distrust her experience as secondary in importance — whether or not her work brings in dollars?

Why does a woman feel she had better not permit herself to excel?

Why does a woman allow herself to be put in a position of dependency, submission, and worthlessness?

These questions are not new.

A hundred and fifty years ago, Margaret Fuller said it all in thirteen words:

"'Tis an evil lot to have a man's ambition and a woman's heart."

HOW I GOT TO HARVARD

It was April, 1979.

I was about to call it quits with Margaret Fuller because throughout my presentation at a Great Neck, Long Island high school two students had been "making out" in the back row.

Secondly, the Brighton Senior Citizens talked and ate so loudly during my performance that I broke off in the middle of a sentence and said, "I see you are not interested," and stepped off the strange, little corner, triangular platform, and went home.

Then someone named Anne Vendig called me. Wouldn't I do my drama for the Sunday-morning worship service at her church, the prestigious Unitarian Universalist [UU] church in Plandome, Long Island. On her second call she invited me to hear Fuller's great grandnephew — the nearest living relative — R. Buckminster Fuller, speak at a church forum.

R. Buckminster Fuller — the "R" stood for Margaret's brother Richard — had been thrown out of Harvard twice. I learned that he'd entered the University in 1913 in the grand tradition of all the male members of the Fuller family since 1760 (including Margaret's father and brothers), but he was dismissed because he'd spent his tuition money on a wild spree for the cast of the Ziegfield Follies. The second time he was labelled as having a "lack of sustained interest in the processes of the University."

He went on to write twenty-five books, held twenty-six patents, and won thirty national and international awards, as well as the Presidential Medal of Honor. President Reagan awarded him the Medal of Freedom. Her Majesty the Queen of England awarded him the Royal Gold Medal for Architecture. He was appointed University Professor at Southern Illinois University, and was nominated for the 1969 Nobel Peace Prize.

He was often called our contemporary American Leonardo da Vinci, esteemed as a lecturer, architect, philosopher, poet, environmentalist, and mathematician. His best-known invention was the bubblelike geodesic dome (a linking of triangles which covered more space without internal supports than any building designed).

Bucky — as he was often referred to by friends and press — had in the 1960s become a popular cult figure, especially among the young, because he believed that humankind possessed the technology to provide for everyone's needs on Earth. He said there was no Third World or First World, only One World. How remininscent this was of great grandaunt who often quoted an obscure poet, "Mankind is one and beats with one great heart."[*]

Buckminster Fuller began his lecture by mentioning his most admirable relative, Margaret.

Can't you imagine her, a hundred and fifty years ago, stepping into Harvard's hallowed halls? Imagine, the first woman, sweeping into the magnificent, newly-built Gore Library and asking for books for her research on her book about the West, *Summer on the Lakes?* I can see her sitting with quill pen at one of the long wooden tables in a beam of light streaking in through a high, narrow window, amongst the male scholars who were pouring over the thick, oversized volumes bound in black leather and feeling rather uncomfortable in the presence of an unorthodox female whose superb brilliance and self-esteem threatened.

It is phenomenal that in 1843 Margaret Fuller crossed the Harvard library threshold. It wasn't until 1967 that the Lamont Library opened doors to women. Though as early as 1643 women donated money to enable poor and worthy students to attend our oldest and most

---

[*] Quoted by Margaret Fuller in the *New York Daily Tribune*.

distinguished educational institution, no women students were accepted into Harvard until 1920 when they were admitted to the School of Education. A special nondegree program for female students was developed in 1879, named after Harvard's first woman benefactor, Anne Radcliffe. In 1894 women were admitted to a restricted number of Harvard graduate courses, but were not granted doctoral degrees. In 1919, when women were just getting the vote, Harvard seems to have been forced to appoint a woman professor — she was denied admission to the Harvard Club, tickets to football games, and at Commencement was not allowed to sit on the platform. In 1943 women were admitted to all Harvard courses. Two years later a dozen women were admitted to the Medical School; in 1950 some entered the Law School. The first Commencement for both men and women occurred in 1970. In 1975 an equal access admissions policy was adopted.

In the early 1900s when Bucky walked into the Harvard Library no questions were asked; he researched the phenomenon of time as a separate entity and in 1927 discovered a book by Margaret Fuller, and he began to read and collect all the works of his celebrated relative.

At the North Shore Unitarian Universalist church forum Bucky covered two ice ages, the abacus, the cipher, the limitations of Malthus, solar energy, Copernicus, Kepler, Galileo, Newton. He was thinking "out loud," about the world's greatest resources: human intelligence, ingenuity, and imagination. He described the problems of the riders on Spaceship Earth and how these problems could be solved with the knowledge and technology we already have, by harnessing the unused sources in gravity, the sun's radiation, and the power of the tides. "We want to have a design revolution, not a bloody revolution," he said.

Listening to him was an absorbing experience. He regretted it was muscle, not mind, controlling the universe, but that we were "all geniuses," with the option of making it if we all pulled together and used our capabilities for solving problems.

He talked about his own personal crisis in the 1920s: bankrupt and having lost his four-year-old daughter after a battle with several illnesses, he stood on the shores of Lake Michigan, ready to throw himself in. As he looked up at the stars, he realized he had no right to eliminate himself because he did not "belong to himself"; he belonged to the universe because human beings had been introduced into the universe for an important reason. The universe exhibited a mathematical orderliness, which naturally implied a greater intellect at work, and human beings were a part of that design. He resolved to convert his experience to the advantage of others. He would search for the principles governing the universe.

I couldn't help but recall the story of Margaret Fuller's comment to Thomas Carlyle one night at dinner: "Mr. Carlyle, I accept the universe." Reportedly, he retorted, "By gad, Margaret, you'd better!"*

The phenomenon of hearing Bucky and performing my drama in front of a SRO (Standing-Room-Only) audience at the Sunday-morning-worship service at Plandome church heartened my Margaret Fuller quest, and then Anne Forman's husband, Jules, handed me a Unitarian bulletin with a front-page article about the Margaret Fuller birthplace in Cambridge, Massachusetts. Enchanted to learn of its existence, I arranged a trip as soon as I could desert my family. I would stay with my sister who worked in Boston.

As I stood before my mentor's first home, I tried to garner the sentiment and emotion I'd anticipated would overwhelm as soon as I came near something that had belonged to Margaret Fuller. But Seventy-One Cherry Street needed paint. It was in the low-income Lechmere section — multi-cultural, largely Hispanic. Tall, plain, wooden, typical of the neighborhood's largest houses at turn of the century. The large rectangular backyard was dreary, cracked cement — nothing like the lovely garden painstakingly cared for by Margaret Fuller's mother and so beloved as a quiet refuge by the precocious youngster. A heavy wire fence enclosed a weathered basketball court and a few beat-up garbage cans. It was a settlement house — Margaret Fuller would be enthusiastic about this.

But I was an outsider, the stranger who didn't belong, who had little interest in perceiving the present value of the house. Where were the two elms Fuller's father had planted in the front yard in honor of her birth. Wouldn't the paved streets meld into rutted, dirt roads. Couldn't the cars dissolve into a lone carriage pulled by a

---

* Buckminster Fuller was certain this story was not true. *See* B. Fuller's letter towards the end of this chapter.

horse. How I wished the dingy crowded abodes on the adjacent streets would vanish and turn into green fields under a brilliant, red, setting sun.

Assuredly I was being ridiculous.

I would go in and find the director.

A large center stairway. Fireplaces. But uneven floors. No curtains. No carpet. Broken-down sofas that weren't early Americana. Scarred wooden tables and straight-backed chairs. Messy bulletin boards. Torn posters. Low-budget community space, unexciting, uncommodious, pitiful even for a settlement house. Where was a picture of Margaret Fuller? Where were people?

In the front room I found a woman who was packing to leave. She was aware that Margaret Fuller had been born in this house. "It's listed on the National Register of Historic Places," she said without ardor, "something about the fireplace upstairs, and the windows." In a flurry to be off — perhaps she was a volunteer — she motioned me to the director's room further back.

Helen Stempkowski was gracious, yet showed little interest in Margaret Fuller. "Did you know that someone from Cambridge or Concord wrote a play about Fuller — only it had many characters."

"No, I didn't know. Who was that?"

"Oh, I can't remember her name, but a lot of people went to see it."

"That's interesting, I'll ask around." Bare walls, devoid of bookshelves. "Doesn't the house have information on Fuller?"

"Oh yes." From a drawer she pulled out two thin manila portfolios. "It's not a lot." She handed me three badly stencilled pages and a small cheaply produced booklet. "You can keep those if you want."

Looming up at me on the booklet cover — I bit my lip in order not to explode — was a portrait of the *wrong woman*. Jane Carlyle, I was almost certain.

The poorly stencilled pages offered a capsule history of the house. Built in 1807 by Margaret's father, it had later served as a YWCA, then was turned into a settlement house. Programs for all ages were now offered: basketball, amateur theatrics, music, bingo, socials, etcetera. Almost nothing about Margaret Fuller.

"Why don't you talk to Liz Kovac," said the director. "She's the historian."

Liz would meet me the next day in Harvard Square at 1:00 P.M. in Brigham's, the famous ice cream parlor a few doors down from The Coop.*

By 2:00 P.M. I should have given up. But I was to be in Cambridge only a few days.

"Sorry," said Liz over the phone that night. "I couldn't make it. You should talk to Ramona Barth."

"Who's she?"

"A lady who does publicity."

"How do I reach her?"

Ramona Barth was about to return home to Maine, but she'd give me an hour in Brigham's, before catching her bus.

You would disregard her if you passed her on the street.

"Please notice I did not make you stand on one leg after another waiting three hours."

Her words spilled out fast, in a high musical register, in humor that bespoke simultaneous frivolity and seriousness. Sixtyish, thin, medium-tall, frail, pale, with no makeup, she was dressed in black from turbaned head to toe-hugging skirt. Grayish wispy hairs frayed out of her black turban.

"Don't worry your pretty little head about Liz — She's doing her history. Let her do it. And good luck. We have other irons in the fire. We will relate with good vibes. Boston and Cambridge is our turf. I've been out of it for a few years, but I can still whip up interest, resurrect energies. Diddling dollars, not our priority. Our motivation is action, not roadblocks. The world should be yours and Margaret Fuller's, everywhere, everywhere."

Arms rigidly close to her sides, she sipped a lone tea, having refused to order one of the restaurant's divine ice cream sundaes. "Younger, I was a bit more radical...But the 'oldie' women — women from the nineteenth century — were great, and they're safe. I can 'do' them. I've written many articles, *scholarly* — and they're all in Harvard library, yes indeed — in the basement somewhere...probably

---

* The Coop, pronounced to rhyme with "loop," was founded in 1882 as a small corner grocery store by Harvard undergraduates who sold stationery and second-hand books.

the mice are eating them right now — but they're there!

"Are you on a diet? I starve one day and lose only one pound, gotta keep it up though. Jesus, we do have our similar patterns."

For one hour she did not stop talking.

"How old are you and are you menopausal? I'm not hot on ERA. I'm a founding member of Boston NOW and Maine NOW, but they are too tame, myopic. J'accuse! The sin of omission makes NOW as crassly racist as was the DAR refusing to let Marian Anderson sing in Washington, D. C. Women and blacks had their chance to bond in a common humanity, but NOW thinks only of the election. NOW has missed the boat, the real gut issues."

In her cultured voice, she demonstrated such originality of expression and humor that I was drawn, amused, shocked, inspired, flattered, always encouraged.

"It can be done! I'm so revved up! I'm salivating! I get locked in Maine, laundry, food, ugh! I freeze spinach. Hausfrau housewife. Wife of a house. I'm married to a house. Take laundry twelve miles away. Get stack of fourteen cent postcards for what we have to know about each other. I'm not as neat and prizzy as you but I love bulletins. I'm limp but livin'!" And forth came ten dozen ideas, one possibility following another.

When I attempted to get in a word, she interrupted, flowing onward, naming names and happenings I had never heard of: The Dante Center...King's Chapel...I listened, mesmerized.

"Boston is my millieu. I have a history here — after all, I wasn't a great lady for ten years on Beacon Hill for nothing. My papa — poor clergy, but famous on Beacon Hill twenty-five years as representative, was founder of national Thoreau Society. I went to U. of Chicago-Theological....I got Betty Friedan to Franeuil Hall....Also Flo Kennedy — I'm National Chaplain for The Feminist Party.* I had an exhibit here. 'Stamped Women' — women on postage stamps. Boston City Hall. The Mayor's Office.** I've been away from it four,

---

* At the New England Feminist Party Convention in Boston in 1973, Ramona Barth, among other contributions, arranged for the presentation of keys to the city by Assistant Mayor Eves of Boston to Feminist Party founder, Flo Kennedy.

**"Stamped Women, Another Revolution, a Two Part exhibit about Women." Also, *see* the chapter entitled "Ramona X."

five years, but I can ressurrect the scene. Doors will open. It only
takes one person, and we are two. We can do more than all those
people who sit behind desks and shuffle papers. The world is
open...."

She gleaned that I had had five children and confessed to having
five herself, clucking like a hen about their problems and personali-
ties and cackling of how she, a bachelor of divinity, was a "kept"
woman, how she married a now-retired Doctor of Divinity minister
and had lived as minister's wife in Miami and Boston.

Too quickly she admired and espoused my drama on Margaret
Fuller, I thought, for she had neither seen nor read it. Still, her
conversation was loaded with expectation. She assumed I would
agree with every idea, and how could I not? She said what I wanted
to hear.

She had to rush off to her Greyhound. "I'm off on knees to wild
blueberry scene...my true place...on knees? You can write to me,"
she said. "My address is Alna, Maine."

"What's the street?" I asked.

"Just write A-L-N-A." She checked the letters off on four fingers.
"It'll get to me."

She was gone.

I was faced with twenty assignments.

Suddenly I felt abandoned. How could she light a fire and then
leave? Sitting across from her, a new future had seemed accessible,
but without her, I immediately experienced a wave of dis-
empowerment.

Could I believe her plots and plans?

What was her motive?

Who was she really?

She was like no one I'd ever met. She didn't sound or act like
any administrator or creative professional; in fact, she'd time and time
again put down high-powered individuals who were in decision-
making positions. Did she just love to bamboozle people, like so
many loud-mouths I'd encountered, or did she truly mean to take
action — and, if so, was she able to do what she said?

And how could she do all she claimed to do in Boston while she
lived off somewhere in Maine?

All her talk seemed an impossible dream. But I wanted to believe.

And what was there to lose besides shoe leather.

The people at places like the Historical Society were behind closed doors, "in meetings," but at the elegant Unitarian Universalist headquarters on Beacon Hill, at the mention of Ramona Barth's name, the Religious Arts Guild and Worship Arts Clearing House executive director came out of her office and sat down with me on a highly polished bench in the traditionally furnished, wide, carpeted, and half-dark hallway. Seemingly impressed, Barbara Hutchins examined my papers, then popped the question. "Are you Unitarian?"

My heart dropped to basement level and my stomach twisted into a pancake, but I did not blink as I answered untruthfully, "Yes."

Of twenty thousand thoughts: *Couldn't I, for a moment, be my mother for she had been Unitarian.*

Now how to reconcile this major breach of honesty to my husband, who was so proud I never told lies.

As scarlet letters formed across my chest, and as perspiration broke onto my brow, Barbara Hutchins smiled and calmly commented about how nice it would be to get to know me.

How to face Nancy Prichard, executive director of the UU Women's Federation?

She wasn't in. Relieved, I left materials with her secretary.

Why hadn't I ever become Unitarian?

My next stop was down the hill to 64 Beacon Street where I was to knock on the door and ask to see the elevator, the chapel, and the wine cellar that didn't have any wine. This was the five-story, twenty-eight-room home built in 1825 where for ten years Ramona had been addressed as "Mrs. Joseph Barth, Sr." (she hated the word Mrs.) while her "man-of-God mate" preached at one of the most historic churches in Boston, King's Chapel. She preferred being called Ramona and I was to find out much later that she had been named after the Indian maiden in Helen Hunt Jackson's immortal love story, *Ramona*.

I'd never known the magnificence of a Beacon Hill home, and the exterior, the door, the halls, the servant's quarters, the exquisite wallpaper with tropical foliage, the parquet floors, the original purple-paned windows, the high-ceilinged rooms in this classic, best of mansions drew from me an inward gasp. It was nearly impossible to place the lady-in-black Ramona as the matriarch.

I never got to see the wine cellar that had no wine.

"I knew it! I knew it!" burbled Ramona when I phoned. "They never give a grand tour! And now they have someone to clean the twenty-eight rooms. Can you imagine — there are four maids' rooms but I didn't have a maid. I carried the garbage out. I'll bet you didn't see the safe in the butler's pantry where you're supposed to keep your silver but that's where our sons kept their marbles. I'll bet you didn't get to go up in the elevator?"

"No, I didn't."

"I knew it! Did she show you the Chapel?"

"Yes — certainly impressive."

"They have to show the Chapel!"

My next stop was at Radcliffe where I was to ask for Pat King, director of the Arthur and Elizabeth Schlesinger Library on the History of Women in America. I stumbled about trying to find the unmarked Radcliffe Yard — assuredly everyone is just supposed to know where it is. At the mention of Ramona Barth's name, Pat King came out of her office briefly. She was as reserved and shy as I, but friendly and obviously capable. (Later, on the phone, Ramona cooed that King had given me two minutes.)

Back home on Long Island, as I wrestled with my guilt for the sin I had committed, I realized I was, had always been, Unitarian. I joined the North Shore Unitarian Universalist Society, Inc., in Plandome and started associating with soul mates. Long-distance to Ramona, I confessed. She laughed and shrugged it aside as though it were the most unimportant thing that had ever occured.

In "Laurie Logs" — missives from Ramona — I got my next commands. I must re-enter Cambridge. Helen Stemkowski, director of the Margaret Fuller House, had taken Ramona to see Francis X. Hayes, executive director of the Cambridge Community Economic Development Corporation. He referred her to David Kronberg, artistic director of ArtiCulture, a Cambridge arts organization.

Ramona had them "salivating"; she handed out copies of Paula Blanchard's biography, *Margaret Fuller from Transcendentalist to Revolutionary,* brochures on the Margaret Fuller House, and I imagine she often uttered the magic words "Harvard" and "Buckminster

Fuller."

David Kronberg talked to Ramona about an outdoor performance. She wrote me that making things happen made her manicky, so if she started to break out in geriatric "tics," I was to tell her I'd carry on but, in the meantime, to send my best "brag" sheets to Kronberg. Brag sheets were flyers, newspaper articles, and resumes which described a person's work favorably.

Kronberg was a history major and did not need to be educated about Margaret Fuller. He was the personable administrator in a sparse office. He said nothing about an outdoor performance. Why didn't I take a walk over to Longfellow Hall at Harvard, take a look at it and let him know if I liked it.

I summoned enough poise not to fall off my seat. *If I liked it.* That's true, perhaps Harvard was not up to my accustomed standards. Perhaps I could conceive of a better place. After all, anybody could perform at Harvard any time they wished, couldn't they? Just snap your fingers, and you'll be there, with an audience.

Well, I said I'd go over and take a look.

If only I had the irrefragability of Margaret Fuller. She must have stepped inside Harvard with confidence and verve.

Not even a janitor was about as I and my old friend Trepidation climbed the steps of the Greek-columned building named after Fuller's contemporary.

The rectangular lecture room did not come close to being a theater. But it was pretty, had red carpet, steeply tiered, comfortable seats that would accomodate maybe 200 people, and floor-to-ceiling windows at the back that let light flow through. The area where I would be performing was long and narrow, conducive to lecturers who used the long, tall blackboard on the wall. I would discuss with David Kronberg the possibility of covering the blackboard, bringing in a screen for my slides, and setting up lights and a platform. There was no dressing room or holding room; I would have to arrive at Longfellow Hall in costume ready to go "on stage."

Ramona started sending me tons of paper. Articles with notes. Background info about Radcliffe and Harvard. Letters from important people I was to try to get to know. Flyers of events with names which she'd label "The cerebral boys!" Unitarian newsletters and pages from past General Assembly programs with briefs that these people were "my pals," or "I spoke here — you next!" Orders of services with notes telling me to write a person or to look him/her up at GA (General Assembly). Pictures of people which she'd circled and told me to "Meet at GA," "Get her quote," "Do meet," "Please, via a letter and telephone follow-up," "Pursue her for our West Coast tour," "Very, very important," "Hope you meet."

"You must meet Rosemary and Howard Matson" — and she sent me literature on Rosemary's work — "Rosemary's baby," as Ramona called it — a new, nonpatriarchal ministry to women, a national network across ecumenical lines to explore the creative process of transition, called Women in Transition (WIT). It had been born, in part, out of the need for the denomination to correct inadequacies in hiring, appointing, and accrediting women in leadership roles and in developing materials, programs, and policies that overcame traditional sexist attitudes perpetuated by patriarchal power. In 1977, at the Unitarian Universalist Association General Assembly in Ithaca, New York, a Women and Religion resolution had been put on the agenda which had been unanimously passed, and the following year Rosemary Matson was named co-chair of the first Continental Women and Religon Committee with the task of carrying out the intent of the resolution.

The sparky, eight-page WIT newsletter which Rosemary wrote and edited, focused on women's issues and contained news of European women as well as WIT women, conferences, workshops, etcetera, and it featured dynamic pictures of mid-life women who had vital inner strength evoking life affirmation. Immediately, I wanted to capture and retain the vibrancy and self-activation these women exuded.

Meanwhile, in Maine Ramona had organized a Silver Tea at the Newcastle home of Rosie Fuller Kenison, sister of Buckminster Fuller, as a benefit for the Cambridge Margaret Fuller Neighborhood House. She got Anzie Andrews, a resident of Wiscasset, to review Paula Blanchard's biography on Margaret Fuller, after which Ramona led a forum, "Meaning for Modern Women." Furthermore, she, with the help of Barbara Warner of South Bristol (founder of mid-coast chapter of NOW), announced the opening of our newest idea — The Margaret Fuller Women's History Research Center — along with a celebration of the United States Mint release of the new Susan B.

Anthony dollar at the Center for Being in Boothbay Harbor. It was open house from 9 A.M. to 9 P.M. on July 2. "Yesterday's kooks and crazies sometimes are on coins tomorrow," Barth was quoted in the *Lincoln County News*, and she called for volunteers, noting that similar women's history centers had achieved success from humble beginnings. Her theme for the day was "Failure Is Impossible!" — a quote for which Susan B. Anthony is best remembered.

More Ramona commands. I must write many letters and make several calls in order to attend and present my drama at the upcoming Unitarian Universalist Women's Federation Biennial Convention at the National 4-H Center in Chevy Chase, Maryland, and I must drop a note to Buckminster Fuller and invite him to my May 27th performance at the UU Fellowship in Morristown, New Jersey. I must also go to the UU General Assembly (GA), a week-long national Conference to be held at Michigan State University in East Lansing, to which thousands attended. Between these dates I had a couple of Long Island high school commitments.

This flurry of activity was good, because these performances served as previews for our big July 19th date at Harvard, chosen to commemorate the day Margaret Fuller died. Ramona wrote of telephone conversations about finances with David Kronberg, quoting him saying, "'We shall see who puts $$ where their minds and hearts are!!'" She finished by adding, "Pray a bit until I call you, Saturday, 9-10 A.M."

Shortly, the reply came in from R. Buckminster Fuller:

April 26, 1979

Dear Laurie James,

I find it extraordinarily gratifying to learn that you are dramatizing Margaret Fuller through your own appearances. I am sorry that I will not be able to attend your Morristown presentation. I'll be in China at that time. But I do look forward tremendously to meeting you sometime in the not-too-distant future.

I am sending you a xeroxing of a set of all the letters exchanged between Emerson and Carlyle that contain mention of Margaret. These letters were collected by Charles Eliot Norton a number of years ago, when he was professor at Harvard. You will note that there is one important letter which was left out, which was the letter written by Carlyle to Emerson on the occasion of Margaret's first calling on him. It was on that occasion that the, to me, probably falsely formulated anecdote occurred in which Margaret was said to have announced to Carlyle that she accepted the universe and he was said to have responded, "Egads, ye'd better!" I would say from the tenor of the letters exchanged between Emerson and Carlyle that Carlyle was a much better and more understanding friend. Quite clearly Emerson "chickened" when he was misinformed that Margaret had an illegitimate child, which misinformation also occasioned Horace Greeley's firing of Margaret as his foreign correspondent.

I'm also sending xeroxes of items of recent years that I feel are very important for your information. You probably have discovered them yourself, but just to be sure, I think you ought to have them in your research files. These latest items together with actual statements by the Ossoli family to members of my family make it clear that the Ossolis now acknowledge that the proper wedding did take place, and that Margaret was truly the Marchioness Ossoli, and her child was completely legitimate. At any rate, the misinformation showed who were Margaret's real friends and who were not. I'm saying this because I think it could color your own dramatization of Margaret.

> Faithfully,
> Buckminster Fuller

How thrilled I was to receive his letter and the packet of xeroxes verifing his opinion that the Carlyle/Fuller story was just a story, and that the Ossoli/Fuller marriage did take place and their child was legitimate!

One morning at about 6 A.M. I was awakened by a phone call from Rural Ramona, as she now identified herself.

"Hold on to your hat!" she bubbled as I shook my groggy head.

Ramona almost never called, rather she'd scratch notes on postcards, backs of old form letters or flyers, or on envelopes or torn bits of paper or cardboard, even on napkins or matchbook covers. So I knew, at this god-awful hour, before the peak telephone rates applied, that something big was afoot.

"Radcliffe is going to give you a reception!"

"What?"

"I've been talking to Pat King. I'm glowing!"

Then, within a few days Ramona informed me that the mayor of one of the most politically astute cities in the U.S. — Cambridge — was going to proclaim a Margaret Fuller Day. (It was her idea; she'd been working on the wording of the proclamation with David Kronberg. "I'll type it up neat, prissy, and professional!") The Dante Alighieri Society of Massachusetts, Inc. and McDonald's of Central Square, Cambridge, were providing funding, along with the City of Cambridge, Office of Manpower Affairs, Community Development Block Grant Program.

David Kronberg of ArtiCulture along with Francis X. Hayes of the Cambridge Community Economic Development Corporation, and Pat King of The Schlesinger Library were offering production and promotional assistance.

The Schlesinger Library was to arrange an exhibit of the papers and memorabilia of Margaret Fuller.

And, yes, there was to be a press conference prior to the reception, and the Dante Alighieri Society was to stage a dinner.

Unbelievably exciting: Deane Lord, director of Information, Harvard Graduate School of Education had arranged for R. Buckminster Fuller to introduce my drama.

There followed a flurry of notes and instructions from Ramona — letters to write, people to call. Her notes were entangled with her everyday life of tending to visits of children and grandchildren, laundry and "shit work," as well as roofers on her 1790 farmhouse, who had pulled the roof off over her bedroom. She'd say "'I'll transcend, per my fifty years experience."

David Kronberg phoned me. "This thing is growing. You'd better come up here and give us an audition — otherwise I might have to call it off — after all, *I've never seen your work!*"

As I'd been sharpening my drama, I was close to being ready, but his questions to Ramona which she relayed to me — "Is it a fabulous magnetic theater piece? Does it have theater charisma?" — caused my nervous consciousness to surface, and anyway, how could I get to Boston? This added trip would mean I would spend more money on this one performance than the fee I would earn.

I flew up on the least expensive airline I could find, a scary plane seating about twenty persons, a single row of seats on each side of center aisle.

At Longfellow Hall there were a handful of people I'd never seen, as well as David Kronberg and Ramona, who was as stylish in a pixie haircut and in beiges and lilacs as any good Newberry Street consumer. Especially animated, she insisted I meet a millionaire friend, her former Beacon Hill neighbor, Susan Storey Lyman, chairman of the board of Radcliffe College. There were more introductions and I must say I started to feel like the all-important star.

I began to plow the deep for the authority of Margaret Fuller.

Surely I would forget all my lines.

Couldn't they see my stage fright?

I threw myself into it.

What I did, do not ask, for I do not know.

Did they like it?

No one complained.

I went home.

No one called to cancel.

I continued working on my drama every day.

Moments when you feel dry — nothing coming alive — it's just words, words, words. Your impulse is to walk away — not to touch any more, give up, trash it all. The advise is, choose a private space that deeply affects you that relates to the material and be in touch with that. And/or select object(s) meaningful to you that will evoke a similar reaction you are seeking in the material. This is the work of the actor that the audience does not see.

Ramona assured me Radcliffe would assign a special room about a block away from Longfellow Hall for me to use as a dressing room.

Meanwhile, I picked up my high school dates (which confirmed that students of that grade level have little interest in historic re-creations), and drove about six hours to the 4-H Center in Chevy Chase, Maryland for the UU Women's Federation Biennial Convention. There, I found my performance space, but where were Nancy Prichard, the executive director, and Natalie W. Gulbrandsen, the president, and where were the participants? Nancy had agreed to run slides. I set up everything myself, got into costume, then stood around the hallway waiting for people. Finally, Nancy and about five people showed up, looking cheery.

"I'm ready," Nancy exclaimed, as though everything was perfection. She went right to the projector.

How could she run the slides properly when she'd never seen the script? It didn't matter, I told myself, because it seemed I was to have an audience of five. But suddenly from out of nowhere came a steady stream of women. They lined the walls. Sat on the floor. Squeezed space. My stage area edged smaller and smaller.

I began. The women laughed and empathized in enjoyment. The slides clicked into place as needed. Everyone congratulated me afterwards. Then these women disappeared down the hall, as quickly as they'd come. When I thanked Nancy for handling the slides without a rehearsal, she said, "That was nothing — I used to be a schoolteacher."

I got out of my costume, carried props to car, and found I'd locked my keys inside. Poking away at the lock with a wire hanger, I was finally saved by a young man who showed me how cars were broken into.

My next trip was a three hour drive, car loaded with props, to Morristown, New Jersey, where I stayed overnight with the coordinator. The performance at the church was fine, and I came home exhausted, realizing I'd been "on" for twenty-four hours, from the moment I'd left home until the moment I returned home.

Ramona continued pushing me to go to the UU General Assembly in East Lansing, Michigan. She sent me what seemed like hundreds of notes and a xeroxed Conference program, with circles around the many workshops I should attend. I found out that these huge Conferences were planned a year in advance. So, at this late date, there was no time-slot available for my presentation. Another major setback was that I couldn't be listed in the printed program, a document of some fifty pages, describing the two hundred or so presentations and workshops, all conflicting since ten or more were scheduled simultaneously. Furthermore, this trip would be expensive with costs of the flight, the rather steep Conference fee, the room at the college, and food for a week. I hardly knew anyone who would be there, though a group of about ten or more were to be there from my church.

"You'll go ad hoc," Ramona wrote blithely. I gathered she considered it more exciting to go ad hoc than like the unprogressives who planned a year in advance. I had qualms. Who would consider barging in on a Conference with a major presentation at the last minute?

Ramona told me exactly what to do. "GA is the biggest COUP — all YOU!!"

As soon as I arrived on the first day, I was to find the program coordinator in the GA office and ask for a time-slot and space. This flexible gentleman turned out to be a Margaret Fuller devotee and he placed me on the crowded schedule. I had to ask him if tables, chairs, spotlight, and slide screen could be rounded up and in the room at the proper time. He connected with the theater department of the University and arranged for some strong arms to put them in place and for someone to run the spotlight and slide projector. These arrangements took a couple of days to confirm, and I anxiously awaited while hundreds of Conference participants rushed off to plenary sessions and other events that drew my curiosity.

Ramona primed me by sending me UU newsletters from around the country with announcements of various events and pictures of people which she'd circled in red with advisory notes: "Crash this party," "Study," "Not interested," "So periphery," "Send $10 and join this group," "Be sure to meet," "The King," "He's scared of women's movement," "He remembers me fondly," "Forty-year-old good friend," "Does not love me," "This group talks and talks and does nothing — Laurie, we are the cutting edge!"

Ramona had told me to have flyers made up in advance — "We do have our 'Old Girls Network'" — with spaces left blank so I could fill in by hand the room number and time. She had sent me lists of names of hundreds of her friends, many of them ministers and their wives, and told me "Don't take time to pee." I was to write a note to each of them on a flyer: "Down Memory Lane — Ramona commands that you come and hear Laurie James — Obey! Important!"

I got writer's cramp a couple of evenings. I folded and thumbtacked my little memorandums to the bulletin board set up in the main hall; what an amusing maze of white paper covered every inch of space! The following day most had disappeared, so I knew they must have been picked up.

Next, as Ramona had commanded, I scurried around and taped flyers on all the walls of the Conference. Of course, standing in line at meals, everywhere I went, I spoke to whomever was around, told them what I was doing, and handed out flyers.

One of my most vital commands was to go to the Women's Room and meet Rosemary Matson. Ramona had long been pestering me: "You and Rosemary will be in love! Rest assured!"

The room had an inviting character of its own, tastefully hung with eye-catching women's posters, filled with hard-to-find books on women of achievement, stacks of free flyers on upcoming events, and chairs that bespoke "peace be with you, relax and enjoy."

Rosemary was busy sorting papers, but she stopped and came forth with heartening energy. Rosemary is the kind you want to hug immediately...looks like the warmest woman on earth...light hair cut short to her round head...blue eyes sparkling with merriment...naturally rosy cheeks as wholesome as a youngster's...a welcoming smile that brightened her entire persona.

Nothing about her belied her radicalism: She and her husband, Howard, had hidden Cesar Chavez and his staff in their Carmel Valley house for ten months during the tumultuous lettuce strike of the United Farm Workers' Union. She was a lay minister licensed by the state of California and he, minister of the First Unitarian Church in San Francisco, had joined Martin Luther King on his marches in Selma, Birmingham and Alabama, and, after retiring, had gone to jail for the United Farm Workers' movement.

She'd changed her name on the roster at Starr King School for Unitarian ministers where she worked, from Mrs. Howard Matson to Rosemary Matson. In those days that was a major achievement. Later, as co-chair of the UUA Continental Women and Religion Committee, she helped to revise hymns into non-gender-specific words and prepared guidelines for non-sexist language in speeches, news releases, and church bulletins.

"At last we're meeting," I said in exhuberation.

I did hug her.

The worry that pierced my mind as I stood in empty lecture hall in costume and makeup, was what was I going to do if the furniture and volunteer tech people failed to show for my performance. Sure enough, five minutes before I was to begin, two men I'd never seen entered with spotlight, screen, table and chairs. So, as the audience was trailing in, I set up my props and directed my technicians on what to do. Total confusion.

The audience crowded closer together; a few opted to stand. Three hundred was an unheard of number for an event not publicized in the printed program.

How was I going to get through my drama properly without a technical rehearsal? There was no turning back; I could only hope. I said the first line, then the second. I was into it. From then on I could only push forward.

The trick is to *be* Margaret Fuller, to enjoy standing there, talking. To visualize what she visualizes, to make her relationships, feelings, thoughts, my own. Taking each sentence, moment-to-moment.

My "crew" made not a faux pas.

I got resounding applause.

The delegates from North Shore Unitarian Society were amazed. They had attended, they told me, because they'd figured very few would come.

People invariably ask me how I memorize so much material. Frankly, it is not inhumanly difficult. You select a section to work on: Today you are working on Margaret Fuller's childhood. You ask yourself, what is the information to cover? An early part is when her father admonishes her. So you read over the first paragraph. What does he say to her? What kind of a man is he? You visualize him. You improvise a bit, parapharsing his words. You put yourself in his shoes, and try to see him as the little girl would. With script in hand, you try out several ways of saying what he says. Then, you go back to the text again. You stumble, because the words are not your ordinary kind, but soon you'll have memorized them — for today. By tomorrow — but tomorrow you'll refresh your memory. Each day is easier. The technique is visualization, association, repetition.

After working on portions, you string the scenes together. What follows what, logically? You open with Margaret Fuller working on the *Dial,* this is followed by a headache, after which she launches into her childhood, next her teaching experience, then her Conversation, etcetera. At night, lying awake in bed, you silently name the progression of the scenes. Often a scene is triggered by an action: One scene ends with a headache, and the next begins with Margaret trying to get rid of it, and progresses from there.

Finally, you have it. Not that you don't keep practicing. You must repeat your words daily, sometimes twice or three times, aware that the words are not the sensory work. Sometimes you just say the lines for the sake of saying them. A few times you say them as fast as you can to see how readily they come to mind. You are quite aware that the language springs out of the emotion and the circumstance, but the exact phrasing must be on the tip of your tongue. In performance the words must be so solidly in your mind that you are freed to imbue your character with all of life's passion.

The Harvard date drew nearer. Ramona sent me bulging envelopes: torn pieces of Boston newspapers and magazines marked with her encouraging and spirited comments, as well as publicity as it appeared. In the *Cambridge Chronicle.* there was a huge front-page picture of me as Margaret Fuller with a small story, and the *Boston Herald-American* featured a picture and story on Bucky. David Kronberg had turned out an attractive, hand-written flyer which, I supposed, was posted all over the city.

I think no one who has not gone through a day of performance can conceive the pressure.

You try to sleep in late. You wake up. You are at once happy, yet full of nerves. You go over some lines. You do not focus. You move through the morning with such tasks as brushing teeth. You answer the phone. You listen to a sales pitch and get rid of the salesman. You become aware that somebody in the family wants something, like food, maybe a Band-Aid. You go to the store. You iron your costume. You pack a prop. Somebody turns on the TV. Rings the doorbell. You consult your script a dozen times. You forgot to pay a bill and if you don't get it in the mail today, you will have to pay a lot of interest. Your long-lost cousin calls you from the

Midwest. You realize that the hem keeps coming out of your costume; you must find a needle and thread. The point on your brown makeup pencil breaks off.

The hours flit by as you deal. You figure the moment you must leave to arrive on time. You schedule your eating. You do not want to eat before the performance because you can't digest and perform at the same time. You can't eat. You try to rest.

The dawn of July 19 was warm and as the day progressed the heat thickened in multifolds so that city movement decreased to a near standstill.

I was to be at the Radcliffe Margaret Fuller reception, in costume, at 4:00 P.M., so I was in the dressing room putting on makeup about 3:00 for a 7:30 P.M. performance.

Ramona and her granddaughter were already in the cement-walled cubicle — you could barely turn around or stand up straight without hitting your head on the ceiling. Ramona suggested I might want to stay overnight in this William Ellery Channing-like cell (it did have a small cot). Channing, the "father" of Unitarianism, had lived in just such a stifling box, when as a youth, he'd meditated and developed his theology. I declined the nostalgic honor.

There was hardly a spot to hang a costume or set up a mirror. Granddaughter was combing grandmother's hair and doing her makeup. Both were giggling like teen-agers. The closeness of the room radiated the Fahrenheit like an oven.

Tripping, costumed, across the Radcliffe Yard — deserted because of the scorcher of a day — I arrived at Schlesinger Library miraculously without my makeup melting — to pass a glass-enclosed Margaret Fuller exhibit of first editions and original letters and to encounter air-conditioned rooms with all sorts of animated people holding glasses of champagne. Ramona, simply stunning, was a combination of pixie and mother goddess in a long, earthy, muslin-type gown. About her neck was a unique and lovely, silver, feminist medallion specially designed and made by the Reverend Randall Gibson, of the Charles Street Meeting House. Her short gray hair highlighted her face like a halo.

I spotted R. Buckminster Fuller. How could one miss him? He was the center of attention, smiling and gracious, surrounded and trailed by the guests. People glanced oddly at me, as if saying Who Are You and Why Are You Here Dressed in This Way with Your Hair Like That. But their focus quickly shifted back to famed Buckminster Fuller.

Soon all hushed while introductions and thank-yous-for-your-hard-work were made by the Schlesinger people, Pat King and Barbara Haber, curator of the archive, and a few other important people I did not recognize. Nice things were said about Margaret Fuller, and someone read aloud the Mayor's Proclamation. Ramona managed a humorous few words and announced the establishment of our Margaret Fuller Research Library or Foundation. (We weren't sure what we wanted to do with it.) She'd commanded me to rough out some primitive flyers and she'd left them around so people could sign up and become members.

It was a gala occasion. Ramona's handsome son, Roland Barth, professor at Harvard School of Education, and her daughter, Vanessa, a computer expert, attended. Bell Gale Chevigny, author of a new biography on Margaret Fuller entitled *The Woman and the Myth,* was there, as well as Sam Ussia, president of the Dante Alighieri Society of Massachusetts, and Francis X. Hayes, president of the Cambridge Community Economic Development Corporation. Then someone mentioned Margaret Fuller's relatives, and I went over and met them: Bucky's wife, Anne Hewlett Fuller; Constance Fuller Threinen, great-grandniece, outreach specialist in Women's Education at the University of Wisconsin; her husband, Bill; their son, Thomas Fuller Threinen; and her step-mother, Ruth Fuller. Also, there was Harvey Fuller, an artist who'd painted facsimiles of two of the portraits of Margaret Fuller and his wife Polly. How I envied them! To be a relative of Margaret Fuller, how fantastic!

Soon I slipped away. I needed to pull myself together. The crowd would be going on to a restaurant down the road where the Dante Alighieri Society dinner would be served.

The temperature did not drop. Longfellow Hall was not air-conditioned. I was sweating — even before going on stage. Thank goodness I had brought along a mini-makeup kit. I kept dabbing my brow with a Kleenex and re-plenishing my makeup base. Hopefully, the sweat under my arms would not soak through to my costume and my skirt would not stick to my legs.

Standing outside the lecture room, waiting to go on, I thought it sounded as though the house was full, lively, and eager. At the opposite end of the hallway I glimpsed Bucky surrounded by David Kronberg and others I did not recognize. Within moments, they exited. There was a hush from the audience and Kronberg was introducing. I paced the floor.

Next came Bucky's muffled voice. I later read that he said: "Although I had heard stories about my great aunt Margaret, I did not meet her until I was already thirty-two, when I was undergoing a reorientation of my life. I was trying hard to play the game humanity was teaching me to play. I saw I was going to be a complete failure in the world I was brought up in, so I experimented on ways to do away with myself." He talked on. I practiced my breathing. I mentally said my opening lines. I said lines in the middle that I frequently stumbled over. I rearranged my silk shawl several times. Finally, there came a lull; I got a signal. I forgot the torrid heat.

When you stand in front of an audience, with the lights pouring on you, you cannot see the people. What you see is a black vastness. You know the audience is there. You can hear breathing or coughing or foot movements, or programs rattling. You try to disregard distractions, to personally relate in character through that black void to the audience.

That first laugh. That's what you wait for. Then you can relax. Strange how you work for months for one moment in time when you will present your drama in which you so deeply believe and then that moment comes. There is a surrealism to it all. You focus on the "moment-to-moment." How fast it goes — much faster than during rehearsal. Before you know it, the first scene is over and you are into the second. You concentrate like you've never concentrated before.

You are aware of yourself as an actress: gestures, voice, breathing, physical movements, did you do this right, did you do that right, not really aware of the audience as you will later learn to become. Then suddenly you're into the last scene, and it seems too soon. It is over. You move off the stage and...applause. You take a bow. A woman is rushing out of the black vastness — you recognize the executive director of The Margaret Fuller Neighborhood House. Into your arms she thrusts a sheaf of soft tissue wrapping a dozen long-stemmed silver roses of the most delicate shade of lavender you've ever seen. Lovely surprise.

For the first time you realize sweat has been running down your back. And that it has been sweltering for the audience, too.

Ramona disappeared. I had seen her only for an instant afterwards. She slipped back to Maine.

David Kronberg called the next morning. Did I want to ride to the airport with Buckminster Fuller and his wife, Anne?

Yes!

In David's old van, taking every bump, we picked them up at a private club where they were staying. More or less the same height, they looked as though they were made for each other. He was eighty-four; she was eighty-three. Bucky, so strong and quick in body and mind, was solicitous of her comfort. Anne smiling, nodding, indicated she was doing fine in the backseat which seemed to be falling apart. The noise from the engine made it difficult to carry on a conversation. Sitting closely, they touched; they held hands all the way to the airport.*

I returned to New York. You live over every moment in your mind, not once or twice, but many times. You walk around the house, your hands floundering. You were a star for a night. Now your audience is on to other interests. The emptiness.

Over the phone, Ramona affirmed, "Harvard publicity is worth thousands." She assured me that everyone connected with Margaret Fuller Day at Harvard considered the event a total success. Her friends said I belonged in academia. "We'll just launch and launch." Her words were food for the soul. But an actor cannot be satisfied without another performance date, to prove to herself she can do even better the next time.

Magnificent articles and pictures came out in *FYI*, the Harvard Graduate School of Education magazine; in *Centennial News*, the Schlesinger Library newsletter; and in the *Harvard Gazette*, where

---

* R. Buckminster Fuller died July 1, 1983. Anne Hewlett Fuller, his wife, was in a Los Angeles hospital in a coma after suffering complications from a stomach operation. Fuller flew from Europe to be with her. Within a week, the doctors told him there was no hope. Bucky collapsed, was rushed to intensive care, and died. Anne died thirty-six hours later, July 3. On the notice Bucky's grandson, Jamie, sent Ramona and me was an excerpt from a poem, "Nearest," which Bucky had written to Anne on July 16, 1967: "Eye to eye we are nearer/But we truly enter each others/ Metaphysical immortal beings/Only through thought/And forever/Only through utterly/Unselfish love/Self is infinitely lonely/Love is infinitely inclusive."

the smiling Bucky, Bell Gale Chevigny and Sam Ussia were shown
with cocktails in hand.

Shortly, I received four letters. The first was hand written on Mrs.
R. Buckminster Fuller's letterhead:

Sunset, Maine
August 1st, '79

Dear Laurie James,

My husband, Bucky Fuller, and I enjoyed our evening with
you, in Cambridge <u>very much</u>. Since then we have been in Maine
as he had to have some corrective surgery at the hospital in
Bangor. He dictated the following to me when I was visiting him
the other day:

"I have been deeply involved in Margaret Fuller's life, not
only disclosed by a host of books I have read about her, but also
in her motivating philosophy. When Margaret is said in the never
authenticated statement to Carlyle - that her philosophy began
with "acceptance of the universe," I could not be more interested.
My own life philosophy centers around synergetics. Synergetics
means behavior of whole systems unpredicted by any of its parts.
I'm concerned with the relatively small family of scientifically
generalized principals which govern all known physical inter-
relationships, intertransforming of our 2,000,000,000 galixied
universe. I've learned that by being master of the generalized
principals, I can readily comprehend the behavior of any special
case applications of any or all of the generalized principals. Tho,
in Margaret's time, physics knew of relatively few of the presently
discovered generalized principals, I feel sure that she was deeply
aware of the cosmic significance.

In Margaret's day, as even today, humans, if educated at all,
were trained to become specialists. Comprehensively of education and growth, concern can only be attained thru synergetics.
The power of her approach to all subjects was not a matter of
specialized knowledge but a matter of her comprehension of the
intercomplimentarily of a vast array of experiences. Dear Laurie,

I was afraid your discourse no matter how superbly monologued, might give the impression of an obnoxioulsy egotistical character.

For all the foregoing reasons, I assure you Laurie, that I was impressed by the confidence of your acting - its many thoughtfully planned stages, with the fact that you are a powerfully courageous and brilliant individual struggling in the pre-dawn of terrestrial accord to woman, of all the freedoms here-to-fore historically staked out for men.

There is much more important data which has come to my attention and which I would like to inform you. I think she would be greater and certainly more lovable were this information incorporated with her life history.

Warmly and faithfully yours,
Buckminster
Dictated to A. Fuller

Another letter arrived from Pat King, director of The Schlesinger Library:

August 9, 1979

Dear Laurie James:

We all very much enjoyed the whole Margaret Fuller Day celebration. In addition to its helping to make Fuller better known, for the Library it was important in putting us in touch with Cambridge organizations with which we had had little or no previous contact. We hope that we will be able to cooperate with them in the future for other women-focussed events.

Clearly your script on Margaret Fuller represents a great deal of research and thought. Many of the passages you have chosen illuminate aspects of her life about which even those of us who had done some reading about her, had been previously unaware. We all learned a great deal from your presentation, and I wish only that the climate had been a more "temperate" one for your dramatization.

We look forward to learning about the progress of the Margaret Fuller Foundation. Do keep in touch.

Sincerely,
Pat King
Director

The third letter was from Inabeth Miller, librarian, the Monroe C. Gutman Library, Graduate School of Education, Harvard University:

August 9, 1979

Dear Laurie:

I want to tell you what a great pleasure and opportunity it was for Gutman Library to participate in Margaret Fuller Day, July 19th in Cambridge. I am most pleased that our contribution was the provision of a facility for your presentation. The day itself was a tribute not only to Margaret, but to all those who are perpetuating her heritage. The participation of Buckminster Fuller and other members of the Fuller family lent an aura of excitement that was contagious. However, I think that the climax of the entire day was your presentation of the early years of Margaret Fuller's life. This woman was an inspiration to all of us today. Through your characterization she emerged as strong, as independent, as a recipient of education and a transmitter of ideas. The electic quality of her learning, the way she exemplified ideas well beyond her time, and the challenge to other women to be brave, daring, thinking individuals is something I will long remember. Your performance was poignant. Your performance was compelling. I thank you for being there and for sharing your talents with us.

With warmest regards,
Inabeth Miller
Librarian

My fourth was a "To Whom It May Concern," dated August 10, 1979:

As the founding chairman of the Cambridge Arts Council, I was pleased to learn that Cambridge celebrated Margaret Fuller Day to commemorate the death of this great American lady who helped to lay the groundwork for feminism in the United States, and am pleased that we helped sponsor Laurie James' performance.

At the recent performance of "Still Beat Noble Hearts" about the American years of Margaret Fuller's life, I had the pleasure of getting acquainted with Laurie James' work. She is the author of this captivating one-woman drama, which she has thoughtfully synthesized from letters and books by and about Margaret Fuller. This "labor of love" for the past ten years captures beautifully the wit and dignity of Margaret Fuller's life as an early feminist and new-ager critic and conversationalist of her time to a fascinated audience in a convincing way. I am looking forward to seeing the European part of Margaret Fuller's life which contains all the ingredients of a Greek drama.

Yours sincerely,
Ronald Lee Fleming

My great adventure isn't complete without these anecdotes which didn't come to my attention until much later:

(1) Backstage, I'd missed seeing Buckminster Fuller's introduction when he'd held up, for the audience to see, the original Thomas Hicks oil painting of Margaret Fuller. The twentieth-century relative, Constance Fuller Threinen, had brought it from Wisconsin, especially for the event. What a disappointment not to have seen it.

(2) Ramona Barth had been the author of the Margaret Fuller Neighborhood House article in the Unitarian bulletin that Jules Goldin had given to me — the one that had inspired me to travel to Cambridge in the first place.

(3) Ramona was the mover behind the dozen long-stemmed,

silver roses presented to me at curtain call. She had asked Helen Stempkowski, executive director of the Margaret Fuller Neighborhood House, to buy and present them.

(4) Before I'd met Ramona, she and a man who'd written a one-woman show on Margaret Fuller had made "the rounds" of the Cambridge/Harvard/Radcliffe community, proposing that <u>he</u> perform the Margaret Fuller role. After I visited the Schlesinger Library, the director, Pat King, had remarked to Ramona, "Well, at least this time you have the right sex!"

So that's how I got to Harvard.

RAMONA X

She called herself a housewife, a polemicist, a mutant.

"I'm a coalitionist. The more fiery feminists rub elbows with Presbyterians the better. I identify with both the crazies and the moderates. I don't want to disown anyone. I want to prove I can do what I want to do without a title or money vis-a-vis people who use both."

I'd write, "I struggle day & night on my book. It is the hardest thing I ever tried. Wish I were brilliant like you but I aint. I go nowhere — sit in silent house in front of typewriter."

She'd write, "World won't crash if your book falls through. I am not brilliant. If I were my genius wd have come out!!!"

I'd respond: "I'm going to become a character like you."

"Use me as a reverse role model. You know all my sins. I'm skidzoid + a brain + a soap addict. Soaps really lull me @ 68 yrs." Everything stopped in the afternoon while she watched "All My Children" and "General Hospital" on TV.

We were called "two crazy ladies" by friends of Fran Hayes, our friend from our big Harvard gala.

"That means you and me," Ramona wrote. "Amen."

When we'd get put down: "We must ignore all these normal put-downs. I do better I think than you but I get <u>zapped</u> continually as do you. <u>Aversion</u> therapy & transcending is best. Brooke Shields & your mama (me) will make waves!"

We were having appointments with bankers, looking at theaters in the John F. Kennedy Library and the Federal Reserve, and pushing to have "Jackie O" attend my performance (which never happened). When we'd make our "re-entry" or "normal transition" back into our homes and laundry, she'd write, "We're in motion....My plot to mix you up with Cambridge claque, if my flotsam-jetsam style (or lack of) hasn't offended your 100% professional expertise.".…."By now you have blue letter trying to structure you <u>Mon</u> & <u>Wed</u> <u>ad</u> <u>hoc</u> & Gwen will bark & Clift [my husband] feel neglected.".…."Sift & sort and we'll launch our revolution like Tom Paine with TRACTS!!" "The sisters will salivate!"

"Obey! Obey Sol, please!" Ramona identified herself with Sol Hurok, one of the greatest impresarios of her generation.

"Get the best brag sheets we have." (She meant past publicity.)

"Groove in and use energies only for what is important."

"File her name for our Boston blitz." "Don't pursue her." "She's my favorite sociologist." "I gave her a Sarah Bernhardt T-shirt." "Have been on phone with her." "Cerebral...Dullesville...." "How can we horn in here....Great bases..." "Maine thots, my milieu — anything can happen." "Buttering up local big wigs." "Three letters and three phone calls." "I'll get a mailing list from Buckminster." "I sent goodie box to kinfolk in Las Vegas and tell them you may want a bed. I got great lecture there, plus a hotel! You gotta see the STRIP." "I'll have to go grab some more Harvard *FYI*s [magazine in which a great article appeared on our Harvard gala] — my son could pick up but I'm properly careful not to overlode the famous!" Her son, Roland, was director of the Harvard Principals' Center.

Once she sent me a picture of a monkey playing, with the caption, "Monkeying around in Boston." On the bottom she wrote, "Yes I deserve it. I've been <u>grounded</u> and <u>dutiful</u> and <u>normal March & April & half of May</u>. Have You? A. R. Q." This meant A Rhetorical Question. We often used initials as shortcuts in our communications.

So while we were "monkeying around in Boston" she sent me "crashing," by myself, a fancy Radcliffe garden party so I could meet the president, Dr. Matina Horner.

Another time, Ramona had me meet her in Boston to "crash" a

press conference at the Arlington Street Church where a Coalition for
the Affirmation of Women in Religion was staging a protest against
the patriarchal structure of the Catholic Church and the invisibility of
women in the Catholic community. I was the only woman sitting at
that press table loaded with microphones who did not have a Divinity
degree. Ramona was Bachelor of Divinity, 1934, University of
Chicago Divinity School, where she'd been the *sole female*, B. S.,
magna cum laude, and Phi Beta Kappa, Tufts, 1932.

Except for me, each woman spoke out, affirming the full right of
women to participate in the religious sphere. "Equal Rites for
Women." "If Women Can Bake the Bread, Women Can Break the
Bread."

Ramona identified with religious radicals Paul Tillich and Mary
Daly. To her the crucial theological issues were male-female vibes
and the phallic imperialism in religion. She concurred with Victor
Carpenter, minister of Artington Street Church, when he said, "Let us
cease being a church where the bland are leading the bland."

She even had me writing the White House. I received a nice letter
back from Sarah Weddington, Special Assistant to the President,
saying, "I don't see where this would tie in with the work of the White
House...but I would like to keep the materials you sent in case a
suitable occasion presents itself."

Ramona urged me to see Shirley MacLaine's one-woman show:
"Is she ever terrific — her comments, livestyle, marriage, the free-est
female I know, sex life +++....'Deserved the Oscar.' — <u>Pushy
unhumble broad!!</u> How I love her!"

Once she addressed a "Laurie Log" to me: "Dear Sol AND Sarah
Bernhardt, How can you be hustler and artist both!! You are a
mutation as I call myself. Laurie, great our mutual reenforcement —
Do continue to be your <u>accepting</u> self. I do head work — plottin n'
plannin' (I fear too much hustling & not enuf contemplative as should
be more befitting to a sexagenarian matron) — I do it 5 A.M. to 9 A.M.
or less than (the usual of 1/2 century). Joe Sr. sleeps late — genius
style — I'm peasant, so this semi-legible aging legibility dependent
on degree of excitement <u>your</u> input produces....I'm so impressed with
<u>your</u> feedback!! — in an era where 'the past gets buried fast' & we
thrust on & on with no (phallic symbol) regurgitation!! I guess our
common housekeeping milieu helps! <u>PICK Up</u> 1st! UGH — the petty

bourgeoise mentality....'The Play' is indeed 'The Thing!'"

Ramona somehow got hold of Buckminster Fuller's speaking engagement schedule — there were nineteen lectures in two months — and wrote on it: "I want yours to look like this!" Indeed, thanks to her, mine finally did look like that. (See my performance schedule in Appendix.)

"Connecting," as Ramona would say, in Boston and Cambridge she led me through her method of making the rounds. Unbeknownst to me, she'd made the rounds by herself days before, early in the morning, generally before office executives arrived, pushing her scribbled snips and packets under closed doors, to be found and somehow deciphered, perking interest, confusion, and attention.

Showing me off was next: She had a *bona fide* actress. Never setting appointments, we whizzed through offices, gaining open doors past secretaries she'd befriended, taking two minutes here, five minutes there, to meet and greet the person in power, to make jokes and to re-iterate ideas and plans which enthused and generally set about a chain of action.

We were finished by noon, so she'd be home in time to watch her soaps. She'd be in bed by 6 or 7 P.M., because she'd be up again at 5 or 6 A.M. Her daily patttern drove me batty; I liked to stay up late and get up late. But "when in Rome" I tried to do what Ramona did.

One time, late in our "tandems" as she called our get-togethers, she convinced the "gutsy" college women at Maine's Bowdoin ("the Harvard of the North") to accept her "pedigreed" papers and boxes she'd collected for about fifty years. The women from the Bowdoin Women's Resource Center Collective came to the "famed" Margaret Fuller Women's History and Research Center and said, "What a treasure lies here!" They received a grant to sort, sort, sort. "So," wrote Ramona, "all the Barth family put downs come to such an ending!"

The Bowdoin women came to her home to tape her words and ask her to plan an event of her choice. Ramona said, I hate saying no can do but now I DO. "I haven't decided what my message is this season...cleaning out pantrys, knitting, or coming on both feet so I'll be exiled??? from Maine...for marital rape." Anyway, she asked her California friend, Laura X, director of National Clearinghouse on Marital and Date Rape, to take the stage for her, but Laura X couldn't make it. So Ramona asked me. To make a long story short, she spent a whole letter telling me every detail, everything I should do, plus I must bring up a Magic Marker, and then she set the date at a time when all the students were off on semester break. "If I can undig Vanessa's [her daughter] barrell of spring clothes and look 69 instead of 73 pushing 80!" she wrote. "I want an E. to E." — Eyeball to Eyeball. The Bowdoin people paid my way, I brought my costume, dressed in it, did makeup, went to the afternoon lecture, and no one showed up. Not a soul. But we did have our E. to E.

Ramona is famous for setting up meetings. One story was that once she convinced a number of top people at the Unitarian Universalist Association to convene; however, she did not attend nor did she set an agenda. So when everyone met they looked blankly at each other, "Why are we here?" And they disbanded. Ramona's perspective is, "Just imagine, all those smart people getting together and they didn't know what to talk about!" That occurred before we'd met. Or B. L. — Before Laurie.

One of Ramona's earliest outrageous acts — B. L. — was to defy the dress code for women at the Ritz Carlton Hotel in Miami. She, Gloria Steinem, and thirty other women wearing pants, were barred from entering the restaurant in which hung a sign saying turtleneck shirts, pantsuits, culottes, and miniskirts were not appropriate.

She loved to send people xeroxes of Grant Wood's famous "American Gothic," a painting of a farmer standing with pitchfork, looking straight ahead, with barn in background and wife by his side, both glum as can be. As she saw it, this said it all about the typical marriage, even her own. She'd ask, "'Tis God's way?"

Ramona caused the "Great Feather Duster Debate" of 1984. The *Maine Coastal Journal* published a parody, a picture of a woman with a mop, and a man with a paint brush. Ramona chastised the editor for not picturing the woman doing something more constructive than holding a feather duster. A series of letters poured in; her picture appeared with the editor, Jeff March, whom she'd talked into posing with a feather duster. The fracas was enjoyed by all readers.

In 1986 there was a tiny item in *The Boston Globe*: "Prince Charles of Britain will not bring Diana, Princess of Wales, with him to Cambridge Sept. 2." Ramona's incensed retort was published: "I doubt the prince 'brings' the princess anywhere without her consent....To refer to the latest star in the royal family as a piece of baggage is bad for whatever loosening-up is possible in the staid, uptight, royal family."

B. L., she made *Time* because, as a pastor's wife, she joined a Vietnam Peace Walk with her three high-school-age sons, zapping Harvard's President Nathan Pusey, who'd complained on TV that his best men had been called to war — "That leaves us here with the lame, the halt, and the female."

On the day before Easter, 1970, she masterminded the picketing of the Park Square Boston Playboy Club. Her group plotted carefully at the Charles Street Meeting House, whose minister, Randall Gibson, with her son-in-law, led a march across the Boston Garden to the Club. She toted a cage containing her granddaughter's pet rabbit and a placard, "Trapped By Our Culture." Other signs they carried read: "Hugh Heffner, why don't you wear a pom-pom on your behind?"; "Down with women as sex-objects"; and "Women are people, not animals." Two or three NOW sisters knocked in a lady-like fashion at the door of their target citadel. "Would the manager like some carrots to give to his bunnies?" The manager would not. "Would he welcome us to sit down for a civilized dialogue?" No, he would not. They dialogued by marching around the building with their picket signs.

She made headlines in the Miami *Herald:* MINISTER'S WIFE RAPS SEX SYMBOLS. In the article, Ramona compared the Playboy Club with the Pentagon: "Both are symbols of what's wrong with our society — women are not chicks, quails or bunnies. Women are not playthings. Men are not playboys."

She and a group stormed the office of a Boston disc jockey, who had referred to women as "chicks." The women let loose live chickens with shouts, "These are chickens. We are women. Do you see the difference?"

Another time Ramona and the sisters picketed the U.S. bride's show in Madison Square Garden — they unleashed one thousand white mice to break it up. They saw these acts as consciousness-raising devices to exorcise demons who stunt, humiliate, and degrade women.

"John Wayne and Brigitte Bardot have got to go," Ramona is quoted as saying. "They're anachronisms, a dying breed. The fragile male ego must be toughened. For every man who feels castrated and put upon and demasculinized and hurt by what women are saying they want, there are 10 who want their wives off their back, emotionally and financially independent."

I must say I was amazed when she — a mother of five and grandmother several times over — said if she had to do it over again she'd be a lesbian. "Because it's so *eeeessy!*" she'd vent, indicating how complex heterosexual relationships were. She was waiting for a new book that Barbara Haber, curator of books, Schlesinger Library, mentioned was to be published showing Margaret Fuller to be a lesbian. (I've never heard of this book being available.)

On Women's Equality Day during the Bicentennial year, 1976, she was chair of a Faneuil Hall Marathon in Boston to which Flo Kennedy and Betty Friedan came to speak for the ERA under John Adams' and Sam Adams' statues — in the "Remember the Ladies" style of Abigail Adams in 1776.

Nineteen seventy-six was the 350th anniversary of Anne Hutchinson's banishment, and Ramona got Governor Michael S. Dukakis to issue a proclamation exonerating her. (Ann Hutchinson was an early American "battered woman" banished from the Massachusetts Bay colony in 1637 for daring to declare her religious views.)

Ramona had her picture taken in front of the statue of Anne Hutchinson, and then mailed off xeroxes of it to countless addresses on one of her ingenius, overkill paste-up collages: paper over paper, crookedly laid out, badly inked, confusing but always amusing. She'd say, "The word is out, my style!! Tom Paine's tracts started American revolution. They were not *objets d'art* brochures!!....AD HOC paste-ins show we LIVE."

She had Governor Michael Dukakis proclaim August 23, 1977, "Nicola Sacco and Bartolomeo Vanzetti Memorial Day" and to declare that stigma and disgrace should be forever removed from their names.

One time — B. L. — she stood outside the Charles Street Meeting House in Boston getting passersby to sign a petition to have February 15th proclaimed Susan B. Anthony Day. "George Washington has been the father of our country for 200 years. It's time we had a mother of our country."

When the Susan B. Anthony $1.00 coins were released by the

United States mint in 1979, she and Barbara Warner (a dance instructor from Bristol, founder of Mid-Coast NOW) hosted a Maine celebration with an open house at the Center for Being Foundation in Boothbay Harbor, Maine. The theme of the day was Anthony's famous line, "Failure is Impossible!"

"ERA," Ramona would say, "is a piece of legislative deception. We, my deah, will highlight the GUT issues." Those issues, she said, were in the bedroom and kitchen. Women getting the vote did not really resolve matters or make people better human beings. She used the "old gals" — "and I'm one of them" — as springboards to call attention to rape, abortion, feminization of poverty, the double whammy for black and ethnic women. "I'm no threat if I fête those now dead. Margaret Fuller is safely in her watery grave."

She pressured governors to proclaim days honoring Florence Nightingale, Clara Barton, Eleanor Roosevelt, Sojourner Truth, even a Maine Women in History Month.

Speaking out in pulpits energized her and she'd have on her agenda such lectures as "Women's Liberation — What's It All About," "Back to the Streets," "Eleanor Roosevelt — Global Humanitarian." She first lectured at the age of twenty-four when, pregnant, she proclaimed, "Woman — Paragon or Parasite." She loved to give Mother's Day talks about God, Motherhood and the American Flag. In these she'd sweetly blast the "sentimental shit" permeating the myths and realities of being a mother.

She boasted that hers were the first women's studies courses in Boston and Cambridge in the second wave of feminism, 1968-1972.

You can find her biographical sketches of nineteenth-century women in the *Journal of Liberal Religion* at Harvard Theological Library. She wrote a wonderful monograph on Edna St. Vincent Millay which received a good review in the Maine Writers and Publishers Alliance newsletter, and she'd written a book, *The Fiery Angel,* about Florence Nightingale, published by the University of Miami Press.

Her peppery articles appeared in the Wiscasset newspaper, about Mercy Otis Warren, Abigail Adams, Sojourner Truth, Molly Molasses, Edna St. Vincent Millay, and of course Margaret Fuller. She had an idea of a popular TV series in which great figures met with modern ones: Cleopatra has a dialogue with twentieth-century TV producer

Norman Lear, and poet Alan Ginsburg converses with Queen Victoria, etcetera.

By 1984 Ramona had lively columns with her byline in Maine's *Lincoln County News* and *Wiscasset Newspaper*, in which she regularly reported on her experiences at the People's Convention, an alternative to the Democratic national convention in San Francisco. She was supporting Jesse Jackson. "For me, the Geraldine Ferraro Phenomenon is tokenism.* An omen of progress, perhaps, but Jesse Jackson is still the winner and the real political phenomenon of the century....NOW did not even invite Jesse to its Miami national convention. Jesse's Rainbow Coalition alone can combat the WASP mentality from sea-to-shining-sea under the Red, White and Blue-and other Rainbow hues."

In a two-year study during Maine's snowed-in winters, B. L., she unearthed cogent quotes denigrating women from all the "bibles" of the world. Accompanying her quotes are plans for a worship service which could occur in pulpit, podium, or street. She entitled it "Exercise in Exorcism," and it included a ceremonial heaving and burning of these texts into a beat-up, smelly, egg-smeared, buggy garbage can. She took this "act" all over the country. "Good theater and good theology," she said.**

In 1976, along with Randall Gibson and the co-sponsorship of the Mayor's Office of Cultural Affairs, she compiled and hung a "Stamped Women" exhibit in the Bostonia Gallery at Boston City Hall. Called "Another Revolution," this was a series of enlarged U.S. postage stamps picturing American women. Gail Bryan photographed the three-cent stamp of Elizabeth Cady Stanton, Carrie C. Catt, and Lucretia Mott, and the other stamps pictured Florence Nightingale, Elizabeth Blackwell, Edna St. Vincent Millay, Eleanor Roosevelt, Abigail Adams, Sojourner Truth, and Frances Perkins.

After our "tandems," as we'd take leave of each other just before she'd whiz off to her free beauty parlor — Ramona had her hair cut by students at a Boston training center — she'd hand me "Laurie

---

*Geraldine Ferraro ran for vice-president of the United States with Mondale as presidential candidate in 1984.

**Ramona's "Exercise in Exorcism" is further detailed in the chapter entitled "More Memorable Moments," and the entire "Exorcism" is included in the Appendix.

files." These were bulging Maine Kitchen packets, extra heavy, oversized, brown grocery bags, (or Copley Square white bags) marked in Magic Marker green, "Grandma's Goodies" or "Lest You Forget." Once I got a big yellow envelope with the red printed message: "Does your Organization NEED MONEY?" She circled this and wrote her answer: "No Just Motivation."

Inside these bags there'd be scribbled notes: "I wanna hear what gives," advice on promotion, "They need us — Gotta get there," "Get four letters out to..." mixed in with news of her family and words of encouragement — "Hope you can be a DIVA like Maria Callas," "The world is yours, if not $$," "Stay monomaniacal on what you think is priority," "Do have tunnel vision in March for your book", her guilt in not "being in love with house" — "I fight black flies, garden, barns," "God, an empty house is like a spa" — ideas (jokes) to get media attention, such as, "Dive into Walden Pond" — diet articles, books to read such as *Married To Tolstoy*, a picture of James McNeill Whistler's famous painting of his mother *(The Artist's Mother)* with the words, "I know I fragment," and "Laurie, please post."

Whistler's portrait has traditionally been revered as a representation of the dignity of motherhood, but Ramona considers it symbolic of the patriarchal "tucking the old woman away in black." It is a profile of a sixtish woman sitting quietly in a chair with her hands folded. She is dressed in a white cap and a floor-length black gown. She is looking ahead at nothing. Posting this picture, I would be making a statement against the stereotype of an old woman who has nothing more to live for.

There were also intimate notes about sparing me "familial, normal crap NUTH new but my FURY to self & his method of relating," which referred to Joe, her husband: "He happily entraps me in Dullesville and my work camp UGH UGH UGH." She sent me a clipping about a research study proving that married couples have nothing to say to each other after eight years and she scribbled her note on it, "I muse, will you & Clift be like us?"

Joe, Ramona's husband, loved his acres and plow — Earth Man, Ramona called him. According to her, when he retired, he bought some three hundred acres in Alna, Maine, without consulting her. A farming community on Sheepscot River settled in 1663, Alna encompasses a 1789 meeting house, an eighteenth-century church with box pews, another church which is the smallest in the world, a one-room schoolhouse with a cupola, a jail, and homes of eighteenth and nineteenth century structure. Currently, the community has a population of 428.

Ramona sent me a local newspaper clipping about how the Barths celebrated the holiday season with sixteen family members "fêting and feasting" at the long, board table constructed from old Head Tide Mill lumber. When I wrote that my dining room table was covered with my book manuscript, she replied, "Love using dining table for important things!! Is Clift pushing your papers off table for food!! as would my mate."

"Joe's just a farm boy from Kansas," Ramona would tell me. They'd met at Chicago Divinity. "All the girls wanted him, but I got him!" On their wedding night they apparently had a knock-out fight which Ramona will not detail, but she shivers when the memory hits. It was her, not his, intention to share a pulpit together.

With his degrees from the University of Chicago and Tufts, he first served Channing Church in Newton, Massachusetts. Then they went to Miami, Florida to help found the First Unitarian Church, which led to his position as senior minister at King's Chapel, Boston, after which he became director of the Department of Ministry, Unitarian Universalist Association.

Ramona claimed she didn't read the King's Chapel prayer book for solace — she read Simone de Beauvoir's *Second Sex.*. She'd quote: "'Why is it a woman feels like a human being only outside her home and family milieu?' Simone has been my 46 yr scream."

She often wrote: "Can I now retire?" "Aint it awful...when we each hit our houses, it gets depressing...our work camps our concentration camps...Ugh...that has been my association for so long I doubt it could ever change. I'm learning to be messier and messier and figure this is the year of Hannah etc." Her son, Ben, had slipped a disk in his back and couldn't walk, so her daughter-in-law, Barbara, had to work; Ramona — in her seventies at this time — took on the job of caring for the two-year-old Hannah during the day. "I can't get detrapped — nor can you when need calls — but she's cute and I love her — 'hooked on Hannah' — Is this masochism or is it not?"

"Ben and Barbara's pipes freeze!! Someone has to go to their very rural road - ice - nonplowed - and stoke fire. I lug huge can of kerosene for heat." "My Xmas structure - Hannah & H-earth So WHAT is new!!" "I SLEEP IN FREEZIN' BEDROOM UPSTAIRS - MAKES FOR <u>VIGAH</u> I GUESS." (One time she froze her feet.)

"I now freeze corn and tomatos and am in kitchen still."

"I demuck....I fight filth....I look like woman on dutch cleanser can."

Often she signed off as Ramona X, her preferred name.

She used whatever postcards she could get gratis, such as the ones from hotels or the Unitarian Universalist Association. The only ones she paid for were those picturing historic women and, whenever she could — which was often — she stamped them with postage picturing women. Then, too, she'd squeeze her message over the white space or the colorful print on Radcliffe or museum brochures that printed the box saying "No Postage Stamp Necessary if Mailed in the U.S." She mailed packets at library rates because, after all, she was the Margaret Fuller Women's History and Research Center. To prove it, she had her bank print her checks with her name and the words "Wiscasset Women's History Research Center."

She addressed envelopes to me with "Dynamic Woman Laurie James" or "Marchessa Laurie James," referring to Margaret Fuller, who became marchessa in Italy through her marriage. Or to my husband: "Clifton James & Rib" (shades of Genesis!). "Clift," she'd write on a torn-off corner of a newspaper, "a presidential election request! Take the little woman to Burning Tree Golf Course - Reagan plays, Washington, D. C., that has sign out NO WOMEN AllOWED!! Please for her press!"

We caucused by "non-committee meets" — meaning we mailed letters back and forth through heatwave and blizzard "which knocked down all power — but not OUR power." "Stay loose." "Various things trigger me." "AD HOC will shake them out of rigor mortes & uptightness." "I feel like Joe Kennedy behind the scenes getting JFK elected." She would have a spasm because she needed fifty-cents worth of manila envelopes and stamps and her "dump of a town" had closed the Post Office. "So I don't chicken and use my age as an excuse to fade out — don't worry, I won't. Don't stop until you drop is a good puritannical adage." "All nitty gritty will be done." "Anything can happen anytime anyplace anywhere to anybody my age." "Anything or nuthing can happen when we meet AU PAIR."

"Im an egalitarian bus rider — YOU be the star!"

Ramona wrote me that she was planning on posing nude for art students at the Maine Art Gallery in Wiscasset. She was to have stripped for four dollars an hour. Later she wrote: "I posed with clothes on or I would have had Asian FLU."

Only I could read her scrawling handwriting, sometimes coded in several colors of ink. "Simpler to be wifie and grannie?? As I muse to self how I can get so integrated. I can't." "I am wearing out. I plotted like Eleanor McGovern 'not to run this year' — the long hot lily summer, but as she said its really simpler to run! (by our mate's side) or for whatever." "We move to rhythm of our great men."

One time I gave her a gift of status stationary with her name printed on it. She laughed and said many of her friends had given her elegant writing paper, but she never used it. Bits and snips was her way of making a statement against hypocracy and pretentiousness.

"Oddsends." "Keeping good vibes nurtured, yes?" "Glad I bugged you and you didn't swat me for _____"

Snips: A newspaper article with words circled: "Her voice is shaky; her face is wrinkled." And her note, "That's us!" Sometimes a Greyhound baggage tag with its band encircling torn bits of papers. Flowers carefully preserved in plastic. Notes clipped together with a wooden clothespin. "I sort and sift and use up another pk of clothes pins," and she'd send along the empty clothespin package. Ashes wrapped in plastic from her wood stove for me and Clift to make the cross on our brows.... "Hope you are grooved in for whatever fulfills YOUR body and psyche." She'd send travel and vacation articles, sometimes about Maine: "I muse if its for you and if you reenter as a Jewish princess with nuth to do." She sent scribbled first drafts of articles she was writing. She'd tear out quotes from newspaper columnists. She snipped off the side of a publicity page from the Boston Museum of Fine Arts and wrote: "I tarried @ Mummy's wing! I guess we are both hooked on our mummy-ism!!!" Often she'd send a note on the back of a cancelled check — this proved she'd spent her "diddlin' dollars" for something.

"Repeat — $$ never been my goal never had none never will have. Motivation not Money — Yours must be money!" "God my blood boils at these poor up-tight institutional churchmice." She never had patience with people or organizations who were always "bleating & moaning." "If you FEEL poor, I guess you are....I do NOT feel poor....I know what can happen nikkles and dimes and lots of motivation I still have." "Dollars are never an excuse." "I won't bleat and moan for $$." "So degrading to be a 'kept' woman - the power of the purse we don't talk of." "Never talk on $$ as my shrink said, 'more painful than phallic talk.'" "Filthy vulgar disgusting money," she'd quote Edna St. Vincent Millay. When I found it impossibe to answer everything she sent, she'd respond, "Here I am - with guilt!"

She sent me Flo Kennedy's brag sheets, maps, walking guides, book reviews on books that caught her eye, horoscope projections, articles on prominent women like Patricia Schroeder, Matina Horner, and Mary Daly, articles about the Transcendentalists, notes and articles about marriage and men/women relationships, theater articles, articles about stars she liked, the most humorous Ellen Goodman columns, articles about disappointed moms, cartoons, a Collegium membership directory with a list of prestigious names from Harvard, the Farmers' Almanac — the 1975 edition carried her insert of Irene Davall's Feminist Party Prayer and the 1981 edition contained her article on Susan B. Anthony and the dreadful catastrophy of the new $1 coin minted in honor of her memory.*

"I go diggin' — lists, lists." she wrote me. "Something will surface."

She'd draft letters I was to write to people I'd never known or heard about. "Hate to have your strength sapped." Sometimes her rough notes were sketchy; I'd have to fix up and fill in.

"Laurie, I know until you run for pres. USA, the hills of N. H. ain't your turf, but since you HIT academia, please hit with my INS...."

When all this overwhelmed and I faded, she suggested we get volunteers or a CETA** worker to do the "shitwork." "Goddamn mechanics of life." "Congrats, Laurie, on sticking to book despite my plethora of papers."

When she felt "in the pink," she'd write on pink paper.

When she felt down, she'd send scraps from newspaper articles:

---

*People refused to accept the Susan B. Anthony coin because it was too easily confused with quarters. It was one of the shortest lived American-dollar coins ever minted.

**Comprehensive Employment and Training Act, 1973, expired 1982.

"Depression sometimes can be relieved by withdrawing from one particularly challenging situation that highlights the problems." Her handwritten note: "I can't withdraw, nor can you."

"Your monster ain't been my monster, but you must finish!" (My book.)

Her "Hausfrau Dirge"*: When, on his retirement money, Joe bought her a thousand-dollar stove, dishwasher, and radio. "How can I beef. Its his $$$$ he earned.... Kills me when I think of what I'd do with that kitty....Oh well I do fine on $215 a month.... " (Her Social Security check.) She'd send a "S. S.", which meant Sneak Sheet, an extra sheet of paper which was for my eyes only and I was not to leave it lying around in my house for anyone to read. "Destroy."

"We gotta accept what IS without blowing brains out....God I should mellow and mature, but I'll try to convince self I am. Margaret Fuller was an amoeba trying to adjust and never did so why should we. Just IN STRUGGLE as sister salut."

Her dirge about living at 64 Beacon Street when her husband was minister at King's Chapel: "Twenty-eight rooms +++ tons of kids + friction + harrassment + absent mate — absent even when body was there."

By the time she reached seventy years of age, she wrote an article about herself, published in *Kairos*, a Unitarian Universalist quarterly:

> My father, in a familiar familial pattern, disappointed when a hoped-for son to be named Raymond turned out to be Ramona instead, inundated me early with all the pioneer feminists. He would make a minister of me. And he did, up to a point (B.D. Meadville, 1934) when, in another familiar familial pattern, I married one instead.
>
> Women who aspire to the ministry are seen as castrating bitches and witches for trying to invade the most impenetrable bastion of phallic imperialism — the ministry. The impact of Freudian brain-washing in my own "case history" is obvious. I didn't make it in the ministry. My husband did. And now, you say, "penis envy" surfaces? I think not. Pencil and paper envy, no doubt. Radcliffe president Matina Horner has told the story of my life in her thesis of the double bind of success for women: guilt and anxiety during my sporadic sorties out-of-the-nest,

---

*The word "dirge" was courtesy of Edna St. Vincent Millay who wrote a poem with that title.

compulsive motherhood, a page from Helene Deutsch's text, finally, settling for the Substitute-Success Syndrome (the Substitute-Self Syndrome).

"The problem of life is ambiguity." This line, from the gospel according to Paul Tillich, I have chanted to myself for the last four decades to make my painful ambiguities less painful to mate, children and self. Obviously some semblance of integration has held a four-decade marriage and family and self together. Mine must have been a mild case of Anne Morrow Lindbergh's famed description of "Torn-to-Pieceshood."

With the emergence of a "sexagenarian selfhood" unlike that of any of my other decades, yet still with guilt, anxiety, and ambiguity, I now dare to speak out and up. What is distinctive about women in ministry? To me what is distinctive and inspiring about women in the UU ministry is the "new breed" who are combining fiery feminism with their will to minister — not only to women, but to men. This phenomenon is rare but there.

Her father, Roland Sawyer, had yelled at her, practically disowned her, when she'd announced she was getting married — to a *minister* — defying his grand plans for her. He'd made it plain that a minister's wife was a role to be avoided. He himself was a Congregational minister in Ware, Massachusetts, and had made a name for himself as a member of the Massachusetts Legislature for twenty-eight years.

In the late 1980s, Ramona couldn't believe it when King's Chapel allowed a woman to preach on Sunday. "Jesus, a SHE and a MS in this sacred symbol of phallic imperialism." Every once in a while she'd send me pictures of a Mexican statue of a young boy urinating, with the note: "Phallic Imperialism - We need to go to its biological and historical roots."

As time passed, I would receive manicky letters. "The 46th year of NON-retirement overkill work & clutter & I muse as I do each June - will I crack up?" "I figure I should spend all $$$ getting help. Why should Joe when he has an olewoman to do shitwork?" "Heave my badmouthing snips."

I would respond as best I could that she gotta think of herself as #1, etcetera. She'd respond, "Thanx for motherly concerns. Dotters shouldn't have to mother Mothers!"

I kept saying, "Ramona, buy yourself some clothes," because she was always asking me to send or bring up my old clothes. I thought it was an insult to pass along my hand-me-downs. She was very different in figure from me, and my clothes didn't really look that great on her. But she'd laugh and continue bugging. She admired my stylish prairie-denim dress so much that she begged for it and wore it everywhere. Once, when I made the trip to Alna, she took me up to a huge attic room, floor-to-ceiling full of all sorts of used clothing heaped one on top of another. As family and friends needed clothing, she'd go up and sort, sort, sort, and hand out the needed items. On another "bucolic frolic" — as she called my visits — she appeared in a worn-out denim pantsuit that was literally covered with colorful handmade patches and holes and fraying strings. She was making her statement.

Lily Day came once a year. "I wade thru barns to clean up for lily day for 1000 and 3 sets of guests feedin & nurturing! etc. <u>ad nauseum."</u>

Joe had been developing new varieties of the daylily, *hemerocallis,* for over thirty years. His annual July day drew record crowds to visit his stunning acre full of red and yellow clusters, a visual treat that began at the long, winding, dirt driveway leading to their Alna home. Joe gave the lilies free to the public in exchange for a contribution to his various causes.

"I 'receive' irrelevant people. I help hustle!! 3 sets of my media folk come Sat to take photos of 5 granddotters by the lilies named for them!!! Oh to have NO kitchen. Signed Loving wife and community worker."

When I wrote of my new interest in planting and picking flowers, she responded she'd rather be picketing the Playboy Club.

"God - my clergy wife being grateful & beholden syndrone never dies."

"This card is to say 3 sets of Joe's clerics have been here and I cook cabbage and all the ethnic shit to show off...and shine and scintillate per lifetime. Amen JERK JERK JERK...'tis the pattern so what's new."

After forty-seven years in the kitchen her motto was that life's shitwork should be shared.

"My sink, my shrine."

She claimed to be "generationally brainwashed...No division of labor was clearer, as I stuck to *kinder, kuchen,* and *kirche,* and my man-of-God took to the fields or the flock."

She hated being a "kept woman," and in her youth she "struggled not to be," and thought "any female who failed to engage in that struggle was a leech. I prayed, 'Please, God, don't let me be normal.' That was adolescent rebellion, but in old age, along with Elizabeth Cady Stanton, 'I will never, never become conservative.'"*

She and her husband "rarely referred to the power battles between us as such; the normal king of the roost crowed unchallenged." In the earlier days at NOW meetings she threw darts at Freud's photo.

"I would not use my Phi Beta Kappa key to pin the diapers of my babies, did you?" she asked me.

She had elaborate plans for the Margaret Fuller Foundation, which was to be a loosely structured commemorative society something like Friends of the Alcotts or the Willa Cather Pioneer Memorial and Education Foundation or the Thoreau Society. I hoped it would be without walls. Her idea included raising money, ladies lunches, postcards, T-shirts or She-Shirts, as she called them. She had bundles of She-Shirts picturing Lucy Stone, Harriet Tubman, Abigail Adams, Phillis Wheatley, Annie Oakley, Molly Molasses, Edna St. Vincent Millay, Kathe Kollwitz, Amelia Earhart, Sarah Bernhardt, Nefertiti, Victoria Woodhull, and Margaret Fuller.

"Tell Clift I'm sad we can't EXPOSE him (not genitals) but chest with a M. F. T-shirt!!" (M. F. for Margaret Fuller.) We made up lists of charter members and boards of directors. We made up letterhead with Margaret Fuller's picture on it. She found Bambi A. Jones, a Maine lawyer, to incorporate.

As a surefire consciousness-raiser, she wanted the Foundation to pressure Harvard Divinity to apologize to Margaret Fuller and to present her with an posthumous degree, and plotted on several occasions to bring this about.**

---

*Quotes from Elizabeth Cady Stanton.

**She sent me a newspaper clipping about Harvard's president, Derek Bok, who had apologized and paid ten dollars in damages to someone named Oliver Brown because his ancester had written a book that had been burned in Harvard Yard by an order from Harvard president, Increase Mather. The book burned was entitled *More Wonders of the Invisible World,* by Robert Calef, a 17th century cloth merchant in Cambridge. It was an attack on witchcraft writings and Cotton Mather, a colonial clergyman and writer.

She rented the unfinished second-story space over Povich's Men's Store on Main Street in Wiscasset, a few miles from her 1799 farmhouse, and named it the Margaret Fuller Women's History and Research Center. There she piled boxes and boxes of her fifty-eight years of snips. "I heaved 2 tons!" As she attempted to declutter, she'd sing Edna St. Vincent Millay's line of poetry: "I will put chaos into 12 lines & keep him there."

"Anyone wd be crazy to go into bizness with me but I think Id make rent back the season & storage cell too $150. I'll hire my great hi school gal @ $2.50 to wo-MAN it 6 mos 3-5 days a week."

She persuaded Anzie Andrews to open her home for a morning coffee to benefit Ramona's "baby."

She put out press releases stating she gave Margaret Fuller brown-bag lunch "Conversations" and lecture-discussions about Judy Chicago's *The Dinner Party*. "As Maine goes, so goes the nation," she'd write on the back of a paper placemat from a Maine restaurant. "From Bangor to Berkeley/From Maine to Miami."

The notice came: "These items will have to be removed within forty-eight hours," signed by the Wiscasset Fire Chief who saw the Center as a hazard because it contained nothing but "garbage." Not without nervous trepedation did she stay one step ahead of the local authorities.

"Consider me a facilitator deah & implementer - whatever grabs. - Skim & waste no energies - replying only to what grabs."

One of her dreams — "we persevere" — was to get Margaret Fuller on a postage stamp and she sent me tons of material on how this was to be done. It never materialized, though she was able to tour her stamped-woman exhibition for display in U.S. post offices in Damarascotta and other places.

We talked about holding Margaret Fuller gravesite ceremonies at Mt. Auburn cemetery in Cambridge where Fuller has a commerative marker to make the statement that "all women are buried in history." Another plan was to take a Literary Tour to Italy. "To keep us in our upbeat momentum and not badmouth our lives!! & droop. We'll make waves!"

"It will all have an accumulative effect...."

"I learned a lot observing my mate — we must caucus and politic...to get what WE want."

"My prediction that the heavies will help the sisters in struggle."

"My Karl Marx theory — to run a revolution, confuse!"

"Put the past to bed...We can THRUST to use penis envy Freudian & YOU must thrust."

"On with my MOP!!!"

"I'll hug phone."

DRESSING ROOMS
I HAVE KNOWN

Nobody knows the dressing rooms I have known.

Maybe you don't think about dressing rooms.

Dressing rooms are half the battle. They do more than provide environments to make the body beautiful. They offer mental support...the self-confidence and courage it takes to face five hundred pairs of eyes.

Maybe you haven't been in one. But you've probably seen Joan Crawford or Bette Davis or Barbara Streisand or other stars playing parts where they put on makeup at mirrored vanities loaded with perfumes, powders and paints. Walls are covered with photos and feathery things. Maids in the background are hanging up fancy dresses and answering the door to handsome men bringing gifts of flowers or jewelry. Actresses slither behind elaborate screens while other characters — immaculately groomed producers, directors, actors, or husbands — wait patiently in overstuffed chairs.

Stars in hit shows do indeed have elaborate dressing rooms, one/ two room apartments with essentials — bars, saunas, showers, sofas, etcetera.

Broadway stars tend to be awarded with less luxurious trappings than those in Hollywood or on TV, but they are still honored with creature comforts. Supporting actors are endowed with less space but they can boast the basics in which to greet visitors graciously. Extras and walk-ons generally share accomodations but they're decent enough with adequate, safe long-term storage for vitals, such as costumes and makeup.

But bathrooms so small you hang your costume outside the door which you keep open to achieve a decent level of oxygen?

Or bathrooms so truly public that while you're pulling a silk nineteenth-century gown over your head, women ask, "So you're the performer tonight?" "Don't mind me, but where did you study?" "Is this the only play you've done?" "My niece was an actress but the going was too hard, don't you find that so?"

Then, dark areas behind curtains, without hooks, furniture, water, or mirrors, where doing makeup and hair becomes an incredible challenge.

Dusty classrooms with walls of windows without shades — you keep the faith that no one passes by.

Or how about meeting rooms with sofas (sans water and mirrors) up stairs and down long hallways so when you come out you don't know which way to go to be where you must be in one minute.

Storage rooms piled with boxes.

Minister's chambers piled with books and papers.

Library rooms that serve as offices during the day.

Kitchens.

Dirty niches other actors use in other hours in other plays.

Of course, make-shifts are preferable to no dressing room at all. Which happens even to this day. I "buckle on my armor" at home or in someone else's home or in motels or hotels, and drive myself, in costume, to the performance. This includes getting out of the car and running to the stage area through rain, sleet or snow. On-lookers exclaim to each other, "Look, there goes the actress — just look at her hairdo!"

At the Quaigh Theater Dramathon, an Off-Broadway house in New York, we were forewarned there was no prop room, no waiting room, and no dressing room. During another person's performance I had to scoot along the back row *behind the audience* carrying a suitcase full of props *in makeup and costume!*

It is unnerving, to say the least, to experience, just as you are bracing to go on stage, the public seeing you in various postures of grooming and to be proffered questions such as "What made you take up this kind of work?"

One time I shared a large church room where a magnificent new organ was temporarily stored. I was in my bra when the door suddenly opened and in walked the minister and three male visitors all impeccably clothed in black suits and ties.

Since I'm a solo performer, I'm usually the only one in a dressing room. Things changed when I entered the Thirteenth Street Theater in New York* where one show went on after another in rapid hourly succession. There you quickly got rid of inhibitions. The one and only dressing room was the size people from suburbia would consider appropriate for a small child's bedroom, and it served a maximum of fourteen actors. Rather quickly I learned the skill of whizzing bottom layers of clothing off and on before top layers. The younger, more curvaceous actresses felt no qualms about stripping to their panties and bras with male actors a few feet away and, likewise, vice versa. With each new cast there would be a few jokes, after which no one thought much about it. Theater is a business and you do what you have to do to prepare. For the most part there was a spirit of friendly cooperation in that tiny room.

The Thirteenth Street Theater dressing room was a carriage house in the nineteenth century. Filthy windows along the far wall are covered by long, black, raggedy, dusty curtains because, as a sign says, "ROOM MUST BE KEPT DARK IF A SHOW IS IN PROGRESS."

Where do you think the furniture and props for the five or six repertory shows have to be stored? In this dressing room — except the bulky flats for the children's shows are kept in the deep dark depths of the basement below. Two or three actors lift up the old carpet that you have been walking on, pull up a large trap door and carry the flats down a ladder to a cement-walled cellar, packed with all manner of interesting things.

Still, no matter how furniture is stacked in this dressing room, there has to be enough space so the actors can get to the makeup counters, the costume rack, and the two stage entrances. No one is

---

*The unusual Thirteenth Street Theater is described in detail in the chapter entitled "Gambling Off-Off Broadway."

allowed to hang clothes on the pipes which stretch out below the low
ceiling, though sometimes I've seen costumes on them temporarily.
In one area a canvas sling droops between the ceiling pipes and a few
boards jetty down from the ceiling on which you can place some odd-
shaped and over-sized props, like swords. There are small lockers
in which to store makeup. The clothes rack was not high enough for
my long costume so I always climbed up on an unstable box to reach
a hook in the wall on which to wedge my extra-long garment bag
which also sequestered my high-button boots and white stockings.

The makeup counters consist of rough boards fixed to the wall
which run across two sides of the room. You sit on uneven wooden
benches. Above the long cracked mirror is a high shelf on which can
be stored, in cardboard boxes, the small props for each show. The
part of the mirror you use you have to clean before each performance
in order to see into it. It is surrounded by bare light bulbs, quite
atmospheric. Of course, you have to "TURN OFF LIGHTS IF SHOW
IS IN PROGRESS." One bulb has a blue gel over it, so you can "TURN
ON IF SHOW IS IN PROGRESS"; then you can avoid knocking into
bulky items.

I grew accustomed to disorganized cubbyholes and corners. In
fact, dingy closets were my friendly pavlovian signal that I was to be
rewarded with an audience.

So I find myself at City Hall Theater in Hong Kong in 1983. As
I approach the huge building, there are wonderful posters of me as
Margaret Fuller everywhere, outside the theater and in the lobby, half
in English, half in Chinese. I am thrilled.

I am met by a smiling Chinese woman from the Hong Kong Urban
Council Cultural Presentations, who leads me into a back office
where another smiling Chinese woman welcomes me warmly. Do
I want to see the theater?

Yes!

I am led into a vast, dimly-lit space with no furniture. I peer into
a black void where a fourth wall would be, grasping that there must
be about two thousand seats out there. I am standing in the middle
of a stage larger than most Broadway houses. Then, before I can ask
myself how I'm to put on an intimate show in so immense an area,
(not to mention how I'm to command an audience to fill all those

empty seats), there steps around me ten eager and ready-to-do-anything Chinese men who, I am told, are technicians. Only one can speak English.

When I ask in English for a table, a command is given in Chinese and the table comes. Everyone jumps.

Finally I ask where is the dressing room.

With enthusiastic aplomb the stage manager leads me behind the curtains and down a wide, clean, well-lighted corridor and opens a door. As if a lightning bolt has hit me — I suppose that is how to describe my instantaneous feelings. Goose bumps break out. I suck in my breath. For the question is, at which makeup table will I sit? In front of me are about six long tables, each with ten individual surfaces with ample mirrors surrounded with dozens of bulbs — enough for a cast of sixty persons!

There are ten showers!

Twenty stall toilets!

Everything clean as a whistle!

Light as a solarium!

Latitude commodious for walking around!

Overwhelmed, I almost feel lost.

Consumed, small.

What decisions I would be forced to make, like which toilet to use.

It had taken over a year to get there. I had written to almost every American ambassador's office throughout the world. With about fifteen responses, I contacted the theaters and presenting organizations on their lists. One response. The Hong Kong Urban Council was celebrating their centenary and we began to negotiate. Each letter seemed to take a couple of months for an answer. My performance date was set a year in advance, two performances on one day, and I would receive a flat fee of about $800 (which would just cover my airfare) and the administrators at City Theater would try to arrange another date at another venue. They did: Scheduled was Hong Kong Baptist College on the Kowloon side, across Victoria Harbor. Furthermore, the administrators put me in touch with an English professor at a university who agreed to provide me with a room in her apartment if I would lecture for her NOW group.

The publicity people did their work. I was in newspaper listings, had my picture and a blurb on the front page of a section in *City News* and in the major daily, *South China Morning Post.* Reading the listings, I saw that I was following on stage in the footsteps of the internationally renowned mime, Marcel Marceau. What an hour in my life!

Through the pit of darkness, I could see legs and feet. The two thousand-seat City Theater was filled with, maybe, five hundred people. Not bad, considering not a soul in Hong Kong knew me. At least the audience was in front and middle, so I thought I would feel their vibes.

But how to make this infinite universe my own! I had closed off the back of the stage with a curtain and extended the reach of my furniture so I would use the width with sweeping walks. With the experienced technicians I had set up every lighting effect I could desire, but since my script was in English, how could I feel confident the buttons would be pressed on cue. There had never been time to "feel" the spots, to experience the tactile sense of the furniture, to pace my larger movements. As I stepped on stage, I could not see one technician.

Well, I would try my best.

I plunged forward.

The people out front seemed like ice. I could not get them to laugh or make a sound. I knew the words backwards and forwards, but my mind was drawing blanks. I stuttered a couple of times, not like me. The audience seemed uninvolved as I continued on. Again I stuttered. I slowed my pronunciation. I was just repeating lines. I was not summoning my Margaret Fuller.

"Dry" moments inevitably happen. What actors are supposed to do is stop, breathe as deeply as possible without allowing the audience to notice, then relax by consciously and gradually dropping the tension in your neck, shoulders, arms, fingers and any other place of which you are aware. How to relax is a major technique actors spend hours learning and perfecting. Actors who are tense — and who isn't when you appear in front of others — block the imagination and five senses, the tools of our trade. Those who relax open sensory avenues, even to new heights. The trick is to do it while staying in character and continuing the dialogue so the audience doesn't know you are doing it.

Relaxation did help. I seemed to get back on track, at least my thoughts started flowing, though the audience remained quiet and, I thought, untouched.

I took my bow, walked off the stage amidst light applause. Suddenly I heard my name called urgently.

I turned around, looking beyond the black curtain into the auditorium where the lights were now up. To my amazement, in front of the orchestra, stood Ramona "Sol" Barth and a man I'd never seen before (her "travel package" tour guide). Ramona was holding high a bottle of champagne and making some kind of announcement to the audience who seemed enchanted by her remarks.

"Laurie!" she beckoned to me. "Come on out here!"

She continued her speech and presented me with the bottle of champagne. Then she walked down center aisle and out the door. That's the last I saw of her in Hong Kong.

The next day a full-page review by Deborah Singerman came out in the *Hong Kong TV and Entertainment Times*. This was the first professional review I'd ever received! Some excerpts:

"It takes brave people indeed to dedicate their lives to propagating that of another. American actress Laurie James is one such person....80 minutes of keen Fuller wit and poignant Fuller insights....Laurie James' dramatic portrait requires extreme concentration from her audience. The spoken word is barely enhanced by any theatrical props. James, in a demure dress and rather stern bun, rarely moves. Two tables and various household items are the only visual objects....James said in an earlier interview that far from being lonely on the stage, she likes to develop a rapport with the audience. Unfortunately, for someone used to loudly appreciative student audiences in the United States, the stunned silence that greeted most of her evening performance here must have made her wonder why she bothered to travel half-way round the world. She definitely appeared to be affected by the reception her show received; often her mind seemed to wander unaccountably and she stumbled over several lines.

"Yet, in a way, the small but diverse audience paid her one of its finest compliments — we all stayed put. It is well known that one of the few uninhibited pastimes of local audiences is their preference for showing disapproval with their feet. Not only did no one walk out, but the more readily understandable sections confirmed that we were all with James, if somewhat quietly....

"Much as the Urban Council is to be praised for bringing *Noble Hearts* to Hong Kong, its decision to stage it in City Hall Theater is questionable. When Frank Barrie brought out his one-man show on the 19th-century British actor, Macready, last July, he filled the small Recital Hall. If an actor acting an actor can be given a sensible-sized venue, why can't an actress acting a writer be treated likewise?"

The reviewer had been insightful. She'd been sensitive to my problems and feelings. She'd been responsive to the audience's reaction. It was clear that she appreciated and was empathetic to the work. Her review was honest, constructive, and actually highly complimentary. I'd challenged audiences to *listen*, to *think* — as Margaret Fuller would want people to do. If so, I was satisfied.

I stayed in Hong Kong a couple of nights to fulfill my obligations to Hong Kong Baptist College and to lecture for my British hostess's NOW group. The lecture audience was to be made up of professors from Australia and England; I figured the questions would be complex. Publicity had gone out; there were to be up to fifty people.

Frankly, I was totally unprepared. I had constantly postponed working on it. I had never lectured before and the thought of it rather threw me. I kept trying to jot some ideas down on paper but they never jelled. Perhaps I could turn the session into question-and-answer — if only I were better at clever articulate answers.

So on the morning of the big day I hoped for a miracle to take place in my mind. Instead, the miracle occured out-of-doors. In late afternoon the heavens opened. Rain poured down. Thunder cracked; lightning broke. Wind twisted through narrow streets. Radio announcers declared a hurricane. Telephone calls were desperately made. Stores and offices closed, cars cleared off roads, people scurried to their homes. Program after program was cancelled, including my lecture. Two NOW women made it over to my hostess's apartment. We decided to make our way to a nearby bar and talk about Margaret Fuller.

The hurricane subsided after rupturing daily routines, capsizing boats, and turning over trees and earth. But it saved me from a mortifying predicament.

Assuredly, in Mexico in 1980-81, I had dressing rooms. However, I don't remember them, which signifies they had to be of the type you block out of your mind. But I did have a couple of amusing experiences.

Ramona, who kept admonishing me that I needed to "'Seize the Moment - Seize the Hour!' as Chairman Mao would say, without which NUTH will happen," had everything to do with getting me to Mexico. Her best friend, Alexa de Payan, who was writing a biography of Flora Tristan, taught in one of the universities there, and she served as our networking contact. The story Ramona told me was that she, Alexa, and another close friend, Kaye MacKinnon,* had been in Paris together in their youth. As they started to run out of money, they were offered jobs — as nudie dancers. Just as Ramona was about to embark on this new career — outrageous for a daughter of a minister — she was rescued by a shining knight. Joe Barth saved her the awful fate by offering her marriage!

In Mexico City Mr. Felipe Garcia Beraza is a most welcoming English-speaking director of cultural activities at the Instituto Mexicano Norteamericano de Relaciones Culturales. He is a warm devotee of all things dramatic — colorful posters of theatrically posed stars cover his office.

With gusto he leads me into the spotless presentation room. We set up the slides. No, he will not run them — his facial expression conveys that dignified administrators do not operate machines. Such tasks belong to the lowly technician. When he enthusiastically introduces him to me, it is clear this smiling man speaks Spanish only. Thus, during my performance, Mr. Bereza holds my script and points his finger to "cue" the Mexican technician. This results in every slide reaching the screen about *five seconds late.* It wasn't funny; it was nerve racking since the sense of the drama depended upon the lines being said in exact timing with the presentation of the slides. But, looking back, I have to laugh.

The next year I was asked to tour the other institutes in Monterey and Guadalajara. In the latter city I was in for the greatest challenge

---

*Kaye MacKinnon de Pacheco became founder and director of the Ballet Peruano in Lima, Peru, also known as the National Institute of Ballet. In Paris she was studying under Olga Preobazhenskaya, former *prima ballerina assoluta* of the Russian Imperial Ballet. Ms. MacKinnon danced and choreographed professionally and also founded her own school of ballet as well as the Ballet Peruano.

of my life.

The marvellous purpose of English-speaking programs is to provide Mexicans with opportunties to hear and practice our language. Of course, my drama consists of English words and sentences that I am sure would be considered advanced by persons speaking another tongue. In Mexico City I was tied in with Americans who lived in and near the city, and I'd been interviewed by top bilingual journalists so my picture and story dominated two front-page articles in both English and Spanish in *Excelsior* and *El Norte* and there were articles and pictures in *The News* and *El Sol de Mexico*. So we pulled an appropriate audience.

But in Guadalajara, where I learned the population is about 100% Mexican, I seemed to have no press.   Nevertheless, the earthy activities director knew how to reach the ordinary guy and there was a sizable audience. From backstage, I could hear him orate a fabulous introduction.   What he was saying, I did not know, for he was speaking in Spanish, but I did hear "Laurie James" so I knew he was talking about me. His vigorous words excited the audience to a noisy pitch; in fact, the longer he talked, the more boisterous they became. I even began to wonder if he was setting up the audience for a stripper because when he left the stage, the audience was clapping, *stomping their feet*, and *whistling* .

I came on to a hundred happy faces. The poor lighting enabled me to see every person in the audience. I readily launched into Margaret Fuller's words. Within five minutes, five people got up and walked out. *Never mind, Margaret Fuller is not everyone's cup of tea.* Within ten minutes, three more persons got up and walked out. Within fifteen minutes, fifteen persons disappeared. Within twenty minutes, a third of the audience was gone, and within thirty minutes, half the auditorium had emptied. By the time I finished, about three people out of a hundred remained.

Your heart sinks when you watch people exit. You try to rev energy and make your material more interesting. But no way can you turn what you do into burlesque or whatever it is they want. You walk off the stage numb.

They caught me backstage — the three who had stayed to the end. Very good, they said, and the reason so many left was that they were just beginning to learn English and my presentation was completely beyond them. Hearing this, I felt better, but could any-body encounter a worse experience?

In New York I had another dressing room no one has ever had, one I will never forget.

Travelling into New York City can be a brutalizing experience, as those who drive the Long Island Expressway know. Every Sunday afternoon I allowed myself a two-hour leeway to fend my way to the Thirteenth Street Theater, even though I made the expected one-hour trip when traffic was anticipated to be comparatively light. *Just in case,* I always said — *I'd rather be early than late.* Early, I could have a cup of coffee before makeup and performance. My routine was one to two hours commute and one hour to make up and set up.

Well, one Sunday I used up my entire first hour approaching the 59th Street bridge which would take me into the city. *Thank heavens I always allow extra time!* My car and I sat rigid in the most horrendous gridlock I've ever experienced.

The time ticked away.

I did not move.

I could not move.

None of the cars around me moved.

As horns honked and furious drivers stuck their heads out of windows and yelled, I began to realize my makeup hour was coming to a close. I was going to be lucky to make it to the theater in time for curtain. Inching along erratically.

Since I'd had a college performance during the week, my makeup kit was in the trunk of the car rather than at the theater. At the next logjam, I opened my door, walked around to the trunk, and pulled out my kit. Back in the driver's seat, I pinned up my hair and started smoothing the base on face and neck. The problem was having only the tiny rearview mirror. At every standstill, I did another eye or cheek until I finished. I paid no attention to the people in other cars, who were looking at me as though I were some sort of crazy. What a challenge to drive and arrange my elaborate hairdo. Luckily there was a lot of halting on that bridge.

I arrived at the theater about five minutes before curtain time. The stage manager held the waiting audience in the lobby. Somebody helped me set up the stage. I literally jumped into my costume.

Curtain was about eight minutes late.
After all, the show must go on.

There are so many moments and memories. It is impossible to write about all of them, but it is impossible not to write about some of them.

MORE MEMORABLE MOMENTS

Ralph Waldo Emerson often wrote that if you throw a rock in a river it will radiate outward in influential circles.*

That's what I hoped I was doing.

No sooner did I finish one platform, I wanted to be on another.

It was dynamite when people told me my "mission" was first-rate and I should carry on.

But complimentary remarks and splendid audience reaction never satisfied.

Always another performance would be better.

The more I did Margaret Fuller, the more perfect control and results I obtained.

Finally, I could make an audience laugh, then listen so intently you could hear a pin drop.

All was a learning experience.

---

*"Throw a stone into the stream, and the circles that propagate themselves are the beautiful type of all influence." — from *Nature*. "The life of man is a self-evolving circle, which, from a ring imperceptibly small, rushes on all sides outward to new and larger circles, and that without end." — from *Circles* by Ralph Waldo Emerson.

Memorable moments:

Cutting the Cake at Margaret Fuller's 169th Birthday Party (May 23, 1979)

Ramona and I met with three or four others at the Margaret Fuller Neighborhood House and cut into a huge sheet cake with a hundred candles — enough for about fifty people.

Where was everyone?

Hadn't invitations been sent?

Didn't anybody *care*?

This was a lesson in the necessity of promotion. The great work lay before us.

The Lincoln Center Blast (December 29, 1979)

I knew that performing "next door" to the world-famed Vivian Beaumont Theater at Lincoln Center in New York was tantamount to Nick Carraway's viewing of his millionaire neighbor's mansion in *The Great Gatsby* — it was merely a partial taste of something much more elegant and lavish than what you could ever hope to be a part of.

Nevertheless, when I signed for a date at the Bruno Walter Auditorium in the Lincoln Center Library & Museum of Performing Arts — a year in advance — I easily conjured the fantasy that being "under the umbrella" of one of the world's greatest stages would bring about a major turning point in my career.

As the date approached I reminded myself that the Lincoln Center/Bruno Walter people gave you two things, stage and printed program. That's it.

My advice to solo performers who must turn producer and promoter: KNOW YOUR LINES. Because once you start producing and promoting you will have no time to be doing anything but producing and promoting:

Go to City Hall. Request Mayor Koch to proclaim Margaret Fuller Day.

Arrange for technical crew: Naomi Kaapcke of Wantagh Community Arts Program to run lights. Peg Spies to run slides. No one minded not being paid; no admission could be charged. All advocated survival of the arts.

Put together a panel, for a Margaret Fuller ceremony. UUA

Moderator Sandra Mitchell Caron to introduce. Dr. Marcella Maxwell, Chairperson, New York Commission on the Status of Women, to read the Proclamation. Ramona to moderate.

Contact Anne Vendig, president, Women's Group of North Shore Unitarian Universalist Society, Inc. Wouldn't she, Toni Hoak, and Pat Ashley like to hostess a reception after the performance?

Wouldn't Marjory Sharp, church member, a descendent of Henry Hedge, like to read her two never-before-published Margaret Fuller letters?

Wouldn't Anne Forman unveil her painting of me as Margaret Fuller? Her husband, Jules, offered to tape my drama.

Write dozens of letters.

Make dozens of phone calls.

Paste up and print flyers.

Write news releases.

Draw up a list of contacts and mail flyers off. Think New York, such as New York Council for the Humanities.

Arrange for a photographer.

The day before the big day, phone call from Pennsylvania. Someone named Margaret Vanderhaar Allen. She'd just written a book, *The Achievement of Margaret Fuller*; she'd seen the tiny notice in *The New York Times*. I told her, bring copies of her book.

Technical rehearsal had to be on the same day as performance, and all furniture (which I brought from my home) and props had to be moved in and out on the same day. In about two hours, Naomi had to figure out the awkward lighting board in the booth at the back of the auditorium, from which she could hardly see the stage.

No dressing room. There is an adjoining room, but that was where Anne Vendig and committee were setting up the reception. With suitcase and long dress on a hanger, I raced to the public bathroom downstairs and across hall.

Racing back across the hall and up the stairs, *in costume,* I saw the SRO (Standing Room Only) audience. *Oh, my God, am I up to it....Did anybody see me....*I slipped through a side door, and stashed the suitcase in a dark corner.

All proceeded as planned. The presentation of the Mayor's Proclamation — from backstage I couldn't hear the announcements. The drama — only a couple of light cues were missed. The reception

— the crowds made the wine and cheese disappear too fast but people stayed and talked. The unveiling of the oil painting and the reading of Margaret Fuller's letters — I was changing clothes. But Anne Forman later consented to have her picture taken alongside her painting.

Ramona had great fun being moderator and afterwards meeting a boyfriend from years back. Margaret Vanderhaar Allen had her moment in the sun and sold some of her books. Herb Vetter of the Cambridge Forum showed up and we had a chat. Phyllis Chesler, author of *Woman and Madness,* came. I brushed elbows with Martin Bellar, program director, New York Council for the Humanities, just as he was leaving. He had a twinkle in his eye.

And so, Lincoln Center did become a turning point. The event laid the groundwork for our Margaret Fuller Foundation's winning five state Humanities grants.

Coasting California (January 12-29, 1980)

It doesn't happen often that you can tour nine Unitarian Universalist churches down the coast of California — Palo Alto, Marin, Monterey, San Francisco, Berkeley, Santa Barbara, Palos Verdes, Los Angeles, and San Diego.

Rosemary Matson of Carmel Valley, California, put me into this enviable position. Her organization, Women-In-Transition (WIT) sponsored the tour. Rosemary made phone calls and did all the publicity. I had "home-stays" with UU's whom I'd never met before.

My husband, Clift, had the brainstorm that I should take along our daughter because, actually, she was a young woman in transition. Having just graduated from high school, Mary was working as a waitress. A trip down the West Coast might be broadening; she could run my slides and lights, and we could rent a car.

The best part about it for Mary, who'd earned her license about a year earlier, was driving along the trecherous, winding, scenic Pacific Coast Highway, passing by the world-famous Pebble Beach golf course, Monterey Peninsula, Big Sur, and Carmel — sometimes with a two hundred-foot drop into a hungry ocean. In mortal fear, I could barely look out the windows at the unparalleled beauty, but daughter had no problem whizzing around the curves.

Margaret Fuller Day was proclaimed on the day of my performance at the San Francisco church. Rosemary and I had sat in Mayor Diane Feinstein's office waiting for the official Proclamation. We were jubilant when it came through, and I've since followed Feinstein's skyrocketing career into the Senate with a great deal of warmth! Rosemary obtained press in all the local newspapers and another coup came in the form of a half-page article in the *San Francisco Examiner.*

In Los Angeles where people like Philip Berrigan, Dr. Benjamin Spock, and Maggie Kuhn* had graced the pulpit, an older crowd sat scattered in a caverous, traditional church located in the downtown, low-income section. In Palos Verdes the president of the Unitarian Universalist Association, the Reverend Dr. Eugene Pickett, attended with his wife, Helen. San Diego, the finale, one of the largest churches, exuded energetic activists in the women's movement and we received good press in the *Los Angeles Times* and a lead article with picture in *Reader's Guide.*

What a pleasure to be among audiences that *listen.* UU's understand every nuance...laugh at every joke. They enjoy the history, comprehend the relevance, are full of questions, and want to discuss. Further, they honor your effort, even with flaws, allow for imperfect conditions. Standing in front of them, I give to them, but they give me more.

It is audience reaction that has encouraged me to travel my long Margaret Fuller road...though, looking back, it hasn't seemed long. Every step has been a step forward...my journey of growth.

Sharing The Spotlight on TV and Radio with Shirley Chisholm, James Luther Adams, Kurt Vonnegut, Sissela Bok, Helen Caldicott, Buckminster Fuller, and others (March 23, 1980)

I arrived at Agassiz Theater, Radcliffe, to find an excited overflow audience stepping over huge cables running in and out the doors. For over an hour, in a cavernous, cold, basement dressing room, a makeup artist I'd hired did a superb job. Afterwards, people said the video looked splendid.

---

*Philip Berrigan, Roman Catholic priest and anti-war activist jailed for civil disobedience; Dr. Benjamin Spock, renowned pediatrician and peace movement activist; and Maggie Kuhn, founder of Gray Panthers.

My drama was one in a series of videotapings for the Unitarian Universalist William Ellery Channing Bicentennial Celebration, entitled "I Call That Mind Free," sponsored by the Cambridge Forum, the First Parish in Cambridge, the Lowell Institute, the M.I.T. Chaplains, and the United Ministry at Harvard and Radcliffe.

Geared for intellectually thirsty audiences, these forums were aired on TV and radio across the continent under a grant from the Veatch program of the North Shore Unitarian Universalist Society, Inc. Production supervision was by award-winning producer Pamela Bullard. Print materials were superb, generating national press of the most impressive kind.

Except mine was a *drama*. The other programs featured prestigious guests who *lectured*. Themes covered racial equality, liberalism, and social progress.

We also taped a discussion on Fuller. I sat and talked with Dr. Jack Mendelsohn, minister of the First Parish in Bedford, and Barbara Miller Solomon, Harvard senior lecturer on history and literature. The Reverend Herb Vetter served as moderator.

The day after I did Radcliffe I was handed a contract by Herb Vetter. Payment was the best I'd received but, considering the hours I'd invested, you could compare the pay to slave wages. Furthermore, I was to sign away all rights.

I said I couldn't give away rights because I wanted to continue performing my drama wherever I could.

Herb Vetter informed me that this was the usual contract — all persons who did a Cambridge Forum signed.

How could I sign?

Herb Vetter told me they had invested a great deal of money in my drama already.

No one seemed to understand that writing and presenting a *drama* is entirely different from writing and presenting a lecture.

I connected with a theatrical lawyer who suggested I make a counteroffer, giving Cambridge Forum a time limit, one to five years, after which all rights would revert back to me.

Herb Vetter turned this down.

The Cambridge Forum finally produced a video including two scenes from my drama, with cuts to the slides I provided, and the discussion.

I know they were disappointed, but it would have broken my heart to call an end to my work on Margaret Fuller.

Headlining in a Church in Des Moines, Iowa (May 22, 1980)

The minister turned on the available lighting — a spot directly above my head. During the entire performance, the top of my head was highlighted while my face was in shadows.

Keynoting with Dr. Kenneth Patton at the first National Symposium on Humanism, Kansas City, Missouri (May 4, 1980)

I kicked off the program, then came Dr. Kenneth Patton, nationally recognized as a compelling liberal religious leader, writer and organizer. He was the *first* recipient of the Bragg Award for Distinguished Service to Humanism.*

Did my performance inspire the selection committee to vote Betty Friedan the award the next year?** I may never know, but it's divine to speculate that I paved the way for Friedan, who became the second recipient!

Making Front Page News With Flo Kennedy in Boston (July 3-4, 1980)

Ramona badgered me to send Florynce Kennedy $50 for her bus fare to Boston. She also coerced me to put down, in the name of our Margaret Fuller Foundation, $50 for two nights at the Ehrlich Theater in the Boston Center for the Arts (BCA), a rarely used downstairs tumble-down space in a huge building on Tremont Street in the derelict-ridden South End — or as some have preferred to describe it, a neighborhood in transition.*** I had baulked — how could we get audience? — but, like the good little girl, did as I was commanded.

---

*Raymond B. Bragg was the first person to sign the Humanist Manifesto. He was minister, scholar, teacher, orator, world traveler.

**Betty Friedan, author of *The Feminine Mystique* and founding president of NOW.

***The Center has since been completely renovated as well as the corner on which it stands. The theater is now named The New Ehrlich.

94 HOW I GOT TO HARVARD

The first I heard of Florynce Kennedy was when Ramona told me the story that, in the days when Harvard was opening its doors to women, there were insufficient rest room facilities for females. So, in and around the statue of John Harvard, Flo and her coterie, including Ramona, organized a Harvard Yard pee-in. Needless to say, proper accommodatations were then furnished.

Ramona sent me a flyer of the M.A.M.A. rally (March Against Media Arrogance) which Flo Kennedy pulled off annually in New York City. The moto "KICK ASS in '79" appeared on the top of this National Consumer Coalition paper commemorating the fiftieth birthday of Dr. Martin Luther King, as well as honoring "Hooker and Housewife dress-alikes," "Kids who do something" and the "Feminist Party's Ms. Understood, Ms. Guided, Ms. Appropriated, Ms. Taken, Ms. Laid, Ms. Placed, Ms. Nomer, and Ms. Anthropy." Honors and prizes were to be awarded after which there was to be a film festival and a Freedom and Disobedience Fair.

Flo's group annually marched with their biggest banners past the offices of Viacom, CBS, ABC, NBC, AP, and Warner Communications. They hit Dag Hammarskjold Plaza by noon, boycotting Procter and Gamble, SAMBOS, J. P. Stevens, General Foods, Florida Orange Juice, all states holding out on the ERA, and they protested nucleur testing and landlord ripoffs.

Sponsoring organizations were Black Women United for Political Action, Feminist Party, Coalition Against Racism and Sexism, COY-OTE, PONY, N. Y. Prostitutes Collective, N. Y. Women Running, N. Y. Wages for Housework, Black Women for Wages for Housework, Who's Whore, Cambridge Women's Center, Queens Collective: Women's Action Group, Kids Into Doing Something, and *Majority Report*, the Women's Newspaper.

Flo's credits ran a mile long: Founder of the Feminist Party in 1951; coordinator of the Coalition Against Racism and Sexism; director of the Media Workshop of the Consumer Information Service; delegate to World Conference of Women in Copenhagen, 1980; author of *Color Me Flo,* published by Prentice Hall; 1978 recipient of the National Conference of Christians and Jews' award as one of the fifty Outstanding Women in the country.

Flo'd been "roasted" at the Playboy Empire Club. Many promi-nent people such as Phil Donahue, Dick Gregory, and Bella Abzug paid tribute to her.

Still, I was totally unprepared for the dynamic, larger than life lawyer and activist. Flo was in the kitchen of her modest mid-Manhattan apartment cooking a ham or roast beef for the five or six guests — I always saw there five or six diverse persons of all colors.

Strong. A street-wise intelligence, as well as a learned one. Looking about forty years old — but I think she was in her late sixties. Skin black as night, it shone like illuminated ebony. Exuding a love of flamboyant color, original dress. Piercing eyes that sized you up to your depths. Wild earrings, long false eyelashes, three-inch false fingernails painted bright red. Red, red lipstick. Energy and independence. Forthright. The ability to face and fight inequity. You also felt a certain vulnerability, a large heart.

Journalists have reported that Flo was one of five girls who grew up poor in Kansas City, Missouri. When she was three years old she watched her taxi-driver father chase the Ku Klux Klan from their property. Getting into law school was a fight. She had to threaten to sue on the basis of racism. "That's when I learned you don't have to be liked and loved," she has been quoted as saying, "— just so you can get what you want. The best thing I like is to have a bad reputation with my enemies." She was one of the first black women to graduate from Columbia University law school.

She got a job in a law firm, had been married three years when her husband died, then went on to write and speak, to champion and generate media coverage for causes.

"If you get headlines," this trail blazer says, "you've done something substantive. They want to keep you out of the media. The point is, you want to embarrass people and get their embarrassment into the streets."

Here are some of her trademark sayings:

"There are very few jobs that actually require a penis or vagina. All other jobs should be open to everybody."

"Unity in a Movement situation can be overrated. If you were the Establishment, which would you rather see coming in the door: one lion or five hundred mice?"

"They call us militants, but General Westmoreland, General Abrams, General Motors and General Dynamics — they're the real militants. We don't even have a helicopter."

"I may seem radical, but I'm not. I'm just a worm, turning."

"If men could get pregnant, abortion would be a sacrament."

"Being a mother is a noble status, right? Right. So why does it change when you put 'unwed' or 'welfare' in front of it?"

"If you're lying in a ditch with a truck on your ankle, you don't send somebody to the library to find out how much the truck weighs. You get the truck *off.*"

"Loserism is when oppressed people sit around and think up reasons why they can't do something. Well, just *do* it. Thinking up reasons why you can't is the Establishment's job."

"In a jockocratic society, you can turn on the TV and find out the score of some basketball game in Alaska...but you don't hear how many women died from illegal abortions."

"Don't agonize. Organize."

"I use the testicular approach — put pressure on the most tender part of the anatomy. People aren't ready to deal with testicular pressure."

"I try to pick big enemies. If someone steps on your foot in the subway, don't get mad at the person. Get mad at the subway."

"There's nothing that can happen that can't be made fun."

"The U.S. military spreads more 'pentagonorrhea' than any other country on the globe. And yet, if you fail to acede to a direct order, you get sent to the brig and court-martialed."

Ramona was networking with Flo the summer Mayor Kevin H. White had chairwoman Katharine D. Kane (first female deputy mayor) and staff busily organizing arts groups to stage as many events as possible to celebrate Boston's 350th Jubilee, a five-month, two-million-dollar celebration marking the city's founding in 1630.

Plans were afoot to invite President Carter as well as Prince Charles and many British dignitaries, and to have twelve Tall Ships displays and races in Boston Harbor, as well as parades, historic and ethnic exhibits, special performances, tours, conferences, receptions, dedications, commemorative products, prizes and gifts.

In the building above the theater I'd rented there was one of Boston's largest exhibition halls — a 400-foot-round Cyclorama which was a landmark of nineteenth-century Americana (built in 1884). To this space the Boston Women's Art Alliance was to bring Judy Chicago's *The Dinner Party,* a sculpture advertised as a symbol of America's heritage. This piece of art was causing national excitement and controversy. Institutions were refusing to show it, even though three hundred artists had worked on it for five years. It was criticized because it was "too big," "not art," or "a poitical act." Judy Chicago had sold her own work, lectured, borrowed money and invested everything she had, nearly $85,000, in her effort to ensure that women's history would become a part of human history.

With china, goblet, flatware, napkin and runner, *The Dinner Party* represented the contributions and achievements of thirty-nine famous historical and mythical women from the beginning of time. The place settings were displayed on three fifty-foot-long tables which rested on a Heritage Floor on which were written the names of 999 additional women who'd helped shape the world. Margaret Fuller's name appeared on the Heritage Floor.

Meanwhile, it so happened that Rosemary Matson, who'd just returned from leading workshops at the United Nations Conference for Women in Copenhagen, Denmark, had come to Boston for a Continental Women and Religion Committee meeting, making it inevitable that Ramona would involve her.*

---

* As a result of her work in Copenhagen, Rosemary Matson and a friend, Patricia Schroeder, were founding a grassroots femininist global network called *Continuing the Peace Dialogue.* They organized Peace Makers Travel Tours to the Soviet Union - Women to End War in the World. They took thirty women to dialogue with Soviet peace workers and received free airplane tickets for both in order to meet with Russian women. In 1984 Rosemary Matson was awarded the Ralph Atkinson Award from the Monterey County chapter of the American Civil Liberties Union. In 1986 she received the Holmes-Weatherly Award from the Unitarian Universalist Association. In 1988 she was recognized as one of the ten outstanding women in Monterey County, California. In 1995 she was awarded the American Humanist Association's Humanist Heroine award. By 1996 she had made twenty-three trips with groups of women to Russia, and was planning another. She is active in Women's International League for Peace & Freedom and is on the board of the United Nations Association-Monterey Bay. In 1990, at the age of 74, she was diagnosed with breast cancer. After mastectomy, she performed an outrageous act: she posed for a nude photograph, her arms reaching high towards the heavens. Laughingly, she proudly showed this photo to friends.

My sister, Gwen Harper, with whom I was staying (conveniently located across from the BCA), claimed that everything we were doing was wrong, unplanned, unorganized, and that our event was destined for disaster. Without advance publicity and audience-building, there was no way, she felt, we could expect a walk-in audience on July 4th.

Gwen and I had always been opposites. Her hair was dark, mine was light. She was tall; I was less tall. Growing up we were off in different directions, different circles of friends. For years, we rarely saw each other. She was into management and social services; I put my mind to writing and acting. She travelled a great deal in her job for Camp Fire Girls, Inc., and piloted many outstanding events which led her straight to the top as national director of Program in New York, and she surprised me one day by hiring me as staff writer. For three years I wrote program books under her direction and came to admire her as a highly effective, flexible, and creative thinker.

She was currently director of the Women's Information and Referral Service (WIRE) with the Junior League of Boston Inc., a unique League project that had Gwen loading a Women's Van with informational brochures and driving and parking it in different population areas in greater Boston so women of all ages and income levels could be provided with literature and directed to needed resources and services within the community.

I could hardly discount her opinion.

But we did have advance publicity. Royal Cloyd, the BCA's founder and president, printed up a slick, impressive newsletter of events with my picture on the cover and a nice story inside. We xeroxed flyers featuring "A Day with Fiery Feminist Flo Kennedy." The mayor's office gave us access to their 350th Jubilee logo under which Flo's picture dominated over a picture of Judy Chicago's *The Dinner Party*, with my picture as a small insert. The mayor's office also supplied us with a technician who had a truck.

Flo asked Ramona to get her on one of the Boston daytime TV talk shows and Ramona made the phone call to Channel 5 in Needham. My sister drove us over. Flo wore her cowboy hat, black pants and shirt, and around her neck she had what I thought was a black silk scarf, but soon she boasted that this garment was her pajamas.

"By wearing this around my neck," she explained, tossing the pant legs in a scarflike fashion, "I don't have to bring along a suitcase. I have my toothbrush in my purse." She even wore her "scarf" in front of the TV cameras.

On the day of performance I carried furniture from my sister's apartment across the street to the theater, and the small and polite technician nearly killed himself hefting heavy lighting equipment off his truck onto his back and into the theater.

In the shabby dark lobby Ramona piled a table high with about a hundred She-Shirts. Next to this, Flo Kennedy sat, waiting to greet the public onrush, while Rosemary, our general manager, was away on her Women and Religion meeting. I frantically buzzed in and out, set up props and furniture and held technical rehearsal. At one point Ramona stopped me. I must speak to a reporter. I must stand behind Ramona, next to Flo, for a picture.

The Judy Chicago people ignored us. Every day *The Dinner Party* organizers had long lines of people waiting to get into the Cyclorama.

Our audience members could be counted on your fingers.

There wasn't much to say after my performances.

Rosemary laid out our money in my sister's apartment. "We have $30 after expenses."

Expenses did not include transportation or food for three days or the money I had put up.

What to do with thirty dollars?

"We'll divide it," Rosemary said.

"No, no," Ramona said. "I don't want it."

"Laurie, you have it," Rosemary said. "You are the *star* and paid for the theater."

"No, no," I said. "We're in this together. I can't take it. Let Ramona have it."

"Absolutely not," said Ramona, turning her back on both of us and walking to the other side of the room. *"No, no, no."*

"Laurie, go ahead." Rosemary pushed the bills towards me.

"No, no." I pushed them back.

"You deserve it."

"I got the publicity, that's enough for me."

Ramona said, "Rosemary should have it. She came from California."

I said, "Yes, Rosemary, you should have it."

"Well — I — No, that's not right," Rosemary said.

It took an hour to convince Rosemary.

Two days later we were on *the front page* of the *Boston Herald-American,* with a huge headline reading: WOMEN'S MOVEMENT GETS BACK TO BASICS.

The article by Jean Cole described us as typical of the new wave of feminists who "think that blind devotion to enactment of the Equal Rights Amendment has derailed their cause."

The journalist stated that we represented the grassroots who wanted to put the movement "back on the track" because ERA was continuing "to fall short of approval in more and more states despite a forty-month extension for ratification."

Ramona, as wife of a former King's Chapel pastor, was quoted in lead paragraphs as saying the ERA was "'boringly myopic. We simply have to get back to the gut issues of the status of women and their history, in which the patriarchal power structure has its roots.'"

The article continued with Flo saying she was "'grateful to the troubled amendment for providing one portion of a "laxative" dose the feminist cause 'needed' for impetus it lost over the past couple of years.'"

We were shown to be disturbed by "ERA tunnel vision" and perturbed that attendance at feminist functions had fallen off.

Through my solo portrait of Fuller I was attempting to renew consciousness-raising tactics and my words were picked up: "'Fuller first brought women together back in the 1830s....She called her sessions "Conversations With Women"....And she can do it again for us now.'"

The article went on: "James and Barth envision Margaret Fuller's cultural revival after more than a century of 'being buried in history' as a means of enticing more women into the feminist cause.

"They want to interest women who fear getting trapped in a militant, radical group but want to participate in learning about themselves and inequality in their lives.

"'Women are torn every which way today,'" I was quoted. "'I think Margaret Fuller's life and how she solved her problems and emotional conflicts would help them solve theirs.'

"With this in mind, Barth, James and others have started a

Margaret Fuller Foundation. One center where women meet and talk about issues and themselves is already functioning in Wiscasset, Maine.

"'This is how we get to the basic issues of femininism,' said Barth. "'This is where we share our hurt and anger, the kind you cannot share with a husband or a boyfriend, no matter how liberated you profess to be.'

"'Without wallowing in misery and self-pity, we supply a support system for each other. From here we will go on to confront those problems of women that continue to erode their relationships with men.'

"'ERA and those who mono-maniacally promote it didn't help man-woman relationships.'

"'Battered and raped women are just the extremes of the patriarchal power system and the dominant male,' Barth said. 'The root of feminism is not ERA, but to see how this patriarchal power was shaped around us and do what we must to change it.'

"'The overbearing power of suffragette Susan B. Anthony eclipsed Margaret Fuller and many other radical women of the nineteenth century,' Barth said. 'Fuller, who died in 1850, never would have settled only for demanding the vote as Anthony did,' she said.

"'It's an old bromide, but you can't legislate morality and ERA must not eclipse the gut issues of feminism today. Those gut issues are still in the kitchen and the bedroom.'"

And there on page A12 was our picture, Ramona, Flo and me, smiling broadly.

Months later we all received signed certificates from Jubilee chairwoman Katharine Kane, and Mayor Kevin White, for participating in Boston's 350th Birthday.

What astounding success we achieved in the media!

Making the Rounds of the Libraries with the New York Humanities Grant (November 2 - December 7, 1980)

Grants were things people smarter than I won.

Then I heard about a grant-writing seminar sponsored by Nassau County Office of Cultural Development. I believe I went to take notes for my friend, Anne Forman, who couldn't attend. Something was said by the publicity director of Nassau Library System: It seems the kind of work I was doing on Margaret Fuller was cresting the current wave at Humanities Councils. Gloria Glaser, the publicity director, would help, but as an individual I could not apply; I needed an "umbrella" organization, a sponsoring organization through which the money and paperwork could siphon.

Though Anne Forman had her hands full, she was agreeable that Wantagh CAP sponsor. We set an appointment with Martin Bellar, program officer at the New York Council for the Humanities. He gave us a "go ahead."

I had no idea how to plan. Happily, Gloria Glaser and Anne did. In Gloria's office we got to the budget. Well, I was floored. I never had a budget in my entire life. But Gloria and Anne sat there and figured. How logical it all was. The only part left was to write the body of the grant, the argument. I did the best I could. I turned it in to Martin Bellar about a month before the deadline. Within a week or so he called. He told me point by point what to emphasize. On my rewrite, he called again and told me to change a couple of things. I made the next deadline.

From the Humanities perspective, my drama was a tool to attract audience and serve up the issues for the "heavy" part of the evening —scholars who talked and fended questions. I could stand in front of an audience and speak at length about Margaret Fuller, but the scholars had a far wider range of knowledge. We signed up Bell Gale Chevigny, author of *The Woman and the Myth*, whom I'd met at Radcliffe on Margaret Fuller Day at Harvard; Margaret Allen, author of *The Achievement of Margaret Fuller*, who we'd met at Lincoln Center; and Ramona who qualified with her women-studies papers in the Harvard archives.

We promoted our crew from Wantagh CAP, Naomi Kaapcki on props and lights, Jay Estep on hair — Jay created the sensational style which I now do myself. And my oldest son, Mike, who needed extra money, was on slides.

With the Nassau Library System — Gloria Glaser — we got the best stages in twelve libraries, good printed flyers, and a half-page article by Barbara Delatiner with my picture in *The New York Times*.

Though I thought my performances were good and audiences seemed impressed, I was still "cutting my teeth." The scholars were teaching me too. I was absorbing. It was a process of osmosis.

Flying with the Maine Humanities Grant (August 26 - September 21, 1980)

Ramona had me flying throughout the wilds of Maine in the kind of airplane you climb up into on rickety steps with a bannister of wiggling rope. Once inside, you can't stand up straight because the ceiling is so low. There is one seat on each side of the aisle with a maximum of nineteen. In this "tunnel" you can't hear anything except the roar of the motor. You feel deathly.

Ramona didn't say "No." She was "all fine in her 68 year-old body," and so I signed her up as project director for our Margaret Fuller Foundation grant from the Maine Council for the Humanities and Public Policy.

Ramona had pushed me to apply. One summer, while I was visiting her in her farmhouse, she introduced me to Dr. Spencer Levan, big in Unitarian circles, former professor of religion at Tufts University, and program consultant on the Maine Council. Later she confessed that she didn't think we'd win the grant. Anyway, Spencer Levan called me and told me what changes to make in our application.

Ramona "beat the bushes." She organized financial director, Barbara Warner, and five scholars, including Marie Mitchell Olesen Urbanski, author of *Margaret Fuller's Woman in the Nineteenth Century*. Ramona fixed the dates and locations at Biddeford City Theater, Wieden Hall, University of Maine at Presque Isle, the Hancock County Auditorium in Ellsworth, the Edward Muskie Auditorium in Rumford, and Kresge Auditorium at Bowdoin in Brunswick. Turning out her earthy rural flyers, she got two articles in *The Portland Press Herald,* and interviews and pictures in *The Maine Times, The Lincoln County News, The Camden Herald, The Bangor Daily News, The Rumford Times,* and *The Wiscasset Newspaper.*

Opening on Women's Equality Day, August 26, at City Theater, Biddeford, Ramona had Margaret Fuller Day proclaimed by Mayor John J. O'Leary, Jr.

In Ellsworth, at the Hancock County Auditorium, Ramona had my name up on the marquee in giant letters. What a thrill.

But the small audiences perturbed me. Then I was made aware of the Humanities position: Large groups were never the primary expectation, because follow-up discussions would be carried further, at home and with friends. The goal is to "pioneer," to break into less populated areas where there were voids in programing and where people were afforded fewer opportunties. The Humanities' stance was in alignment with Emerson's belief that there would always be "ripples of waves outward."

Ramona knew we'd be taking our chances in Presque Isle, in the northeastern corner of the state. She was right. Ten people showed up in a thousand-seat theater at the University of Maine. Even so, the director of Theater, John Shordone, sent the Maine Humanities a rave review: "Miss James, a competent actress, kept this audience attentive and, speaking for myself, enthralled....Her sensitive portrait made us all aware of a vital literary historical figure we had hardly heard of before."

The reviewer in the *Maine Times*, G. P. O'Connor, commended the Humanities for bringing me to the state and advised people to make an effort to see valuable historical documentaries like mine.

Towards the end of our run, Ramona "leaked" her honest feelings about being project director. I'd wanted her to have some dollars since she'd done so much for $00.00. But I had assumed too much. I wrote her she should play only those roles she wanted. (Still, I think she was more than pleased to spend her hard-earned money.)

Scholar Marie Urbanski, who taught at the University of Maine at Orono, wrote me I was better than Julie Harris in *Belle of Amherst*. You can see why she became one of my friends.

Reading about "Buckminster Fuller Day" in Wiscasset, Maine (August 26, 1980)

Why Ramona planned events in two different parts of the state on the same day, I have no idea. "Buckminster Fuller Day" in Wiscasset was a real coup, but since she also designated the day "Women's Equality Day" in Biddeford, Maine, where I was performing at City Theater, the following story is vicarious.

"Call Bucky," Ramona said, "and ask him to stop in Wiscasset on his way to his summer home on Bear Island and speak on 'My Great Aunt Margaret' to help perpetuate the first Margaret Fuller Center USA."

Ramona expressed astonishment when he agreed. She had a

marvellous canvas banner made, and promoted a large rural crowd, selling tickets at $10 each, and achieved full page articles in *The Times Record* and *The Portland Press Herald.*

For Bucky, coming to Wiscasset was a homecoming. Wolcott Andrews, a long-time resident, said Bucky had come to Wiscasset in 1921 in an airplane, "something nobody around Wiscasset had seen before."

First Selectman Larry Gordon sent official greetings to "world citizen Buckminster Fuller" at the Municipal Building and Ramona gave Bucky the first incorporation papers of the Margaret Fuller History Center.

Ramona and Anzie Andrews presented him with a large gold key. "For a revolutionary, it seemed more appropriate to give Bucky a key to the Old Jail than to the town," Ramona said. (The Lincoln County Museum and Old Jail, built in 1809-11 of granite blocks from Sheepscot River, is a National Historic Landmark.)

Bucky recalled Margaret Fuller's declaration, "I accept the universe," and gave his usual hour talk.

He said, "Each child born today is born with less misinformation than those before him. I was born in 1895 and thought it was absolutely impossible for man to fly. We have the option to make it on this planet. We can re-design things so that within ten years we can live entirely without fossil fuels or nuclear power."

Nuclear power was a touchy subject in Wiscasset which was next door to the largest nuclear-fueled generating station in New England, Maine Yankee Atomic Power Station.

"Does anybody here know how to design gravity," Bucky asked. "Does anybody know how to design a human being?"

A pregnant woman in the crowd whispered loudly, "Yes!"

Bucky laughed heartily along with the audience. "Well, nobody really knows how to design us," he responded. "Nature designs us. But in order to have people and nature, we have to have energy and all of our energy comes from the sun's radiation."

He pointed to the stars — each a sun — producing heat and radiation from a nuclear reaction. "The stars are collectors of energy, so there must have been some place they collected energy from. When I was twenty-eight, a new galaxy besides ours was found. Now we know there are at least as many stars as a two followed by twenty-one zeroes. Each is an atomic plant running at full blast and they're all arranged in perfect order. Nature knew how close we should be to a nuclear plant. Nature found that humans shouldn't live any closer to an atomic energy plant than ninety-two million miles — the distance from our planet to the sun....Humanity is in the final examination to see whether they'll stay here or not."

But in Wiscasset shutting down the plant would mean cutting 1300 jobs.

The Pennsylvania Grant Disaster (February 25 - May 10, 1981)

The truth is, not everything always went smoothly. The fact is, our Pennsylvania experience turned sour — from the perspective of both Ramona and myself. Assuredly, our project director has her own perspective. I speak out — like Margaret Fuller whose motto was: "Truth at all costs" — to exemplify how one ingredient can spoil the whole.

The Pennsylvania Humanities grant was the largest dollar amount our Margaret Fuller Foundation was allocated; we had eleven presentations in colleges, libraries, and an art museum. Our project director rounded up a crew of friends who lived nearby in Allentown and used mostly local scholars, though she did invite Ramona twice to fly in as scholar. Since dates were sporadically sprinkled throughout the month, I too flew back and forth. The crew shared rental cars.

Right away our director apologized to the crew for being underpaid though, she explained, they did have enough to eat and drink, a legitimate expense, and they were to perceive this grant as a way to have fun. She made similar comments several times.

At the first performance, she celebrated with a bottle of champagne. I didn't have any because she popped the cork when I was out of the room. After the show, though, we all had dinner at a restaurant.

Unbeknownst to me, the routine became the crew having dinner and drinks *before* the show as well as sandwiches and snacks *after* the show, often bringing along wives and husbands. Once I became aware of what was happening, I joined them afterwards, since actors do not do well eating before the show. As the tour progressed, everyone was complaining that they were gaining weight.

In Philadelphia I was instructed to fly in and out on the same day to save the grant money. No one picked me up at the airport. When I arrived at the library in the morning, it was closed. I had to wait in the park across the street with two large suitcases full of props. Two hours later I saw someone walking out the front door. It turned out that the crew had been there for half an hour. They had gone in through a side door. No one apologized. This put me in a foul mood for a performance, but as there had been very little publicity — in fact, I hadn't seen any newspaper articles — so I didn't expect a sizable audience and we didn't get one. Afterwards, everyone had a party. I could not attend because I had to fly home on the same day to save the grant money.

Neither did I attend the party closing night in Allentown, where the director said there was a new restaurant everyone was talking about. The entire crew lived in that town and could have eaten at home. If they had, perhaps I could have had my expenses for my last two performances. The director refused payment. I had written her that if my travel was not to be paid, then I could not travel. She responded that if I did not keep my commitment, she would not send me a penny for any of my performances. I was never reimbursed for my last two flights.

To top it off, a month later the manager of the Sheraton-Johnson hotel called both Ramona and myself. He said our project director refused to pay Ramona's bill and they were taking legal action. After phone calls back and forth, Ramona and I were forced to spend the money from the one and only contribution we'd received for the Margaret Fuller Foundation.

Our director offered the excuse that she had to spend most of the grant money to transport people around the state.

Stirring Controversy in Johnstown, Pennsylvania (February 23, 1981)

In Johnstown, Pennsylvania, Ramona and Gordon Tomb, *The Tribune-Democrat* reporter, caused my play to be more than a one-night stand.

Tomb interviewed us in our hotel and he wrote in his half-page article: "The president's wife [Nancy Reagan] is viewed by the two feminists as the 'typical adoring female' who is the 'antithesis of

Margaret Fuller' and who is 'setting the clock back for women' by her example in the national limelight. In activist lingo, that means Mrs. Reagan is kicking dirt back on the cultural casket."*

The townspeople were up in arms. They called in and sent letters. Doris M. Todorich, President of Johnstown NOW, found nothing wrong with Nancy Reagan's wearing nice clothes and looking adoringly at her husband, but wrote: "It would be refreshing...to read of her concern for those millions of people less fortunate than she who are finding it increasingly difficult to provide the bare essentials for themselves and their families."**

Ramona responded: "We did not soft-pedal our beliefs. To do otherwise is not in the American tradition....We sought and obtained free and open discussion via press and person on the controversial subject of feminism, currently being called the most important revolution of the twentieth century. We think the feedback will continue in PA. In an era of Moral Majority, the Washington Council which funded PA must combat. We felt we must send our message loud and clear. The Hegalian dialectic was put in motion. There was a 'thesis.' Thanks to *The Tribune-Democrat,* an 'antithesis'; we all know the 'synthesis' in philosophy and action is a long, slow and painful process. I am happy to be at the onset."

Gordon Tomb dashed off a note to Ramona: "The chauvinists giggled & the liberated praised. Thanks for an interesting interview."

Kicking Off a Major Wisconsin University Conference (April 24, 1981)

It was so still beyond those white lights, I thought they'd gone to sleep. But no, they were spellbound, I was later told.

This was not a tiny library. It was the largest and best theater I'd been in to date — all the great lights and space I wanted. There were about two hundred people out front.

My drama led off this major Conference whose theme was "Accent on Women" at the University of Wisconsin, Madison, and co-sponsored by UW-Parkside/UW-Extension/Gateway Technical Institute's Women's Bureau.

---

*Gordon Tomb's article, "Predecessor Cheated, 2 Say," appeared February 25, 1981.

** *The Johnstown Tribune-Democrat,* March 4, 1981, Letters to the Editor.

Best was meeting Tom Reinhart, director of the Community Arts Theater. At first I thought he was chauvinist because he created all kinds of difficulties. He delayed my tech rehearsal until I felt my energies giving out. He harped on tiny details that drove me wild. He made comments like "I had to guess what you wanted."

Tech rehearsal was called at 10 A.M. He fiddled, taking tedious pains to get every light area perfect. It wasn't until 12:30 P.M. that we were ready for our run-through. I was to have lunch with the women's education specialists for University of Wisconsin Extension, Connie Fuller Threinen* and Marion Thompson, at 12:00 noon. Since they were applying for the Wisconsin state humanities grant, lunch was important. There was nothing they could do but sit and watch.

We started with light cues and Reinhart made commands to his helper. He made sure he got the "feel" of every scene — without having read a page of script. As we went along he got involved and excited, even though we were only taking cues. He would stop and give me specific moves. Gradually, I became aware that it was a privilege to work with someone so interested and sensitive. We finished at 3:15 P.M.. Connie and Marion had been kept waiting four hours. I apologized, but they claimed they'd been fascinated. I wound up admiring Tom Reinhart, this perfectionist who said, "I wish I'd had more time to devote to this."

Spreading the Word with the Massachusetts Grant (April 24, - May 28, 1981)

If you carried too many groceries, you couldn't unlock the three heavy front doors to get in. If you didn't have your coat hung up in its proper place, you didn't have room to sit down. It had a refrigerator that barely held one can of soda. After the first night I figured out a way to slide the mattress off the divan onto the floor. If I didn't do this, I woke up crippled. I didn't see the people who lived here, but I did see the landlord. He was at the corner supermarket playing the pinball machine.

The grant we won from the Massachusetts Foundation for the Humanities and Public Policy wouldn't pay for my food, but it would

---

*Connie Fuller Threinen, great-grand neice of Margaret Fuller. I had met her on Margaret Fuller Day at Radcliffe.

pay for a transient room, rather than flights back and forth between
Boston and Long Island for twelve performances within a month.
project director David Kronberg found me a tiny, third-floor walk-up
on Commonwealth Avenue.

Would he connect me with someone who could speak Italian, I
asked. For some of the performances I'd decided to present the
second part of my drama, Margaret Fuller's European years. I set an
appointment at City Hall to learn how to speak my Italian words. The
larger-than-life man, Alfred Vellucci, who read the list of words into
my hand-held tape recorder, had been Mayor of Cambridge twice.*
He was proud of his Italian heritage.

I learned he was an independent who credited himself for
establishing rent control and the Cambridge Women's Commission.
He championed the plight of the ordinary guy.

Revered because he always provided Cantabridgians with good
laughs by needling Harvard, he'd been quoted as saying Harvard was
a greedy monolith trying to take over the city's land and houses.
Vellucci grew up in East Cambridge, next door to Harvard, born to
that economic group that could never attend. He'd earned a high-
school-equivalency degree and drove a truck and later was a
sandwich-shop proprietor. At some point he became an accountant
and later achieved a position in City Hall chambers.

The stories abound: When first elected to City Council, Vellucci
was annoyed when Harvard asked the city to help find parking for
students. So he launched a resolution that Harvard Yard be turned
into a parking lot. The next night 2,000 students stood outside the
Lampoon Building and shouted "Hang Vellucci!" In retaliation,
Vellucci suggested that the area be named "Yale Square."

Every night David Kronberg picked me up in his old van. We
bumpily rode for miles; we were visiting all the outlying libraries. The
publicity person did not show up at the Cambridge Library press
opening — no press showed up either. David Kronberg claimed his
press person was great, but after two performances I still had not met
her. I was supposed to do a TV commercial, but that never
materialized. There were superb flyers, but I didn't see articles in the

---

*Al Vellucci finally served as mayor four times, 1970-71, and 1976-77, 1982-83, 1988-
89.

newspapers. I began to have my doubts about professional publicity agents, especially after being spoiled by Ramona-energy.

The person David Kronberg paid to help backstage left before the performance was over; she said she had to go to another job. The person he paid to do slides held three part-time jobs and left as soon as the performance was over because she was studying for mid-terms. That meant I struck the small props. ("Strike" is theater lingo meaning taking down after the show and putting away whatever is on stage.) This was irritating because I'd figured that, with grants to pay for help, I would be relieved of this responsibility which is tiring after a performance. Then, I waited a half-hour for Kronberg to strike the spotlight.

Nevertheless, I was having a great time living in the heart of historic, exciting Boston, walking anywhere I wanted, and during the performance standing beside scholars such as Eugenia Kaledin,* cultural historian, Northeastern University, and Ethel Klein, social historian, Harvard University. Audience questions were driving me to realize the need for a new book on Margaret Fuller, and I was gaining confidence that I could write it.

After one performance of *The European Years,* Al Vellucci congratulated me on my correct Italian pronunciation. "I don't care anything about history," he boisterously exploded in a loud, no-nonsense voice. "But I do care about Cambridge. So the Marchessa married an Italian? Marchesa, Marchesa," he repeated as though he were testing the sound of the words. "Margar-etta, Margar-etta."

Little did I know how beneficial Al Vellucci would become to our Margaret Fuller Foundation.**

Raising Consciousness at a Lesbian Conference (May 30, 1981)

How would heterosexual "me and Margaret" be accepted by lesbian audiences?

---

*Eugenia Kaledin was to become author of *The Education of Mrs. Henry Adams,* University of Massachusetts Press, 1994.

**See stories in this chapter: "Converging Margaret Fuller with Edna St. Vincent Millay and Buckminster Fuller in Camden, Maine," "Dedicating The Margaret Fuller Ossoli Square, Cambridge, Massachussetts," and "The Cambridge Capers: Dedicating the Margaret Fuller Ossoli Plaque."

This Boston conference was a week-long event at Studio Red Top, organized by The Feminist Amerikan Theater, producers of the annual Womyn's Theater Festival along with Women on the Move, Split Britches, Atthis Theater, and Theater of Light and Shadow.

Lesbians show interest in Fuller because she dared, in print, to support homosexuality. That was a bold act in 1845 and Fuller was one of the first to speak out.* These are the words that shocked:

> It is so true that a woman may be in love with a woman and a man with a man. I like to be sure of it, for it is the same love which angels feel, where—

> Sie fragen nicht nach Mann und Weib.

> It is regulated by the same law as that of love between persons of different sexes; only it is purely intellectual and spiritual. Its law is the desire of the spirit to realize a whole, which makes it seek in another being what it finds not in itself. Thus the beautiful; the mute seeks the eloquent; the butterfly settles always on the dark flower. Why did Socrates love Alcibiades?...De Staël for Récamier.**

Applause stopped the show when I said Fuller's words, "I wish I were a man!"

At "curtain," the response was thunderous.

One of the group's leaders came up to me, shook my hand and said "Thank you!" with affirmation that indicated identity with Fuller's conflicts.

She didn't know it, but that handshake helped to launch another journey for me; the homophobia I'd been brainwashed with faded

---

*There is no written proof that has so far been found that Fuller can be considered to have been a lesbian. Some people point out that Fuller did have two female women friends. These close relationships seem to have been "like the angels," as Fuller described. In her journals and letters it seems clear that she was constantly searching for heterosexual love and she did find love with the Italian, Giovanni Angelo Ossoli.

**From Fuller's book, *Woman in the Nineteenth Century.* Socrates was a Greek teacher and philosopher who sustained a friendship with Alcibiades, an Athenian politician. Germaine Necker de Staël was the intellectual French novelist whose friendship with Juliette Récamier spanned twenty years.

into oblivian.

My only problem was their promise of payment of $100 for expenses, but then I know these "womyns" theater groups are idealistically motivated (like me). They create their own works and hope to break even.

Converging Margaret Fuller with Edna St. Vincent Millay and Buckminster Fuller in Camden, Maine (July 11, 1981)

Ramona was going into orbit.

"All the world will come to us!"

Ramona is probably the only person in the world who would think of combining Margaret Fuller with Edna St. Vincent Millay but she did it successfully and the two-three hundred who attended were happy she did.

She honored both these historic women in beautiful Camden, Maine, a seacoast village where mountains meet the sea, a place nineteenth-century Margaret Fuller never saw but where Pulitzer prize-winning poet Edna St. Vincent Millay grew up and wrote her earliest poetry in the beginning of the twentieth century.

Ramona implored me to come up three weeks in advance to "Maine's prettiest village," Wiscasset, about ten miles from her farmhouse. She arranged to have me stay at a historic bed-and-breakfast. I brought books and my typewriter, for I was beginning my book.

Then Peggy Campbell, twenty-nine years of age, came up. I didn't know Peggy but Ramona had written she was in a "slough of despond" during a divorce situation, trying to survive financially, feeding her soul and regaining her strength with a summer in Maine. The plan was that Peggy would organize and straighten the files for the Margaret Fuller Women's History Research Center located in the Wiscasset "garret."

Peggy stayed and earned her keep at Castle Tucker, the sprawling castlelike home occupied by the only surviving member of the Tucker family. There was really no way Jane Tucker could maintain this mansion, but she staunchly did what she could in order that her castle not fall into undesireable hands, at least while she lived. She opened her doors for public tours, and one of Peggy's jobs was to cover the furniture with sheets every evening to keep off the dust.

Peggy also cut the long grass nearby. She slashed it with a scythe.

Peggy, a poet who worked hard at being autonomous, wore colorless pants and shirts without collars. She garbed herself in ugly footgear. She pulled her hair back in a bun. She didn't put on makeup. She had problems seeing and squinted most of the time. With a high, thin voice, she talked in a monotone between closed teeth which made it difficult to understand her. Yet she had one of the most glorious smiles I've ever seen. I liked her the minute I saw her.

Right away Ramona got the mayor to proclaim Edna St. Vincent Millay Day, and the U.S. Postal Service was issuing an Edna St. Vincent Millay postage stamp. For some good reason, Ramona could not arrange our celebration on the first day of issue, so she persuaded the local post office authority to offer a second day issue of the stamp, most unusual.

Next, she organized Buckminster Fuller to schedule another stop on his way to his summer home on Bear Island. He had just written his book, *Critical Path*,* and he could introduce my afternoon drama at the Camden Opera House, and have a book signing at The Owl and Turtle Bookstore.

About a week before this outstanding array of events, we received a call from Cambridge Councilman Al Vellucci, who was driving up from Massachusetts to make the first public announcement that there was to be a new square in Cambridge named after the Marchesa Margaret Fuller Ossoli!

When the energetic Al Vellucci arrived, we all piled in his car and drove to newspaper offices in the neighboring towns. Ramona had flyers and news releases ready and she led the way into the rural offices where she joked with the editors while reminding them of the many local events she'd pulled off. We were sure to get good publicity and we did in *The Maine Times, The Lincoln County News, The Camden Herald, The Casco Bay Weekly,* and *The Wiscasset Newspaper.*

Vellucci seemed to be quite taken with the three of us — sixty-nine, forty-nine, and twenty-nine years of age — coming together in

---

Critical Path by Buckminister Fuller, adjuvant Kiyoshi Kureomiya, St. Martin's Press, 1981.

our own independent and original way. He joined right into the spirit
of it all. He must have found Maine's prettiest village an agreeable
contrast from his Cambridge pressure-cooker.

I showed him the "garret," the Margaret Fuller Women's History
Research Center. He was speechless. He'd never seen anything like
it. Frankly, neither had I.

Next to Povich's Men's Store on Main Street, you opened a door
and faced some wide, steep stairs. Going up, you came to the large
unfinished second floor of roughly hewn studs and openings. There
were piles and piles of bulging grocery- store boxes reaching higher
than your head. Some had been thrown in a side room, and were
carelessly stacked one on top of another. Others were neatly lined
up on the floor. (The neat rows must have been Peggy's handiwork.)
Inside the boxes were clips and snips of newspaper and magazine
articles, letters, posters, envelopes, books, and momentoes of all
imaginable kinds on the women's movement dating twenty years
back, from the 1960s.

The sight was a revelation. You could spend hours here. You
could poke about and come across a familiar or forgotten picture,
pamphlet, or poster that brought to mind another effort made by
other enthusiastic women in another time and place. This was a gold
mine — a collection of rare materials librarians would envy.

When I told Ramona I'd taken Al to her Research Center, she
gasped in horror, thinking he'd surely take early leave of us "crazy
ladies." However, I had a hunch he'd admire Ramona all the more.

"We're going on location," I announced to Vellucci as our day of
days drew near. He seemed surprised but decided to come along.

In Camden we took rooms overlooking the sea at the lovely
Whitehall Inn, where Edna St. Vincent Millay had worked and had
first read "Renascence," which led to her finding a patron and going
on to Vassar.

In our large room, Al came up for a cocktail. For over an hour
he and Ramona sent Peggy and me into gales of laughter, as they
topped each other with stories and jokes about life and politics in
Cambridge and Boston.

Why didn't Harvard separate from Cambridge? Vellucci asked. It
could declare itself a monarchy...President Nathan Pusey could be its

king. Did Harvard pay taxes to the city? No. Yet when dignitaries such as Bishop Tutu visited Harvard — which cost Cambridge taxpayers "muchos dineros" — the Harvardians were angry that the mayor of Boston had his picture taken with him.

"Is Harvard a city like the Vatican in Rome? Is the president of Harvard king or pope?" Vellucci had been asking these questions for years. "Harvard seems to forget that Boston and Cambridge are bigger than Harvard. Bishop Tutu must pass through Boston and Cambridge to get to Harvard. So what if the mayor extends his hand of welcome to such important men as Bishop Tutu?"

On the July morning a raw wind was blowing on top of Mt. Battie, but the sun was out and you could see into the vast distance, the exact vista Edna St. Vincent Millay had written about. We took for our stage a towering stone structure the park department had probably built.

A group of about seventy persons were assembling, including Buckminster Fuller. All were standing, for there were no chairs. Vellucci went about from gathering to gathering, in traditional political-campaign style, mentioning Margaret Fuller's name and her importance.

It was an inspiring moment, on top of that hill, looking down on the stretch of beautiful landscape. We had to shout through the strong wind. But the whipping gusts added to the dramatics of the scene.

Ramona introduced, Bucky spoke for awhile, then I began Millay's famed words from "Renascence":

> "All I could see from where I stood
> Was three long mountains and a wood
> I turned and looked another way
> And saw three mountains in a bay...."

I lost myself in the long poem, lines I'd long loved. It was over before I knew it. I felt the spirit of Edna St. Vincent Millay was living.

Then it was Peggy's turn. She recited "God's World."

> "O World, I cannot hold thee close enough!
> Thy winds, thy wide gray skies!
> Thy mists, that roll and rise!

Thy woods, this autumn day, that ache and sag
And all but cry with colour! That gaunt crag
To crush! To lift the lean of that black bluff!
World, World, I cannot get thee close enough!...."

Coming down from the mountain top, we rushed into the small, tasteful bookstore, The Owl and Turtle, bought Buckminster Fuller's book, *Critical Path*, and stood in line to have him sign it.

I hastened along to prepare for Margaret Fuller. Backstage at the Camden Opera House I listened again as Bucky talked, saying almost the same words he'd said at Harvard. During my performance, since the houselights could not be dimmed, I saw, in the audience, Bucky front and center — sound asleep. I stifled a laugh. Yes, he'd heard me before too, and he'd had a long day. He must have been in his mid-seventies.

As I was taking my bow, Al Vellucci came up on stage, made a speech, and presented me with a street sign reading, "The Marchesa Margaret Fuller Ossoli Square." There was a lot of applause.

Afterwards, I met Bucky in the hall. He energetically started to explain some triangles of the universe to me, but he was soon interrupted by reporters and photographers.

It was lights/camera/action, Ramona style.

Blitzing Fire Island with Flo Kennedy (August 9, 1981)
"I need some money," Flo Kennedy said one day when Ramona took me to her apartment. "Not a lot of money, just a little."

A meeting was held with a number of people at Vi Mendrackia's house on Long Island. Vi was a spitfire, warm, outgoing, organized. She was a widow with six children who was also the Nassau County human rights commissioner. Flo, looking especially chic in white cowboy boots, took out a pad of paper and pencil and started planning. Everyone volunteered to do something. These wonderful women and the Margaret Fuller Foundation staged the first Fire Island Festival of Women in the Arts.

Fire Island is a long stretch of narrow land off the South Shore of Long Island, where Margaret Fuller, her husband, and son drowned in a freak gale storm on July 19, 1850.* Flo had a summer house there

---

*For the story of the drowning read *Men, Women, and Margaret Fuller*, by Laurie James, Golden Heritage Press, Inc., 1990.

— a Buckminster Fuller-type geodesic dome, the only one on Fire Island.

Margaret Fuller Day was declared by Suffolk County Executive Peter F. Cohalan on August 9, 1981, commemorating the 131st anniversary of her death. We activated a bonanza of events, one after another, at the Ocean Beach Community House, a "barn" of a building with impossible accustics. I presented my drama and Flo's group presented *Darling Boy,* a musical adapted from *Cover Girls,* by Carol Conover; a slide show by photographer Bettye Lane on the history of the women's movement; and a jazz tribute to Billie Holiday, Mary Lou Williams and other jazz greats. For children there was a feminist version of "Cinderella." Outside the theater there was a day-long crafts fair. Tied in, at the Hutchins Gallery at C. W. Post College, our Margaret Fuller Foundation mounted a free exhibition, "Barred Art," featuring the paintings, sculpture, and ceramics of New York State women prisoners. This was coordinated by Joan Burton who took an extraordinary interest in our Foundation. She organized this exhibit in association with the C. W. Post Women's Center with the support of the Library Association. The art was assembled by P.A.C.E., the prisoner art project, which works with artists in thirty-nine prisons in seventeen states.

Best of all, Ramona did her "burning the Bible bit, which she'd toured to pulpits coast-to-coast. Ramona had admitted she might "get killed doing it — but how can a pushing-70 grey-haired married 46 yrs mother-of-five be threatening?"

I'd never seen "Exercise in Exorcism." Flo and I pulled chairs up to the platform stage, joining a small audience.

Ramona had rounded up a big garbage can and lined up several women. She opened by saying something about how "demons of sexual prejudice must be exorcised if women are to be truly liberated." She quoted Harvey Cox's* definition of exorcism: "That process by which the stubborn deposits of town and tribal pasts are scrapped from the social consciousness of man." She noted Cox's concern for casting out the demons of racism, but chastised him for his lack of concern when it came to sexism. She mentioned Dr. Mary Daly's book, *The Church and the Second Sex,* which contends that

_____
*Harvey Cox, Harvard University theologian.

both the Eternal Woman on her pedestal and the Girl who is used as a footstool are faceless, passive nonhumans and must be reformed.

From small cards each performer read a historic biblical or theological quote denigrating women. The cards were torn up dramatically and tossed into the oblivion of the dark, dirty, stinking garbage can. One by one the women read the quotations:

"If a woman grows weary and at last dies from childbearing, it matters not. Let her die from bearing, she is there to do it."
—Martin Luther

"Blessed art Thou, O Lord our God, King of the Universe, Who hast not made me a woman."
— Morning Prayer of Orthodox Jewish men

"Men are superior to women on account of the qualities in which God has given them preeminence."
— The Koran, holy book of the Muslim religion

"In childhood a woman must be subject to her father; in youth to her husband; when her husband is dead to her sons. A woman must never be free of subjugation."
— Hindu Code

"Such is the stupidity of woman's character, that it is incumbent upon her, in every particular, to distrust herself and to obey her husband."
— Confucian marriage manual

"Woman is deceptive and misbegotten."
— St. Thomas Aquinas

"...It is a shame for women to speak in the church."
—Paul the Apostle
(I Corinthians 14:35)

The quotes go on and on.* When Ramona was criticized because her Exorcism "smacks of Nazi book-burning," she responded: "We aren't burning the Bible. We're just trying to show how strong the patriarchal structures have been and how influential in brainwashing women they've been."

Ramona's fires are a way of purging attitudes and creating dialogue.

She was pleased when she heard that a woman active in the UUA had published her "Exercise in Exorism" without her permission and was selling it through her organization. Ramona said, "Plagiarism is the highest form of flattery. I'm thrilled someone makes money on it...and it don't have to be me."

The influence of our Fire Island Festival of Women in the Arts radiated outward — we got feature stories in Long Island's *Newsday* and in *The Fire Island Sandpaper.*

Dedicating the Margaret Fuller Ossoli Square, Cambridge, Massachussetts (October 18, 1981)

"I had an age 70 orgasm @ the Sept.15 Council meeting," Ramona wrote. "Now we have bus & my committment is to fill it. Amen. I will."

She claimed our event would go down in Cambridge history just like the unveiling of John Harvard's statue. Yes, indeed, she wrote me, it will be as strong a statement as Yoko Ono's dedication of "Stawberry Fields" to her husband John Lennon in New York's Central Park.

Councilman Al Vellucci opened doors. He took Ramona and me to the First Church in Cambridge, Congregational. The administrator was agreeable to everything.

Street naming was one of Vellucci's specialties. One time he tried to rename Harvard Square after Christopher Columbus. He'd said: "What the hell, that guy John Harvard never did anything for Cambridge except give the city six lousy books on Prostestant theology."

Now Harvard was about to change the name of the John F. Kennedy School of Government to the Harvard School of Govern-

---

*The entire "Exercise in Exorcism" appears in the Appendix.

ment because some people thought the word "Kennedy" would hinder fund-raising. Vellucci, who often boasted he'd walked and eaten spaghetti with John Kennedy, put through an order to name Boylston Street (the location of the Kennedy School) "John F. Kennedy Street" and the park in front of the school "Kennedy Park." Approval was unanimous.

Vellucci had also convinced the City Council to unanimously vote "yea" to naming the intersection at Quincy Street and Broadway after Dante Alighieri, author of *The Divine Comedy,* a literary classic which describes the poet's journey through Hell, Purgatory, and Heaven. Vellucci had discovered that the style of the interior architecture at the Fogg Museum was Roman. On the opposite side of the street was the Harvard School of Architecture, claiming many names of famous Italian architects. Thus, Vellucci decided the name "Dante Square" was appropriate for the Hell, Purgatory and Heaven in Cambridge.

Invitations from the Mayor's office went out.

The weekend was sunny, with fall's crispness. Ramona, Al Vellucci, and I met the mayor in front of City Hall, where there was a tremendous sign reading: Mayor Francis H. Duehay invites you to the dedication of Margaret Fuller Ossoli Square, Mason & Garden St., Sunday, Oct. 18th at 2 p.m., Followed by a Dramatic Presentation by Laurie James, The Life of Margaret Fuller, at the First Church in Camb. Congregational.

Jane Reed of the *Harvard Gazette,* was there as well as Howie Carr of the *Boston Herald* who described the happening in his Sunday article better than I can:

....."Margaret Fuller was the first American feminist," Ramona Barth was explaining, just before the photographer pulled her away to have her picture taken with Mayor Francis Duehay and Vice Councilor Al Vellucci.....

"Smile, Ramona," the photographer said.

"She can't smile," Vellucci told the photographer. "She's a WASP."

"I am not a WASP," Ramona Barth said. "I'm a humanist."

So how did Ramona Barth and Al Vellucci ever get together on any issue, let alone Margaret Fuller, who may be best known for her Howard Cosellian line, "I find no intellect comparable to my own"?

"I was gonna help Ramona on this one anyway," Vellucci was saying. "But then, when I heard they wouldn't let Margaret Fuller into Harvard, boy, that [bleeped] me off. That was when I really decided to stick it to 'em."

Pro-woman and anti-Harvard — in Cambridge, not a bad one-two punch two weeks before the election. So this afternoon, the corner of Mason and Garden streets — directly across from Radcliffe College — will be dedicated in Margaret Fuller's name.

"We wrote Harvard a letter about not letting her in," Vellucci said. "I told 'em they owed Margaret Fuller and every other woman in the 19th century an apology. They never responded."

Over where Al Vellucci lives, in Ward 1 in East Cambridge, hard by the Somerville line, feminism is not your basic hot issue. A coffee shop on the McGrath-O-Brien highway, for instance, begins a hand-lettered order to its help "GIRLS" — a salutation that in some parts of the city, say Inman Square, would get a place torched within hours.

In Ward 1, however, Harvard-baiting is considered great sport, as Vellucci well knows.

"I want us to put up a portrait of Margaret Fuller in City Hall," Vellucci said. "Maybe we can hit up Harvard for the bill. It's about time they started practicing what they preach."

But the ceremony today is more for Cambridge feminists, who more and more outnumber the Al Vellucci types who hang out at Don's Lunch in Cambridgeport and the Abbeyfeale Cafe on Beacon Street.

Check out the Cambridge listings in the phone book — Women Entrepreneurs, Women's Center, Women's Emporium, Women's School...on and on and on...

So would Margaret Fuller have been interested in that sort of thing? Would she have been someone out of a Jules Feiffer cartoon? What would she be doing today?

"Maybe writing poetry, or going for a canoe ride on Walden Pond," explained Laurie James who will perform this afternoon as Margaret Fuller in — where else? — a Congregational church. "Or she might have been having a headache. She had a lot of very bad headaches."

By now the ceremony at City Hall was ending, and everybody was climbing aboard the bus to take them on a tour of the landmarks of Margaret Fuller's life.

There was only one problem, at least from a feminist perspective. The bus — it was from the Boys Club.

Red and yellow leaves were falling to the ground. Under trees on the church grounds, a podium was set up. A band was playing. In costume, I slipped out of my dressing room (the church's nursery). As soon as Al Vellucci saw me, he escorted me up to the circle of chairs already occupied by the honored guests. The music subsided to quiet the crowd for the mayor's tribute, then Pat King, director of the Schlesinger Library, offered long and esteemed praise. Others offered their accolades. Anne Vendig, from my church on Long Island, had driven up and took some pictures. One I especially treasure is of the street sign in front of the Congregational Church. Then I slipped back to my nursery/dressing room, ready to present my drama to the unusually interested audience.

To this day, you can go to Mason and Garden Streets and see, just above the regular street marker, the green and white sign (a bit weathered now by rain and snow) that reads, "The Marchessa Margaret Fuller Ossoli Square."

Touring Concord, Portsmouth, Peterborough, New Hampshire, and Brattleboro and Hartland Four Corners, Vermont (October 23 - 29, 1981)

I got a five-church tour in New Hampshire and Vermont!

I had been working to get tours. I'd contacted the VEATCH Committee, the national Unitarian Universalist funding committee and applied for a grant. What I asked for was turned down. (Ramona wrote, "I can transcend.") But a counter-offer was made. If a church planned an event for my drama as outreach to invite and attract potential members, VEATCH would allocate up to $500 for promotion or ads in newspapers.

I jumped at this idea. Paid ads were something most churches couldn't afford and Margaret Fuller and I stood to gain visibility which could accrue excitement and larger audiences. Of course, it meant extra work for me because I had to teach ministers and committees how to do it. I learned very soon that many churches just didn't have the people power.

I had homestays with Unitarians and a volunteer to drive me from town to town. We led off with a District Fall Conference in Concord, New Hampshire, which was a smash with a large enthusiastic audience. There was good press in *The Peterborough Transcript, Leisure,* and *Keene Shopper News.* Between each engagement we drove for miles, oftentimes in the dark of night — how I remember those long jostling rides — we were indeed *rural.* Most of the time ours was the only car on the road. My prayer was that the car would not break down! — this prayer was answered.

We wound up in Hartland Four Corners, Vermont. Truly, the small, narrow, lonely church, the First Universalist Society, sits at the junction of four roads and there is nothing, *nothing* around except flat land. "Do you think anybody will come?" I asked the driver as we waited in the chill autumn air for someone to arrive to open the church door. There had been press in *The Vermont Standard* and *Momentum,* and ads in local newspapers. There were numerous sponsors, churches in Hartland, Ascutney, and Woodstock. The driver offered me assurances but I privately concluded this location was a dud and I was annoyed to have to summon energy after a long drive, to rush to unpack, set up, get in costume and perform for the straggling group this area would attract.

Dressing in the basement, I could not see what was occuring upstairs. When I stepped into the hall, the long wooden benches were jammed! Some people were poised on shaky, metal folding chairs which obviously had been set up in corners at the last minute. Immediately, I responded to the warmth of the crowd. When I said my opening lines, I knew this was a sophisticated assemblage; they laughed and were intensely fixed on every one of Margaret Fuller's words.

"Where did all these people come from?" I asked after the show.

"Oh, from all around. They're used to driving," was the answer.

So much for the myth that people in rural areas are interested only in cows.

Adorning Red Shawls for Susan B. Anthony in Washington, D. C. (February 15, 1982)

I had not known that in our Washington, D. C. Capitol Building the *only statue of women* is in the *crypt* (or basement) where no one except Congressional staff sees it or even knows about it. Moreover this statue has been dubbed "the Ladies in the Bathtub" — why, surely only its author knows. All of this seems insulting — comparable to the mad woman kept in the attic in the famous story, *Jane Eyre*.

Statues honoring American men — George Washington, Thomas Jefferson, Abraham Lincoln, Martin Luther King, Jr., and others — are to be seen in the upstairs, second-floor rotunda.

On Susan B. Anthony's birthday, Ramona and I rallied in the crypt. Like the early women revolutionaries, we wore red shawls and we stood in front of the trio of America's first suffrage workers, Elizabeth Cady Stanton, Susan B. Anthony, and Lucretia Mott. These women, in a thirteen-ton block of white marble, were looking forward into the future — albeit their future seemed limited by the surrounding cold, cadaverous walls.

We, however, were not arrested as was Sonia Johnson, the excommunicated Mormon who climbed the White House fence to urge President Ronald Reagan to support the ERA amendment.

Ramona had organized the Capitol's photographer and so it was lights-camera-action as we presented Maine Rep. David Emery with a Margaret Fuller poster as a tribute to National Women's History Week. It had been sixty-five years since women had won the right to vote with the ratification of the Nineteenth Amendment to the Constitution. This picture appeared in the *Lincoln County News* in Damariscotta, Maine.

Our rally was not totally in vain. It seems both the Senate and House of Representatives have since voted to put this statue of our suffragists in the rotunda, but final approval was blocked because it was felt the move should be paid for with private funds. Therefore, a coalition of women's groups began a $75,000 fund-raising effort to lift the statue by crane and move it upstairs. Groups involved include the National League of Women Voters and the National Federation of Republican Women.

Wouldn't equality be served if this statue were moved up?

As Ramona would say, Amen.

**Beholding the Thomas Hicks Portrait of Margaret Fuller;
Circuiting Universities with the Wisconsin Humanities Grant
(Nov 2 - 10, 1981)**

Connie Fuller Threinen's words echo Margaret Fuller's: "We need
to be more future-oriented....Women are over half of the population
and the half which is most directly related to the next generation. We
need to make people understand that women's concerns are not a
side issue."

Connie knew almost nothing about Margaret Fuller until the end
of the '70s. "I started reading about her when I inherited her portrait."

Staying overnight at Connie's Middleton, Wisconsin, house, just
before launching our Humanities grant tour, I had the unique
privilege of standing in front of the fireplace and looking closely at
the original of one of three existing pictures of Fuller.* It was painted
by American artist Thomas Hicks in Rome, Italy, in 1848, during the
height of the fighting in the Italian Revolution.

Fuller is central, seated on a red-velvet bench, wearing a lovely,
modest, lilac gown and a cream-colored shawl, her hands in repose
on her lap, with a background of browns through which a light dawn
rises making visible historic Italian landmarks. Her head is slightly
bowed and a trace of resignation crosses her face while a certain
peace permeates her entire being.

Connie, a beneficiary of Margaret Fuller's groundbreaking advo-
cacy for women, graduated from University of Wisconsin-Madison
with a degree in economics, then founded the League of Women
Voters of Middleton, serving as president, and later served on the
League's State Board. She helped to establish the Wisconsin
Women's Political Caucus and Wisconsin Women's Network, a
strong coalition of about a hundred women's organizations in the
state.

Now she was Women's Education Specialist for University of
Wisconsin-Extension. She designed and coordinated noncredit
courses for and about women.

All went smoothly on our ten college stops. Perfect planning

---

*The other two pictures of Margaret Fuller are a steel engraving made when she was
about twenty years old, and a daguerreotype in 1846 at the age of thirty-six, just before
she sailed for Europe.

and organization! We drove through the state; Connie went on half the tour and her upbeat, convivial co-administrator, Marion Thompson, took the other half. Scholars and technical help were recruited from each college. Audiences were sizable, about two or three hundred at each performance, made up of students, faculty, and community. Press was excellent...a full page article in *The Capitol Times*.

Margaret Fuller must be looking down from the heavens with a sense of satisfaction. Connie's granddaughter is named Margaret Fuller!

Talking About Transcendentalists with Dr. James Luther Adams (Exact date not remembered)

No one cared for this conversation except ourselves.

We were both delighted to be so absorbed.

For an hour in a noisy community room in Arlington Church, he and I sat and discussed the Harvard graduates of 1829, all friends of Margaret Fuller.

Ramona "cross-pollinated" me with James Luther Adams. He was one of the most revered persons in the U.S. He was the Edward Mallinckrodt, Jr., Harvard Professor of Divinity, *Emeritus*.

Ramona sent me tons of press on him with one of her scribbled notes: "We have such biggies who love us."

Stepping onto the Famous Hasty Pudding Stage — the Harvard University Theater (March 25, 1982)

Stars have been born on the stage of one of America's oldest dramatic organizations, Hasty Pudding Club at Harvard — which was in full swing during the era of Margaret Fuller. Many an outrageous undergraduate production has been mounted here, and past performers have been Oliver Wendell Holmes, Franklin Roosevelt, William Randolph Hearst, Henry Cabot Lodge and Robert Sherwood. More recently, Man and Woman of the Year honors have been awarded to Dustin Hoffman, James Cagney, Julie Andrews, Ella Fitzgerald, Jane Fonda, Meryl Streep, and Mary Tyler Moore, and others, all of whom were paraded through Harvard Square by Pudding troupers and endowed with engraved brass Pudding Cups. Once, Alistair Cooke, presenter of PBS's "Masterpiece Theater," came complete with red-velvet chair, to award a Fiftieth-Reunion version of the Pudding show he directed as a graduate student, *Hades to Ladies,* based on "the absolutely ludicrous possibility that women would be admitted to Harvard."*

I got onto the Hasty Pudding stage because my sister, Gwen Harper, was organizing a special day-long event for members of the Junior League of Boston, Inc.

It just so happened that, on the day I was to perform, because there was no backstage, the entire set for an upcoming student production had to be stored on stage in full view of the audience — even though the Junior League had contracted for Hasty Pudding months in advance. Desperate, the women draped black cloths over the furniture. But legs of tables and various lumpy things remained stubbornly visible.

Moreover, I got the brainstorm to freshen up the performance. Mary, my daughter, was attending Emerson College in Boston. I rewrote parts of the script so that about twenty Emerson theater department students could voice some lines while they sat as audience members in the theater. And I wrote a small scene for Ossoli, Fuller's lover, ten years her junior. My daughter served as casting agent. Except for the role of Ossoli, the students had their lines written on index cards. It was fun and easy for them; we held rehearsal and they were all charged with enthusiasm. But I went crazy memorizing cues and holding my breath they would say their lines at the proper time from who-knows-where, since I didn't know where the young actors were sitting.

The Junior League women seemed satisfied, and president Betsy Nelson invited Gwen and me to lunch a day or two later. But I wish I could have seen the performance in order to evaluate the effectiveness of this technique. I never attempted it again.

Launching a New Three-Character Margaret Fuller Play, *O Excellent Friend!* (June 9 - 22, 1982)

The countdown was on!

We were rehearsing at my church, the North Shore Unitarian Universalist Society, on Long Island, several times per week and the

---

*From *Harvard* magazine, May-June 1984, p. 86.

Reverend Dr. David P. Osborn was having tremendous difficulty learning lines, largely because he also had duties as minister and couldn't possibly devote the four or five hours per day that was needed for this drama.

But we'd gotten a special grant from the Board of Trustees practically as soon as he'd agreed to play Ralph Waldo Emerson in my play *O Excellent Friend!* to be presented at General Assembly in honor of the 100th-year commemoration of Emerson's death. So we had a budget of about $3,000 for travel, technical help, print materials, and costumes, and we picked up further moneys from The Emerson Committee and the Denominational Affairs Committee. We also had publicity supports from Women and Religion, the Unitarian Universalist Women's Federation, and MSUU (the women minister's organization).

We obtained a good time slot and the best auditorium at Bowdoin College in Portland, Maine, where the national Conference was being held. Locations and scheduling are always highly competitive because all UU groups are vying for them — and I figured my new drama could become one of the outstanding events of the year.

When Anne Vendig learned I'd written a new script, she cornered David Osborn after church services one Sunday and said, "Want to play Ralph Waldo Emerson?"

I was certain he'd say no.

It turned out he'd been an actor and had played in shows Off-Broadway before becoming a minister. He was also a devotee of Ralph Waldo Emerson, and a member of the Alumni of Harvard Divinity School — Emerson's alma mater as well as that of Margaret Fuller's father and brothers.

After David Osborn read the play, he called me and questioned to the effect, "Perhaps your script shows Emerson in a negative light?"

"A *human* light," I responded. "A human being he was."

Whether or not that comment convinced him to take on the role which, as I'd written it, was critical of the ideal image that many people carry of Emerson, I don't know.

As usual, I had overwritten. We sat in David's office, reading aloud, and we cut, cut, cut; probably about half my script went into "the round file." I would never have found the necessary cuts without his eye, knowledge of history, and impeccable taste.

I tried to find a professional person to create David's makeup — he didn't look like Emerson. The makeup artist we went to in New York City turned out to be a fraud in my opinion; however, David was content, and we didn't have budget nor time for another. But where were we to find his costume and wig and pictures.

The artwork was a mess. I'd planned slides of Emerson's and Fuller's houses in Cambridge, Concord, and Boston to be flashed on to help indicate the rapid scene changes, but when we rehearsed, they didn't work and so I cancelled their use.

From Lexington, Massachusetts, Billie Drew, our very special and cooperative Margaret Fuller Foundation liaison, planned to get our Margaret Fuller exhibit up to Bowdoin College — twelve giant blow-ups on foam board, black and white, photographed courtesy of Polaroid to be exhibited in the foyer of Kresge Auditorium where we'd perform.

"These lines are like learning Shakespeare," David Osborn complained in frustration. "I say them without a hitch every morning, but when I rehearse, they just don't come."

The dialogue *was* difficult. I had built from Emerson's and Fuller's letters and journals, so the language seemed stiff and erudite. You had to get the knack in order to capture the conversational tone. One word off and you ruined the flow.

Interestingly enough, David never delivered a sermon from a script. His presentation was always a spontaneous sharing of his very active mind.

I commiserated. "You need to repeat your lines every morning, afternoon and night."

He didn't have time. In fact, church members were complaining that he was neglecting his *real* duties. As we continued rehearsals, I convinced Janet, his wife, that she was needed to sit in and "cue" him.

One of the church members' sons, an appealing eight-year-old who hadn't grown as fast as others his age, was able to take on the third character in my play, Waldo Emerson, Jr., who was supposed to be five years old. His parents were thrilled.

I found a professional photographer, had a superb picture taken of David Osborn and myself, and devised an excellent black-and-white flyer to hand out and post on the walls of Bowdoin.

Run-throughs before audiences were set at the Unitarian Universalist Church of Central Nassau in Garden City, UU Fellowship of Muttontown, and at our church.

We planned a panel-and-audience-discussion afterwards. I wrote letters and organized the most prestigious "biggies" in the UU movement. We were a smash.

We solved Osborn's memory problem by placing his script on the desk amongst Emerson's letters and papers — so he was able to read the tough lines and glance at others.

The applause was deafening.

Everyone loved seeing Osborn play Emerson. I believe it was an experience he will always remember. On the other hand, I am sure he was glad it was over. I have a sneaking suspicion he now knew for certain that, years back, he had chosen the right occupation for himself.

Protesting the Demise of the ERA (June 30, 1982)

I half understood what Ramona was doing.

Connecting in Boston for a tandem, Ramona asked me to dress as Margaret Fuller.

Walking up Beacon Hill, she gave to passersby primitive handwritten flyers announcing that our Foundation was dedicated to the memory of all women buried in history and that our protest demonstration upon the demise of the ERA would be held at the golden dome of the Massachusetts State Capitol beside the statue of Anne Hutchinson.

I followed as she "crashed" offices in the Unitarian Universalist Association headquarters and interested key persons in attending.

I waited while she used the public phone in the building to call the press, and in about an hour we were at the feet of Anne Hutchinson's statue, with the lights-camera-action of five newspapers and TV networks.

That evening we appeared on Jack Borden segment on News Center 5, WCVB-TV. His story commenced with NOW members speaking out and demonstrating in front of the White House in Washington, D. C. Then the TV screen flashed to what was happening in Boston — Ramona making a statement followed by me in costume resounding Margaret Fuller's famous words, "Let women be sea captains if they will!"*

Ramona considered such extemporaneous public protests more effective than all the windy work that organized institutions spent long hours planning.

"The thirty-year-olds take three years to put on a conference," she'd disparage. "Semi-structure; semi-happenings — that's my style. Ad hocs as the vibes dictate."

Upon reflection, I had to agree.

Performing for the Department of the Army, Fort Gordon, Augusta, Georgia (August 26, 1983)

I don't usually care to peform at luncheons while people eat cake and sip coffee, but an invitation from the Department of the United States Army was intriguing.

My drama was scheduled to celebrate the 63rd anniversary of the ratification of the Nineteenth Amendment which gave women the right to vote. Sponsors were the USASC Federal Woman's Program and the Garden City of Federally Employed Women.

Reconnoitering at Fort Gordon in Augusta, Georgia, I met a number of dynamic top-brass men, all perfectly charming, and I performed for women on the narrow apron of a rather high and awkward stage in front of a curtain. There was a good article and picture in *The Semaphore,* a newspaper for the personnel of Fort Gordon, and Major General Henry J. Schumacher wrote me a congratulatory letter wherein he stated: "Your performance was well planned, informative and enjoyable. I have received many favorable comments from Fort Gordon Personel concerning your excellent presentation."

This impressed my husband, who'd served as a Platoon Sergeant in the South Pacific during World War II and was awarded the Silver Star. He said he'd been in the army for five years and had never even seen a general.

Celebrating Peace and Freedom with W.I.L.P.F. (March 11, 1984)

You won't find lovelier women than Susan Blake and Dori Gloria. Both are beautiful and bright, full of energy and charisma.

---

*From Margaret Fuller's book, *Woman in the Nineteenth Century.*

They were the Nassau branch of the Women's International League for Peace and Freedom (WILPF) which believes that peace is more than the absense of war, and requires nonviolent means of conflict resolution. Their purpose reminds me of Margaret Fuller's favorite quote: "Mankind is one, and beats with one great heart."

Susan and Gloria were creating a different scene in the heart of suburbia, Massapequa. Susan was not hampered without a car; she went everywhere on a bike. Both worked out of an old house called Peacesmith House. Their large, superbly lighted basement was wall-to-wall files — cardboard boxes of paper neatly covering long tables spaced just wide enough so you could edge by.

Upstairs, in small old-fashioned rooms, the two women held Sunday-afternoon poetry readings, discussions, and other events. They cultivated a predominently young-adult group, but their audiences were also smattered with the past-fifty crowd, most of whom came in jeans and T-shirts and sat informally on old sofas or floor.

WILPF had emerged from the turn-of-the-century International Women's Suffrage Alliance headquarted in London. It was founded in 1915 when an International Congress of Women met in Holland at the Hague Congress. Jane Addams presided over the first congress and was elected first president in 1919.

I had all this to learn when I picked up my phone and heard Susan Blake's voice. WILPF was celebrating their 75th Anniversary.

They treated me like a star. I had to do nothing but perform. They chose the site, Community United Methodist Church, and connected with co-sponsors, CUMC Outreach Commission, Committee on Role & Status of Women, found people to help, sent out flyers and announcements, and staged a follow-up discussion and reception.

I would have wanted to work with these people if I hadn't felt that my best time and talents served Margaret Fuller.

Cruising on a Ferry to Perform on Star Island (August 19, 1985)

People are rejuvenated at Star Island, named in 1651 because its points stretch north, south, east, west. Star, one of the Isles of Shoals ten miles out of Portsmouth, New Hampshire, boasts historic interest and scenic beauty, rocky land without trees in a vast expanse of water and sky. The beds and chairs in the guest houses are inclusively uncomfortable, but the air is pure. In daylight hours on winding paths you discover geological formations, native plants, and marine life. At night your Schoalers gather in a silent march and carry lanterns to the highest point to enter an 1800 stone meetinghouse for an evening candlelight service.

Coordinators of this UU summer conference were the greatest people you could meet, Paul and Louise Mitchell, who said nothing when, for some unexplainable reason, I went blank on stage, couldn't think of my next line, and stood like a fool, embarrassed, the sweat breaking out, knowing no one in the world could help.

There are many reasons for going blank. Distractions from the audience. Tension in your body. Technical problems. Props being in the wrong place, or not there at all. Your mind wandering.

It is always worse for the actor than for the audience. Two seconds of going blank seems like two hundred minutes. You try not to stumble or stutter, but keep your cool, stay in character, and cover for yourself. You search around for something to do, some action or gesture, to fill up the silence, praying to heaven that the proper words will come. You attempt to focus like you've never focused before but, instead, you notice your hands are beginning to shake. Five lines flit into your mind, but they are ones later in the script. If you're lucky and if you have your wits, you can ad lib until you're back on track. If you stand there in character and make an honest effort to relax — and just try to in that situation! — the words eventually float back, from out of nowhere.

After this performance I learned the absolute only way to handle such disasterous moments. I am Margaret Fuller and Margaret Fuller is a *person* who doesn't always know what she is going to say next. She pauses and thinks. Thinking in character, if real, is often more intriguing to an audience than talking.

After all, do you always know what you are going to say next? Don't you pause and think?

Margaret Fuller *cannot* "forget" a "line."

The Cambridge Capers: Dedicating the Margaret Fuller Ossoli Plaque; Dedicating the Margaret Fuller Ossoli Room at Marriott Hotel (October 20-21, 1987)

I have to hand it to Ramona.

Ramona, of the Margaret Fuller Network — we'd given our Foundation the trendy name of "Network" by now — convinced the Cambridge "fathers" to commemorate Fuller with a permanent memorial plaque to be placed on the wall in the foyer of City Hall. Vice-Mayor Al Vellucci introduced the order to the City Council which voted affirmatively to adopt the measure. The plaque was created by the Cambridge Historical Commission. The mayor's office again sent out impressive invitations.

On a rainy and gloomy night, we attracted a small crowd. Mistress of Ceremonies Ramona introduced Mayor Walter J. Sullivan, who offered his greetings, after which Vice-Mayor Vellucci made some remarks. Then Ramona, City Councilwoman Saundra Graham and Vellucci pulled off the veil of the lovely bronze and wood plaque with Fuller's picture. It reads:

> Born in Cambridge, Massachusetts, May 23, 1810
> By birth a child of New England
> By adoption a citizen of Rome
> By genius belonging to the world
> Educator, Feminist, Journalist
> Died July 19, 1850

Afterwards, the town-and-gown crowd gathered in the red-carpeted, red-velvet, city-hall chambers where Ronald Lee Fleming, founding chairman of the Cambridge Arts Council, introduced my drama, which was video-taped for Cable Channel 8. A reception followed.

Ramona had planned a week-long series of mini-events, "Margaret Fuller Days in Cambridge" which were to have included: (1) espresso at the newly built Dante Cultural Center building and at the Blacksmith House on Brattle Street (now an Adult Education Center) where Margaret Fuller lived for a time; (2) exhibits of photographs and memorabilia at the Cambridge library and at the YWCA; (3) a meeting in the 170-acre Mt. Auburn garden cemetery where Fuller is commemorated with a memorial amongst the winding, green, tree-lined paths; (4) a sermon at the First Parish Church on Harvard Square; (5) a Margaret Fuller "Conversation" at the Margaret Fuller Neighborhood House; (6) a walking tour of Harvard Yard to the location where Fuller first stepped inside Gore Library; (7) a meeting at the statue of John Harvard.

She and I giggled over coffee at the Blacksmith Shop but the rest of the events actually did not happen, though she did donate a part of her collection of women's history books to the opening of a rare Italian library at the Dante Cultural Center.*

"Laurie," she wrote me later, "hold me to 1/10 of my plots OK!! This is to keep our blood circulating."

Ramona was successful, though, in getting the powers-that-be at the newly constructed Marriott Hotel in Cambridge to name a room after Fuller. Don't ask me how she did it. The general manager Bill Munck and his committee already had named rooms after Longfellow and some of the other Cambridge "boys." Perhaps there was guilt about not including the Cambridge "girls."

The night before the City Hall plaque dedication, we went to the Marriott in our best to dedicate the Margaret Fuller Room — which turned out to be a suite luxurious enough for the president of the United States. If you stayed overnight in this room, you would be billed something like $2,500. I'm positive Margaret Fuller had never been in such a hotel room — even when her father had campaigned for John Adams.

We had a great party. We looked out the floor-to-ceiling windows on the Charles River and the glittering lights and stars of Boston. We wandered back and forth in the spaciousness, and gingerly touched the new, custom-designed, ultra-modern furniture. We watched the waiters deftly wheel in a cart of hor d'oeuvres placed perfectly on white cloths. Dramatically, they opened bottles, and we made champagne toasts.

Go and see the Margaret Fuller plaque in the foyer in Cambridge City Hall today, do!

Go and see the Margaret Fuller Room in the Cambridge Marriott!

Encountering Margaret Fuller's Statue in Ron Fleming's Backyard (Exact date not remembered)

"God, what press!"

Ramona was salivating over the thought of a newspaper picture

---

*These books were lost in a flood.

of us standing beside a Margaret Fuller statue in the Harvard Square subway.

Ramona had discovered that Ron Fleming, founding chairman of the Cambridge Arts Council, had commissioned, after seeing my performance, the Cambridge sculptor Penelope Jencks* to create a statue of Margaret Fuller. His idea was to have this statue placed in the newly renovated Harvard Square subway station along with "underground culture" — inlaid ceramic tiles, murals, and massive chimes, dedicated by the Arts on the Line program, which was helping to brighten the station so that the arts could truly belong to the people.

We were overwhelmed when we saw the statue. There was Margaret Fuller, gleaming gold, life-size, lifelike, standing straight and proud, tucked in amongst the bushes and trees of Fleming's backyard.

Somehow Fleming never could pull the strings of the Massachusetts Bay Transportation Authority. We helped by pressuring the MBTA with letters, but Ramona said, "I guess there are some stone walls we wd be immature & adolescent to crash & of course we are mature responsible matrons!!!"

To my knowledge, the golden Margaret Fuller still stands in Fleming's backyard.**

Bringing Margaret Fuller To Life at Flushing Unitarian Universalist Church, Long Island, New York (March 13, 1988)

Steps, podium, and choral area jutted out in all the wrong places for a dramatic presentation, but at the far end of the long, narrow worship hall there was an exceptionally beautiful floor-to-ceiling, stained glass window. During the performance, just after Margaret Fuller's prayer, I looked into the filtering light. The dazzling colors energized me with a spiritual power I'd never felt. I began to live Margaret Fuller with a reality and sensitivity never before touched.

---

*In 1996 Penelope Jencks sculpted a statue of Eleanor Roosevelt which stands in Riverside Park in New York City.

**A picture of the statue appears on the cover of this book.

Shouting Like Liberty Fighters in Old South Meeting House in Boston (April 5-6, 1991)

What made the performance unworkable were the accoustics. Built in 1729 as a Puritan house of worship, Old South Meeting House had "dead spots" and echoes impossible to overcome. I thought by using exquisitely perfect diction and talking slowly I could handle it, but no. Nothing, not even a microphone could help. The audience heard my words drifting in and out like static on a ham radio.

Still, it was nostalgic joy just to be Margaret Fuller in that historic building where Sam Adams, George Washington, John Hancock, and Julia Ward Howe had spoken out, where the Sons of Liberty had shouted in fiery debate, deciding to throw four hundred chests of tea into Boston Harbor in protest against the outrageous English tax.

Weathering a Miracle at the Twelfth Night Club, the Oldest Club for Actresses in America (March 10, 1996)

The sound and lighting technicians — volunteers — were so conscientious that we rehearsed two nights to perfect every cue. Alfred Boone had never run a reel-to-reel tape recorder but he was an actor with good theater background and was well aware of the importance of every detail. That's why it was gratifying to work with the Twelfth Night Club, Inc. members, including Melanie Hill who was on publicity. They were professionals and "ran the extra mile" to ensure success in limited facilities in an apartment on 55th Street in New York City. And the great advantage there was setting up props and equipment days in advance, confident that I could come to performance with everything in position and that the tech crew knew exactly what to do.

On performance day I arrived full of anticipation, but Alfred was in a state of agitation.

"You know" — his forehead was wrinkling in dismay — "I can't get any volume." The reels were turning, but the sound was barely audible. He cleaned the heads and fiddled with all the switches but the tone did not improve.

He talked to our coordinator, Elnora Hayes; she was at a loss. He made phone calls to Curtis Ether, our reel-to-reel expert. In desperation, Alfred shook the machine.

"It's going to work, *I know*," I said, "have faith!"

Still nothing could be heard beyond backstage.

The hour of performance was upon us. Elnora instructed our MC (mistress of ceremonies), Peggy Turnley, to apologize for technical problems — which she did.

I adjusted my Margaret Fuller shawl, picked up my books. Alfred, Mies Ottenheimer who was on lights, and I nodded to each other. Mies turned off the houselights, then turned up the lights on the stage area. Alfred punched the button on the reel-to-reel.

Miracle of *miracles* — the sound blasted FULL POWER!

I made my entrance with the music FULL POWER!

FULL POWER we had throughout the show!

The only explanation anyone can offer was that there must have been a power surge. In this old building power surges *did* occur. But to be rectified *at the very moment* I made my entrance? !

Facing Empty Chairs and Candlelight at the Old Merchant House Museum (November 8-9-10, 1996)

As soon as I entered the Old Merchant House Museum in New York City I began salivating, as Ramona would say. I immediately got dates for three performances.

Merchant House is a landmark rowhouse built in 1832, just fourteen years before Margaret Fuller arrived in the city. It was lived in by the prosperous merchant Seabury Tredwell and family during the years Margaret Fuller was becoming famous for her front-page literary criticisms on Horace Greeley's *New York Daily Tribune*, and for her book, *Woman in the Nineteenth Century*. The Merchant House is one of the finest surviving examples of late-Federal and Greek Revival architecture. Open to the public as a museum, it houses the original furniture and decorative arts of the lifestyle of a typical upper-middle-class family.

To promote the museum, the curator, Mimi Sherman, scheduled concerts, readings, and other programs in the large living-dining-room area. She told me that the person who took tickets and opened and closed the house received $10.00 per hour, so after that expense was taken care of, we'd share profits from the $10 tickets. Fair enough — however I wasn't doing it to earn money; I wanted Margaret Fuller in that superb environment.

The superb environment proved to be technically impossible.

First, we had to dispense with sound effects. Theaters use heavy professional reel-to-reel tape recorders hooked into amplifiers, but we needed the small portable machine — which I learned is no longer made or available to rent. (The old one we'd used at the Twelfth Night Club had been inadvertently given away to the Salvation Army during a clean-up campaign. A reel-to-reel is vital because the technician has complete control in handling the various cues; cassette tape decks are virtually impossible for a performance situation.)

Second, the overhead, period lighting in the room and the four gas lights on the mantle piece were much too dim, and the two availablbe spotlights (the kind photographers use) could not be set up in any way appropriate. I was about to "abandon ship" when the brilliant idea dawned: There were beautiful crystal candelabra throughout the house. How novel to perform by candlelight!

Alfred Boone and Mies Ottenheimer of the Twelfth Night Club had volunteered their technical services again and, as it turned out, I couldn't have performed without them. They entered ahead of me and lit the candles, then, after I left the stage — during the Bayard Taylor letter about Margaret Fuller's shipwreck (which Alfred read) — Mies extinguished the candles with long-handled, brass candle snuffers. How dramatic!

Alfred said he couldn't imagine a better setting. It was truly lovely and intimate, the chairs in a semicircle close to Fuller's table with its lace cloth against the background of the fireplace. I decided to talk to my audience as if Margaret Fuller were sharing an evening with them. "Welcome," I said. "Thank you for visiting me tonight. I always enjoy having visitors...appreciate your stopping by. There is only one problem — I'm on deadline. I must get these articles out for the *Dial* magazine, but please, do stay, and I'll just work along, if you'll excuse me, and we'll have a conversation at the same time...." Then, I launched into the beginning, where editor Margaret Fuller criticizes James Russell Lowell, Longfellow, Thoreau, and Emerson for their inferior work and chastises Henry Hedge and George Riply for not sending in their best writing.

All was perfect — except the first night there was one audience member more than the crew.

Saturday night, with two persons, I felt like cancelling but the curator was absent and no one knew the house policy.

Sunday there were five.

Alfred and Mies affirmed we were pioneers, that the Merchant House was new to programming and hadn't yet developed a following.

I'd mailed out about two hundred flyers — $64 worth of stamps. I'd paid personal visits to churches, and I'd handed out flyers to theater-goers on Theater Row. But unknown Margaret Fuller and me needed something big.

Maybe we needed a Ramona.

Being Awarded Sho-Dan, Honorary Black Belt (December 25, 1990)

Our family was crowded at the long table noisily finishing a tasty Christmas dinner. I had just published my books on Margaret Fuller and had given a few away as gifts to interested people. Suddenly my thirty-year-old son, Hardy, was standing, speaking above the gaiety of forks and knives and voices. He stood straight, looking strong without attempting to, for he had reached the rank of Go-Dan, fifth degree Black Belt, one of the highest achievements in Okinawa Shorin-Ryu Karate in the United States. He'd studied the art since he was fourteen. He was smiling, "And so, for you, Mom —" He held out a long piece of paper and a black belt that was badly frayed on the edges.

I was being awarded Sho-Dan, Honorary Black Belt!

The belt had belonged to Joseph Carbonara, *sensei*, one he'd worn so often that it was threadbare.

The diploma had vertical Japanese writing and was stamped with the official red seals, the symbols of the training school. It was signed by both Chotoku Omine, 8-Dan, Delegate of World Shorin-Ryu Karate Association, who had since passed away, and Joseph Carbonara, Renshi, 6th degree, Chief instructor of the Budokan East Northport, New York and East Coast Representative of (Matsubayashi-Ryu) Shorin-Ryu Okinawin Karate.

Hardy explained that since Chotoku Omine had died a few years earlier Joseph Carbonara *sensei* had only a few diplomas with Omine's signature left in his possession, and he allocated them sparingly. Therefore, this particular citation rendered an absolute token of esteem.

The letter that accompanied the diploma read:

December 25, 1990

To Laurie James

For her dedication and fervor in the research of Margaret Fuller, so that people young and old, male and female can come to grips with at least a starting of understanding of one's self!

Bravo!

This award of Black Belt is for one who I consider at the time of their training pure at heart. Only time will tell if they follow through on the path of the understanding of the nature of self.

For me Karate is in the Heart.

Love,

Joseph Carbonara

It seemed a far stretch to link Margaret Fuller and me with this art form, and so I looked into the reach of spirituality and found that karate teaches perfection of mind-body-spirit through disciplined training. It cultivates right action, respect, concentration, dedication, duty to society. The task is to find truth, enlightenment, and the universal harmony between man and nature. In karate the greatest fighter is he who can win an encounter without violence. Fighting is a strategy to be used as last resort.

I had taken my daily creed from Margaret Fuller, and she and her circle of Transcendentalists counseled truth, beauty, individuality, harmony of nature, and the divinity of mankind.* They were all revolutionaries who revolted without violence.

I learned no other woman in Shorin-Ryu Karate had received an Honorary Black Belt.

---

*If Margaret Fuller lived today, she would substitute the word "humankind" for "mankind."

GAMBLING OFF-OFF BROADWAY

It took forever to drop the idea that, as natural as night follows day, if I was good enough I would be discovered.

Long term results, good or bad, would come only if I boldly took a gamble.

The great gamble — or should I say *gambol* — is Off-Off Broadway.

Off-Off Broadway is theater that is not on Off-Broadway.

Off-Broadway is theater that is not on Broadway.

Broadway in New York City represents large-scale, extravagant productions, the best in the world, in the best theaters with the largest seating capacities, the largest budgets, the greatest names, and it has survived on the heartless vicissitudes of the ticket-buying public — in other words, it is professional, slick, commercial.

The unknown artist driven by a sense of purpose has little hope of working on Broadway.

Off-Broadway is the vitality of New York City's Greenwich Village area — but you'll also find companies off Times Square, on Theater Row, 42nd Street. Elsewhere in the city, too.

You always used to want to work Off-Broadway because that was where, in makeshift, no-pay or low pay conditions, you could get your feet wet doing innovative, experimental drama. You could step into Beckett, or Chekhov. It was beyond the mainstream, more hidden, younger, but you had more freedom, more radicalism. Where you could be in theater for the love of it, where you could fail and grow.

Trace the movement back to 1914 when Lawrence Langner founded the Washington Square Players — this group evolved into one of the most respected producing units in the country, the Theater Guild. The Provincetown Players, founded by George Cram Cook and Susan Glaspell, produced the first plays of Eugene O'Neill and nurtured such writers as Louise Bryant, Floyd Dell and Edna St. Vincent Millay. At Neighborhood Playhouse on the Lower East Side, Alice and Irene Lewisohn concentrated on European plays. In 1926 actress Eva Le Gallienne created the Civic Repertory Theater where she established a low-price ticket policy until the Depression forced her to close. During the 1930s Mordecai Gorelik's Theater Collective awakened social consciousness.

The Second World War curtailed Off-Broadway. Energy resumed in the late 1940s as David Heilweil and Norman Rose opened New Stages, and in 1948 there birthed the Interplayers with Gene Saks, Michael Gazzo, Kim Stanley, and Beatrice Arthur staging Cocteau, O'Casey, and e. e. cummings. Then surfaced the Living Theater, T. Edward Hamilton's Phoenix Theater, and Joseph Papp's New York Shakespeare Festival.

In 1952 Off-Broadway became a viable, recognizable force as Geraldine Page created extraordinary excitement in Tennessee Williams' *Summer and Smoke* at Circle in the Square. In the late 1950s Joe Cino pioneered impromptu poetry readings in his Greenwich Village coffee house. Ellen Stewart, at Cafe La Mama in a cellar on East Twelfth Street, rang her cowbell at the beginning of each performance. Al Carmines opened Judson Poets' Theater, and during the '60s audiences were treated to writers like Rochelle Owens, Lanford Wilson, Sam Shepard, Maria Irene Fornes, Leonard Melfi. The American Place Theater was founded by Sidney Lanier at St. Clement's Church, and Michael Allen and Ralph Cook broke ground for Theater Genesis in St. Mark's Church-in-the-Bouwerie. Off-Broadway was heralding new American playwrights: Edward Albee, *The Zoo Story*; Jack Richardson, *The Prodigal*; Jack Gelber, *The*

Connection; Arthur L. Kopit, *Oh Dad, Poor Dad, Mamma's Hung You in the Closet and I'm Feelin' So Sad;* and others.

From the perspective of the devotee of serious American drama, Off-Broadway has taken on the look of Broadway. In the last quarter of the twentieth century, economics forced most serious drama to transfer downtown, away from Broadway's fantasticly lavish productions which take six months to a year to break even. The musical was perfected and became popular; group ticket sales burgeoned as tourists were bused in. Television, videocassettes, cable edged in. People have rushed to what is hottest, neglecting what is most worthy. Theater unions became stronger and theater people began receiving higher salaries with benefits. Rents skyrocketed. Ticket prices soared. Producers found they can service dramatic production less expensively Off-Broadway.

The biggest Off houses, such as Manhattan Theater Club, and Playwrights Horizons, have acquired more stabilized economic bases, hired business managers and publicists, developed coterie audiences, and have thereby attracted the gifted. Becoming subject to the hit-or-flop psychosis of Broadway, they became cautious in their choices of material, actors, and directors. Hollywood tapped hits and turned them into major films, such as *Driving Miss Daisy, Steel Magnolias, Frankie and Johnny,* and *Other People's Money.* The term Off-Broadway remains, but Off-Broadway has become The Establishment.

So what became the plight of less-commercial, committed artists? They gravitated back to the side streets, in the churches, factories, warehouses, storefronts, cellars, lofts, coffeehouses, restaurants, and shops, in Soho, Chelsea, Clinton, the Upper West Side, and Harlem, where they could be free to take chances, extend their range, rely on their own resources, venture without censorship or coercion. Thus, somewhere along in the late '60s-70s, arose the term Off-Off Broadway.

Off-Off was where I wanted to be.

I started making calls. In the larger houses, you never get beyond the front desk. But in the smaller ones, there are no front desks. One artistic director was interested. She and her male sidekick were ready to set a spring date for a run of my Margaret Fuller drama in their

charming Theater Off-Park, attached to the Community Church of
New York at 35th, off Park Avenue. It could squeeze in an audience
of fifty. She suggested I do a reading for their Monday-night series.

On that sleet-and-snow night a few days before Christmas almost
no one showed up — to my good fortune because that experience
taught me what never to do. Never spit out words in an excruciatingly
loud and dull monotone. It was misery to hear that the artistic director
had left midway through my performance, only to return with a
stricken face after it was over to tell me she couldn't stage my drama.
My confidence was maimed for over a year.

The theater no longer operates, though the name has spawned
in another venue in Greenwich Village. The artistic director has
passed away.

Another method of getting to Off-Off is to be discovered by a
producer or a director.

Once I thought I was discovered. I had written to many theaters
and the Center for Music, Drama, and Art in Lake Placid, New York,
booked me — a year in advance — for a four-week artist-in-
residency. When the long- anticipated day finally arrived, I tramped
through two feet of soft powdery snow and was greeted as warmly
as a star by the publicity director, who was busily arranging an exhibit
of my show in the glass showcase in the lobby. As she showed me
about, I learned that Lake Placid was a superb Olympic training
ground and I was not to be dismayed if the sparce populace was more
interested in skiing than in theater.

The publicity director's husband was one of several directors who
helped keep shows in repertory. After I'd played to half-empty
houses, he appeared and said he wanted to take my drama Off-Off.

A likeable guy, he joked and ate a lot at "get acquainted" meetings
in restaurants. I was even invited to dinner at his home with his wife
and children. He would re-direct the show. He knew important
producers and who did we want?

He arranged for me to do a "run-through" at the theater. I put my
heart and soul into it and afterwards he said he knew I had just been
"walking through it." But it showed potential. He would set up
meetings in New York.

Within a month he drove down to the Big Apple.

Behind a desk with a lot of phones, an energetic wirey guy smiled. He was producing another show Off-Off Broadway, but he could run with our show. As we left, he told me confidentially that I could not expect to make any money, but if I was good, it would set me up to go a long way.

I did not get his name or phone number, figuring that was up to my director. The following week I received a call — where *was* my director? Our producer wanted to set up a meeting with his partner. I called; my director wasn't in so I left a message. Over the next three weeks I phoned every day. After that I wrote letters; I must have written every day for a month. To this day, I have never received an answer.

After a while I began to make a noble effort to study the theater section in *The New York Times*. A respected theater group, The Open Eye, staged Saturday morning play readings/discussions open to the public. For about two months I was part of their audience of about a hundred. At first no one noticed me. The actors and directors, always in a frenzy, communicated in tightly closed cliques. Hanging about, I introduced myself to a director. He nodded as though he were interested in what I was doing, took my materials, and rushed off. Then, one day one of the coordinators asked me to read stage directions. Estatic, I began to feel included and ready to approach the same director again. Can I ever forget his look of revulsion and horror. The walls of that cavernous room echoed his resounding "NO!" so adamantly I wished I could disappear through a hole in the floor.

The women's movement had been accelerating for about ten years and women in theater were building opportunities for themselves. I read about a newly designed laboratory promoting the work of female artists in all disciplines. Since several women from suburban Westchester were presenting an original musical, I rushed to see it. I liked this spacious West Side loft, was sure my work belonged here. I sent a letter with materials and made phone calls. I paid a personal visit and found the atmosphere vibrant with women creating. But I was shunted off hurriedly. Nor was I allowed to see the artistic director. But so sure was I about this place that I decided to aggressively place phone calls every day. Then I wrote a letter, stating that the artistic director owed it to our great foremother, Margaret Fuller, to give me time and space. The next week she was on the phone. "Listen," the harsh voice blasted into the receiver, "will you please desist! I am tired of it! If I am interested in your piece, I will get in touch with you! Don't you contact me!" And I heard a click.

To this day a great many women are busily fulfilling their dreams at this theater which has become a major Off-Off house. I admire their accomplishments; I attend their shows which are good. To this day I feel my work is on a par, and I wish I could be a part of them. I still have to wonder, if supporting women and their work is the basis for this group's existence, how can one woman be treated rudely?

All the while, I was honing and perfecting my script, adding to my slide collection, promoting and staging my drama for churches and organizations. The responses from the various audiences gave me cues as to how to cut, add, and shape. *Finally,* I found a way to combine both the American Years with the European Years, thereby I could tell the entire story of Margaret Fuller in a little more than an hour. Cutting my script was like cutting part of my heart out — but I knew it had to be done. *Part II, The European Years,* which itself took an hour to perform, was actually a history lesson, instead of a dramatic presentation.

I've discovered that I'm a "detail" writer — I like to include *all* the information because I think it is *so* important. Often I say the same thing twice, in different ways. Or I explain too much — fail to allow for audience imagination. Finding the proper "notes" to hit was a revelation, a remarkable achievement.

I also "graduated" to a more sophisticated costume. Many women who saw my show commented on how they'd expected to see a more extravagant outfit and, after all, Fuller had dressed immaculately in New York and Europe when she'd been relieved of helping to support her family. Though she could never afford to spend exhorbitant sums on clothing, she was always well groomed. Since silk was the available and fashionable material of the day, I found a lovely silk-like fabric that was resistant to wrinkling — wine-red with white lace at the collar. And the color went well with my purple shawl (still borrowed from my sister-in-law). When this dress began to show signs of wear, I had another one made of the same material, but this time in forest green.

(As a footnote, this green dress held up though my three summer tours with The Great Plains Chautauqua Society, Inc. when I wore it practically everyday out-of-doors in hot weather. Home from Chautauqua, I had to have a fourth costume made; I chose steel-blue silk. This last dress was the most authentic and elaborate, with the old-fashioned-type bones sewed into the lining and smocking on the shoulders. The steel-blue looks lovely with the purple shaw! Much later Anne Vendig gave me a hand-knitted, circular rust-colored shawl which also looks lovely and quite authentic and which I now use because the purple one actually has holes in it.)

It was in 1984 when I also began to expand my repertoire and adapted for the stage a favorite short story, "The Yellow Wallpaper" by Charlotte Perkins Gilman, and found groups which booked it. I submitted my Margaret Fuller script and qualified for membership in the Committee for Women of the Dramatists Guild, recently galvanized by dramatist/actress Gretchen Cryer to further the work of women playwrights. Another bonus was being in a playwriting group started by actress/playwright Romola Robb Allrud who'd played the nurse in *Harvey* on Broadway in the mid-1940s. All this was food for my soul, but there remained that gnawing ache to be on Off-Off.

Contacts led me to a youthful group called Women in Theater (WIT), chaired by a likeable and efficient Susan Morris who conducted meetings at which I found myself envied because I secured pay for my one-woman presentations. WIT produced a Spotlight on Women Festival at the 53rd Street Y, but dragging my props up and down flights of stairs and performing without lights in front of an audience sitting on wooden folding chairs did seem a letdown. WIT dispersed a year or two later.

I was able to arrange a meeting with Rosemary Hopkins, a lovely person and a major influence with the small Eccentric Circles company that was gaining a good reputation. Over coffee in an outdoor plaza, I learned that her company had lost money and needed to recoup. She was off to Florida to direct a show for another theater, but she felt that any Off-Off would produce for about $4000. But I never heard from her and I never read that this company produced again.

In 1984, with more footwork, I found another artistic director, Bertha Lewis, affiliated with a theater on Waverly Place in Greenwich Village. She took my suggestion to her board. Three weeks later she told me the board had not approved. This group has also dispersed.

Through WIT I heard about the Quaigh Theater's 24-hour Dramathon scheduled over New Year's Eve. Everyone warned me against expecting much from such marathons. But the Quaigh was a *theater*.

I hiked to the address on 43rd Street, one block off Times Square, and was in front of the seedy Hotel Diplomat. Could this be right? The comfortless lobby was filled with characters who might be classified as downtrodden. Walking down the street, I spied Quaigh posters and a separate entrance so I climbed some ratty iron steps which opened into a depressingly run-down dark hall. Peering in, I discovered some half-open doors and a slant of raked seats in a blackened theater. Following one shaft of light, I found an open-doored office, but no one was about. Papers pyramided on a broken oak desk. Soon a man half my size, twice my age, and thrice as full of life bounced in. William H. Lieberson spoke so rapidly that I could barely understand what he said.

The unsolved mystery for me is where all the actors come from who are interested in participating in the Quaigh Theater New Year's Eve Dramathon. All sizes, shapes, and colors sign on. It works as a lottery system. A few days before performance you get a time slot according to your luck of the draw. Think about it: If you get 3 A.M., you know your prospective agent will never come. Who besides drunks will be in the audience at 5 A.M.? Some actors who draw the wee hours just don't show. Mr. Lieberson has stories of how he has had to read poetry for long intervals in order to keep the marathon operating.

You couldn't leave anything at the theater; you had to bring and take away everything the moment you were finished. You had the barest of essentials to work with. Technical rehearsal lasted about twenty minutes two days before the big day. You were in and out before you knew it.

Tech was a matter of selecting what table and chair you were going to use, and there was hardly any choice. You gave your marked script to two people in the lighting booth and you had to use whatever general lighting was set, so you had to re-direct your show to adjust. You were lucky if you could practice one cue.

I phoned Lieberson to tell him I was going to pull out but, before I could speak, he told me I had drawn a nice time slot: 9 P.M. Had he arranged it? After all, he was probably sensitive to the fact that a woman alone wouldn't care to be out after midnight on Times Square on New Year's Eve.

When I climbed those dingy stairs, in Margaret Fuller makeup and hairdo, carrying my costume and small props, I came upon a small crowd in front of the quaint make-shift box office. All were clammering to pay their fifteen dollars.

The spirited audience, which nearly filled the theater, energized me as I quietly jostled my way along the narrow aisle behind the last row — backstage had no other entry. What you have to have in mind when you are doing this with make-up on is this: *It doesn't matter at all. The audience, concentrating on the play, doesn't see you. What they don't see, doesn't matter. What matters is what they see.* If you think like this, everything is okay. The main thing is, don't let little things like this throw you.

There are other little things that shouldn't throw you. Like I was stopped midway in that narrow aisle and someone whispered I had to use the table already on stage — instead of the one I had chosen during tech — because the table on stage was too big and heavy for anyone to take offstage. Indeed, it took up half the stage area. In seconds I had to figure out how I could change my actions to adjust to this piece of furniture fit for a giant's grand ballroom.

Backstage I slipped into my costume and gazed through the dim light into a cracked mirror to see if my precarious hairdo had stayed in place. The people in the lighting booth waved to me. Did they want something? I could not understand what their signal indicated.

As I heard the audience clapping, the actors in the play

preceding mine came offstage shrugging their shoulders. Obviously they were thinking, *Well, it was as good as it could be under these circumstances.* They had five minutes to strike their props. I had five minutes to place mine. *If the audience saw me in costume doing this, then they saw me in costume doing this.* This is another minor detail that you should not allow to throw you.

The stage lights dimmed low; I stepped behind the curtain. The stage lights came up: I stepped onto the stage. I became Margaret Fuller.

When it was over, it was like in the old Mickey Rooney/Judy Garland movies. The audience cheered. Some of them stood up and shouted "Bravo!" I didn't even have friends in the audience! The lighting people in the booth raised their arms, squeezed their thumbs and forefingers into a tiny "o", signaling I had given a great performance.

But there was no time to be thrilled; I had five minutes to grab my props. While someone I'd never seen before whispered that I had been the best on stage of anyone so far, I heard the next group of actors begin their dialogue. I slipped out of my costume and into pants and shirt. Carrying all my props, in makeup and sweatsuit, I eased my way out, along that narrow aisle behind the last row in the audience.

I had had the night of my dreams.

No one called me within the next few days.

I found out later that Lieberson had not seen my performance.

I had not been discovered.

The Hotel Diplomat has been demolished; the Quaigh Theater moved to the Upper East Side for awhile, then relocated to Theater Row on 42nd Street. Now, who knows where it is, though Will Lieberson still produces.

By October, 1986, there arose a question: Should my friend, actress/playwright, Romola Robb Allrud, speak up for me? She was pouring energy into a fund-raising weekend drama festival at The Actor's Outlet, a six-year-old Off-Off in a loft on 28th Street. Eleanor Segan, executive director, and Ken Lowstetter, artistic director, were running about fifteen shows Friday through Sunday evening, offering a pass for $50 and one-shot tickets for $10. Allrud's original play,

Indian Summer, was scheduled, and she was playing a part. Yes, *Still Beat Noble Hearts* could be booked into a nice time slot.

During the frantic hour alotted for technical rehearsal, I was impressed with the two co-directors. One show after another was pushed on stage but their tech crew was good, and my show went well. I approached Seagan and Lowstetter a few days after my successful presentation. For one second I thought Lowstetter, who I believe was a lawyer five days a week, was going to be affirmative. But no, he had always dreamed of doing Euripides' *Medea* with an all-black cast, so he was not interested in my drama. His production was good. However, I haven't heard of this group again.

The person who gave me the inspiration and direction I needed was Anne Vendig, who'd booked my show for that Sunday-morning service at the North Shore Unitarian Universalist Society, Inc., on Long Island and had organized the reception at Lincoln Center.* I had to admire this pert, energetic woman, a former WAVE (USNR), assistant buyer, advertising executive, and kindergarten teacher, who was distinguished by a warm smile that lit up the entire room. She took for granted that anyone can do whatever is desired.

Vendig had presented her own original play at a Great Neck community theater. She had located space, director, actors, props, and had put up her own money. Later she invited me to join a group who were attending her nephew's play at an appealing theater in Greenwich Village. Why, she asked me later, didn't I do my Margaret Fuller at this theater?

So I was inspired to re-visit this theater. Six or seven odd-ball posters plastered a board attached to the attractive iron gate of a brownstone flanked by greenery. I stepped down two steps in front of a large window with a red electric candle, topped with a marquee that read "The Thirteenth Street Repertory Theater," and descended into a tiny court leading to a heavy door.

As I entered, I was assailed with dark muskiness. As my eyes adapted, I saw black brick walls with a few framed show cards of celebrated Off-Broadway plays. In front was a captivating, old-

---

*For these stories, see chapters entitled, "How I Got To Harvard" and "More Memorable Moments."

fashioned, wooden box office with beckoning Victorian glass. To my right stretched a lobby crowded with stuffed sofas — covers faded — and non-matching chairs and tables from flea markets or second-hand shops. On the left wall were grouped some thirty black-and-white, glossy headshots of the company's actors. A narrow, black entryway opened onto a welcoming black bar manifesting the possibility of drinks and cheese, and beyond was a black curtain leading to a small black passageway with narrow, curvaceous black iron stairs winding up to who-knows-where, and another black curtain through which was a center aisle boasting, on either side, black theater seats (some broken), which could minister to about seventy who faced a black brick-walled, black-box stage.

I was standing Off-Off, in the rectangular work space behind the ticket office, and I was speaking to a towering, twenty-five-year-old husky blond who'd tied a bit of hair in a pony tail and looked as though he might perform well on the football field.

"Yes" was a noun startling to hear. Yes, the Thirteenth Street Repertory Theater, though maintaining its own company of actors, directors, and playwrights, was available to rent. Yes, I could rent it for one or two nights, or time slots, say two hours: twenty minutes to set up for a one-hour-fifteen-minute show, then twenty minutes to strike the set, so the next show could set up. Yes, the cost was minimal: $75 for Monday night (when the theater was "dark," that is, the actors' night off), $100 for Sunday at 5:30 P.M. (tucked between their afternoon children's show and their evening mainstage show), and $150 for Friday or Saturday night at 9:30 P.M. (after their mainstage show). Yes, this fee included use of their lighting and sound system. Yes, they could supply a technician for a small fee. Yes, they would provide front-of-the-house (house manager), but I should arrange to have my own ticket seller in the box office so there would be no confusion over money.

The only problem was, on that small stage, I could not project my slides in the way I envisioned. Using slides had always been controversial. My director and some audience members had commented that they didn't care to see a slide show; they wanted a performance. They could imagine Emerson, Thoreau, etcetera — they didn't need pictures. Feedback from others was opposite — they felt the slides helped to create the reality of the nineteenth century.

I always felt comfortable working beside the slides, especially when I could have them imaged giant-size on the wall, serving as dramatic backdrop or set. By now I had almost a hundred; they were professionally produced, and I had perfected the positioning and timing of each. However, not only did I always have to find and train a volunteer to run the projector — and I always had to carry the heavy equipment — but I also had to deal with the projector's light which usually cut straight across center stage — which meant I couldn't perform in it. Center stage had to be kept dark for the slides and the two side areas had to be lit for me, the actress. Problems — you would be surprised how many rooms did not have walls appropriate for slides. Often we had to use wobbly, portable screens. All could be solved with rearview projection (placing the projector behind a curtain behind me), but I was almost never in facilities where this technique could be utilized.

Nevertheless, dropping the slides was like taking a significant prop away. I was nervous about it. Still, I couldn't help but wonder: Had the slides been a crutch?

It was now early September. I gambled six months ahead, during Women's History Month — the most promotive time for my drama.

On Friday nights and late afternoon Sundays

I put up a "Coming in March to Celebrate Women's History Month" sign in the theater. I wrote releases and flyers, compiled lists, offered group discount tickets to church groups, women's organizations, colleges, theaters, libraries, P.T.A.'s, seniors, newspapers, magazines, radio, TV, on Long Island and in the city. A tedious business, I never had enough hands, enough time. When I wasn't at my computer or stuffing envelopes, I attended meetings and tried to mix in different circles.

March cometh, and what trustworthy person could I burden to sit in the box office? My own daughter, Lynn, a former thespian who now had two sons. Of course, I would pay her — a pittance. I was awed by her box-office savvy.

Rehearsing with the tech person whom I paid, and putting on make-up in that crazy, dusty, dressing room for my opening, I must confess I allowed myself to live my fantasy which was easy to create, even though I myself had set up all the furniture and props. (I supplied the small ones.)

I would not let it cross my mind that I was actually fully aware that I was the only one in the world who was enchanted by all this.

The music to my important New York opening began. I stepped behind the curtain and peeped through a little hole torn by actors who'd been there before. I could see a few audience members talking to each other and reading the program I had devised and paid for. I stepped to the side of the curtain and watched the stage lights dim to a solid black. I tiptoed into the creepy blackness and found my place. The lights graduated to full power. I said my first line.

When I said my last line and made my final exit, I felt the slow release of tension. When I re-entered the stage for my bow, I listened to the satisfying applause, and then disappeared behind the black flats and curtain, into the drab black-box dressing room where several young actors were quietly — so as not to disturb the climax of my show — applying their makeup for their show due to start in forty minutes. "Hey, good audience," someone said as I stepped out of my costume and into a smock.

Twenty minutes to get small props packed into suitcase; costume in garment bag, furniture off stage.

Leaving the theater, I knocked into people waiting for the next show. Anyone who'd seen my show had disappeared.

Sunday attracted feminists and students who couldn't allot weekday time, plus commuters who wanted to get home early, as well as an older crowd who wanted to dine before or afterwards. The late night Friday slot drew interested New Yorkers, and young theater people and friends.

As the month of March faded, so did my show. No critics came — but I'd no expectations that *Still Beat Noble Hearts* would be hailed as the "sleeper" of the season. ("Sleeper" is theater jargon for an unexpected smash success.)

How much money did I invest? About $1700. How much did I lose? If you don't count time expended or gas driving in and out of the city, or phone calls — I am always less than great at detailing expenses — about $500.

Sundays when I left the theater I had seen the artistic director, Edith O'Hara, working in her rectangular space behind the box office, but I never got to know her. When I returned one day for a prop I'd forgotten, she was straightening something in the lobby and stopped me.

"Say, would you like to continue presenting your show on Sundays?"

I thought she hadn't even seen my show.

"By the way, did you know I did a paper in college on Margaret Fuller? In Idaho — I come from Idaho."

"My mother's from Idaho, and Montana — I'm a Westerner myself— born and bred in Portland, Oregon."

"Is that so....Small world, isn't it. What do you say? You won't have to pay rent, and I'll supply the technical help. "

I'd hated leaving this quaint theater where actors joked and rushed in and out, and were ambitious for themselves.

"There won't be any money for you, but we'll sell your books at the box office, and you can keep whatever they bring in."

"Sounds great, but I am taking Margaret Fuller to the Edinburgh Fringe Festival in August for three weeks."

"Really — how exciting!"

O'Hara helped to place a new collage of my pictures back up on the wall and iron gate, and my show became a featured attraction.

I used O'Hara's mailing list. She paid postage, saw that my show was included in magazine and newspaper listings, and assigned an attractive young intern named Sarah to help stuff envelopes and accompany me about the city to tape up flyers. Sarah also swept floors and did my tech.

Audiences were erratic, but I hoped for a build.

Soon I expressed concern.

"Put the name Margaret Fuller into the title," O'Hara advised. "That way it will draw those who know her name."

Thus, I dubbed my drama, *Men, Women, and Margaret Fuller,* after Edgar Allen Poe's famed quote: "Humanity can be divided into three classes, Men, Women, and Margaret Fuller."

However, audiences remained about the same.

When I returned from the Edinburgh Fringe Festival, I got to know every hidden recess of this incredible building on Thirteenth Street. A brownstone, built in 1840 (just a few years before Margaret Fuller came to New York), it is four stories high. Up the first narrow flight of steps from the theater lobby (which is the basement), you enter the narrow first floor hallway covered with nondescript dusty and worn-out carpet that runs the length of the building. On your right, there is a door that opens into a rather large room which services rehearsals and readings. It is equipped with wooden fold-up chairs, a broken-down overstuffed sofa, and an upright piano.

Down the hall, on your left, is a rickety door, which opens onto a dark square barely large enough to step into, and there, when you pull the string to turn on the bare light bulb, is a toilet, with a handwritten sign over the bowl which reads: "DO NOT FLUSH IF SHOW IS IN PROGRESS."

Further down the hall on your left is the dark tiny annex which encloses a washstand stained with multi-colored paints, above which hangs a yellowed cracked mirror, and a filthy make-shift stall of a shower. The doors to these adjuncts of necessity, when opened, reach across the width of the hall so that no one can walk past unless the doors are closed.

Beyond, on the right is another corridor barely wide enough to squeeze into, off of which opens five doorless and windowless cubby holes. Astoundingly, these airless five-by-six foot spaces are rented to actors, both male and female, who consider themselves lucky to have found cheap living quarters in the exciting heart of Greenwich Village. They throw down old mattresses, line walls with posters and clothing (there are no closets), and suspend tattered curtains or strings of beads across thresholds.

Continuing down the main hallway, you have a choice of two directions. If you bear to your right, you come to a closed door with a sign with large black lettering: "DO NOT ENTER IF SHOW IS IN PROGRESS." If you step inside, you see you're in the control room with all sorts of light and sound equipment. The technicians sit at a long counter and view the stage through a long glass window. On the far side is that winding staircase which gives access to the lobby.

If, from the main hallway, you go to the left, you climb a wider staircase, and if you turn around as you reach the third or fourth step, you might be startled to see a smiling male sitting on the edge of a five-foot high attic crawl space which stretches above the hall ceiling and is accessible by a rough wooden ladder nailed conveniently to the wall. This young man is perhaps drawing or sewing a button on a moth-eaten coat. His chamber has flooring but the walls are unfinished in the manner of all attics and at the far end is the obligatory air vent. The resident has neatly arranged a mattress, a stand-up lamp, an alarm clock, and boxes to hold clothes. He pays rent for this space.

If you continue on up the stairs, you reach a heavy door which brings you outside onto a porch inside a court surrounded by brick apartment buildings. On your right is Edith O'Hara's enclosed porch. This is the back entrance to her fourth story apartment which spans the entire top floor. Beyond and below is a huge slanting roof with a drop-off to a flat roof with a low railing and a walkway to the opposite building, below which is a courtyard boasting grassy clumps and clothes hanging on a line.

Now if you go down the porch steps onto the flat roof — which, in fact, is the roof of the theater (so IF A SHOW IS IN PROGRESS you are instructed to tiptoe across QUIETLY), — you progress to an opposite building, push a door which is usually open, you immediately face steps which you never go up because up there are rooms occupied by tenants. What you do is bear left down another wedge of a hallway which leads to a precarious hole in the floor. Here you wind down the steepest of steps — *do hang onto both walls* — and ease your way down to the backstage dressing room. This is *the one and only way* to get to the dressing room WHEN A SHOW IS IN PROGRESS.*

For celebrations and holidays Edith O'Hara has pot luck dinners on a big table set up in the lobby, and once a month, on Monday nights when the theater is "dark" (meaning there is no show), she and her general manager conduct company meetings in the theater and I was eventually invited to attend. To me, being included in an alive theater group was what I loved even though the members seemed not to get beyond the mating games. Most had college and some community theater experience. Just about everyone held down menial jobs in order to pay their bills. They regularly sent out pictures and resumes to agents and producers. They talked about their agents and some went on appointments and auditions.

I especially liked Tom Harlan who lived in O'Hara's attic cubby hole. He was ignored or dismissed by most people because he was not an actor, but he was always making dumb jokes and he always

---

*For a description of the Thirteenth Street Repertory Theater dressing room, see chapter entitled "Dressing Rooms I Have Known."

had time for a cup of coffee after my show. I learned he lived at O'Hara's because he had been cold sleeping on the streets. He helped in small ways about the theater, carried heavy things for O'Hara, and once in a while locked up the theater at night, but he never worked steadily at a regular job. Once, he told me he'd had three days modeling nude for artists, and once he wore a chicken or duck outfit as advertisement for a store. He did admit that his mother sent money every month. At Christmas I received a highly original, artistic and complex Christmas Card which he'd made with hundreds of precise scissor cuts. (Years later I revisited the Thirteenth Street Theater and Harlan was listed on the program as one of the company's actors.)

You have to admire the quiet and unobtrusive artistic director Edith O'Hara and the way she keeps The Thirteenth Street Theater going year after year, despite such incidents as a playwright threatening a suit because a director had the female character start to unbuckle the male character's belt buckle. Then there are the inevitable personality, plumbing, wiring, furnace, air conditioning, and fire department problems.

O'Hara's success is due to her independent spirit and philosophy — or is it that number thirteen? In her mind thirteen has always been lucky. The first show she brought to New York, *Touch,* had a cast of thirteen, which ran for a year, as well as another success, *Boy Meets Boy,* a musical spoof on the '30s. (She has a soft spot for musicals with a cast of thirteen.)

The Thirteenth Street Theater is not subject to the strict operating requirements of Actor's Equity (the union), nor victim to the vaccilations of the marketplace or the high real estate rentals that swiftly close non-profits or force groups to function without walls.

O'Hara's aim, unique in all New York City, is to establish a friendly homebase where talented young people can work, develop, and receive recognition. Thus, she has a steady stream of hopefuls who stay for a show or two or even a year or five, and then move on.

Maybe it's her logging-camp childhood in the uncultured wilds of Idaho that is shining through. If you catch her at the theater, you'll probably see her in sweat shirt and pants, painting scenery or adding up a column of numbers.

"The way I grew up," she'll tell you, "you were right down to earth in your approach to life. My father worked hard, built the houses, the roads, the railroad up to his camp, and, you know, you work and get what you want, and you take care of yourself. You don't call for someone to come in and do something for you. You do it yourself. So I did it." Then, she'll laugh modestly and a sparkle will come into her blue seventy-odd year-old eyes.

"We don't go for grants," she says, "because I just feel that if we can do it without, then we should do it without, because then we don't have to depend on grants. To get grants you have to hire a full-time grant writer, so that's a salary expense, and you don't know if you'll get one or not. Because we have the building, we have a little bit of income. We've really been lucky to be able to make it work. The trials and tribulations of making a theater go in New York are serious. It's not that we have overwhelming attendance at the shows. Sometimes we'll have a good house, sometimes it'll be small. I guess the concept of having so much activity is one thing that helps. The more things you do, the more chance you have of income. And also the more things you're doing, the more opportunity there is for the people that are here to learn and develop themselves."

She's run the theater since 1972 when she took over a fifteen-year lease. When the lease ran out she and her company scrambled to raise funds in order to buy the landmark building where *The Drunkard* (a popular old-fashioned melodrama) had run for thirty-five years. She and her actors watched as prospective buyers trooped through their halls. When the owners of the Japanese restaurant next door came to measure the rooms, O'Hara risked the $20,000 her company had raised as a partial downpayment; where the rest of the money would come from in one summer, they had no idea. It must have been fated that she would have this theater, because a benefactor appeared with a sizable donation and O'Hara learned she was the recipient of a small inheritance.

The theater has always been "just *it*" for O'Hara. In fifth grade in a one-room schoolhouse her teacher staged a program. "From that moment on I was never away from persuing theater. After sixth grade I moved into town to attend Junior High School and I was in the plays there. In college I majored in theater."

As a young married in Pennsylvania, she founded a children's theater, for which she wrote, directed and produced. Moving to a town of about 15,000, Warren, she founded a summer barn theater. Since there weren't enough serious-minded people, she recruited college youth and actors from New York. Over the course of five years her company turned out popular productions, improvisations, and originals, while growing their own vegetables. Her son and two daughters grew up, graduated, and found their way to New York and Broadway. (Jill scored in *Promises Promises* in which Jenny eventually took over the role, and later was in the female version of *The Odd Couple*.) O'Hara decided to follow her daughters to New York, bringing in the company's best original musical and, much to everyone's surprise, *Touch* made a splash and ran an entire year. When it closed, she began looking for out-of-the-way corners in which to start a theater. After a year she spotted an ad in the newspaper: "Building for lease; contains small theater."

Her concept was to produce musicals, but she broadened the focus when worthy originals couldn't be found. To find actors she put notices in the trade papers. Eventually, people began to send in their resumes and pictures. Periodically, O'Hara and company begin the process of interviewing, auditioning, workshoping, evaluating. Selected actors embark on a probation period of about three or four weeks, after which they become company members.

Presenting four or five shows fifty-two weeks a year, including a new mainstage drama every three months plus children's productions, O'Hara's had her share of successes. For about twenty years she's staged *Line* by her prolific playwright-neighbor, Israel Horowitz, with different casts and directors. By now it's considered a contemporary classic which is often produced on college campuses and has been translated into twenty languages.

Some rare moments come from that play. It is staged with actors sitting in the audience who, on cue, come on stage and perform their parts. This is done so convincingly that some people watching have climbed onto the stage and the actors have had to figure out how to get them off! One actress just danced a man back to his seat. Another night, when she was dancing someone off, he became so fighting angry that the actors had to stop the show!

Then there's Brother Theodore, now eighty-eight years old, a survivor of a concentration camp, whom reviewers label as "genius of the sinister." His monologue is so pessimistic that audiences laugh.

He has performed late Saturday night for about fifteen years. Norman Mailer also directed at Thirteenth Street, and Bette Midler and Tom Eyre have performed there.

My audiences were just not building — even though I received good half-page spreads in two Greenwich Village newspapers. I re-plastered the city with posters and on my computer printed out discounted tickets and placed them, along with flyers, at the half-price ticket booth on 47th Street and Broadway.

"I admire your willingness to keep working on it," O'Hara said, and she introduced me to Beatrice Da Silva. I liked her immediately. She had an outspoken honesty and sarcastic wit like Margaret Fuller's, was bright, a chain smoker who coughed a lot. Nights, she was a proof reader. She'd had quite a bit of directorial experience in small theaters throughout the USA and had done some work Off-Off Broadway. She lived only a couple of blocks away.

After Da Silva saw my show, I overheard her say, "Why does she want help on it?"

We scheduled time in the rehearsal space upstairs. I began by teaching her about Fuller, and she validated my choices, devised a dramatic ending, and introduced me to Andy Bloor, a musician, who sensitively selected, edited, and recorded background music and sound effects — all of which I liked immensely.

One day Andy Bloor pointed out to me that Da Silva had come to rehearsal even though she hadn't been feeling well. Then it seemed strange that she missed our first performance. Next, I heard she was in the hospital with pneumonia.

One day Tom Harlan stopped me. "Let's go and visit Beatrice. She's on Long Island in a hospital again, and I have no way of getting there. Couldn't you drive?"

"What's wrong?"

"AIDS."

At that time AIDS was considered a mysterious, terminal, male, homosexual disease.

Before being admitted to her room, Harlan and I were instructed to put on paper masks and gowns. What an empty feeling to drape ourselves in that pale green crepe, and then to face Da Silva unable to show our smiles.

She was looking chipper. She sat up, joked and told stories about friends and family who advised her on the latest "cures." She took a couple of phone calls, one which ended with her comment, "Don't worry; I know new things are being discovered every day."

One evening she stood at the doorway of the theater, reached up her arms, and sang out "Voila!" She looked terrific. She had lost weight and had thereby achieved the socially correct figure. Her waistline was cinched with a red belt and her short skirt showed off nicely shaped legs. Her hair was cut in a lovely style.

"I'm in remission," she said ecstatically, "and I'm going to enjoy every minute of it!"

After that I didn't see her for months. Later, reading the theater listings in *The New York Times*, I noted she was directing a play at a Westside theater complex. At the end of her show, I asked for her. "Unfortunately, Beatrice was unable to finish directing the show," the producer told me. "I had to do some of it myself. She's in the hospital."

I called the next day. "Laurie," Da Silva cut me off. "Excuse me, but I don't want to see anyone right now. And I'm just not up to talking. I'll call you back later, okay."

I never got a call; a year later I got a letter. It was a xerox she was sending to friends. Sensitively, without pity, she asked for donations to help pay medical expenses.

Months later, as I opened a squared white envelope addressed beautifully in her own handwriting, out scattered a modicum of lovely colored glitter. I pulled out a stark white card. It was the announcement of her memorial service.

Meanwhile, O'Hara took me aside. "There's a new play one of the directors is doing and it has a part you might be interested in. Don't you want to read and consider it?"

It was to be a mainstage production. It was called *Warehouse Moon,* a Christmas comedy about a young boy and girl, by Adam Kraar. "Rhea," the girl's mother, was entirely different from Margaret Fuller. It was the first time since before I was married that anyone had asked me to be in a play with other actors.

We rehearsed several times per week in the rehearsal room, usually at night because everyone held daytime jobs. Then, it was invigorating to come into the city every night to perform. I thought mainstage audiences would be larger and more receptive than for my one-woman drama, but this didn't prove out. I soon became restless performing a character who did not fulfill my aspirations. I never seemed to tire of Margaret Fuller.

Then suddenly a young man from Tunisia was showing up around the theater, trying to convince actors to attend his workshops.

Here I immediately sensed a unique and superior directorial talent. In my opinion he was far in advance; he had studied and worked in Tunis, Paris, Poland, Rumania, and he spoke Arabic, French, Spanish, Rumanian, plus he commanded a sophisticated English vocabulary. His technique, stemming from yoga, emphasized the physicality of the actor, which was opposite from the emotional base of Method acting in which I had been trained. It took me awhile to pronounce his name — Sassi Brahim. He told me confidentially, "I have the disease of Theater."

His workshops were at first well attended, then as he began to ask for long term commitment, many actors dropped out. However, he kept finding newcomers. Some of them, I later learned, had only casually talked to him on the street or in restaurants. Their inexperience did not worry him; he seemed determined on molding them into a cohesive group based on his technique.

He began to create a drama out of Denis Diderot's famous eighteenth-century French essay, "The Paradox of Acting," which I'd read when attending acting school at the age of seventeen. I wondered just how he could accomplish this out of a ponderous, old-fashioned, intellectual treatise.

"We are a group of European actors," he proclaimed to our group, "who have been ousted from our theater and we are now wandering through cities, acting in streets, in search of a new home." He selected and edited sentences, even footnotes, assigning portions as dialogue, and began to develop plot, theme and action. He titled the play *Paradox*.

Sassi gave us characters that we could easily portray and devised dramatic scenes. Because I'd always wanted to play the part of Medea, he originated a character called "Medea" and put me in a climatic scene which ended the first act.

Sassi was critical of American drama for its overabundance of talk which he considered static, and therefore directed us in group movement — running, leaping, fighting, shouting, even singing. He brought in a musician, an imigrant from the Far East, whose original score was intruigingly different from American rock and roll. He introduced a dancing instructor — thus, even I was dancing (in the back line). Someone else taught us Tai Chi. We were on stage for two hours — there was so much physicality that I had to warm up at home by exercising with Jane Fonda tapes.

Rehearsals over four months presented tremendous obstacles. Actors kept dropping out and new ones joined. Space became difficult because the theater's mainstage productions got first rights to the one and only rehearsal room. Through some connection we found a lecture hall at Fordham University — we were instructed not to tell anyone we were there. Then, just as we were nearing completion, O'Hara heard some false rumors about our group and insisted on sending an emisary to evaluate our results. In due time, we were approved and we opened *Paradox*.

I must say we did it well, and it was the most unusual production ever mounted on that mainstage. People talked about it, but it did not astound. Most thought it was visually interesting but they did not understand it. Some of my friends told me frankly they hated it. Others seemed to catch the *Paradox* spirit.

After that Sassi left the aegis of The Thirteenth Street Theater. He began to live with a young Argentinian art student who received money from her parents and rented a large but ugly dark basement in a building on the unfashionable end of Greenwich Village's Bleeker Street, just off the Bowery. There Sassi continued with a smaller nucleous of actors, some of whom came and went rather quickly.

He devised another drama around the Lebanese poet, Kahlil Gibran, who achieved world-wide fame in the 1920's with his book-length poem, *The Prophet*. I played Mary Haskell, the Bostonian teacher who became Gibran's benefactress. Reading her published letters, I found one where she described her feelings when she had refused his offer of marriage. Sassi set up the scene so I became symbolic of the older woman who remembered and called repeatedly for her lost lover...for her lost younger self. Sassi teamed me with a dancer who symbolized the youth whose movements touched and turned the older self with whom the youth would eventually merge.

Proclaiming Margaret Fuller/ Edna St. Vincent Millay Day on Mt. Battie, Camden, Maine

Picketing the Boston Playboy Club

Vacationing

Honoring granddaughter

Honoring Edna St. Vincent Millay in Camden, Maine

R
A
M
O
N
A

X

On stage Buckminster Fuller introduces and displays the Thomas Hicks painting of Margaret Fuller, July 19, 1979.

Left to right: Buckminster Fuller, great grand nephew of Margaret Fuller; Constance Fuller Threinen, great grand niece; Polly and Harvey Fuller, artist; Thomas, son of Constance.

Paula Blanchard, author of MARGARET FULLER FROM TRANSCENDENTALIST TO REVOLUTIONARY, and David Kronberg, Executive Director of Cambridge ArtiCulture.

Ramona announces the founding of the Margaret Fuller Women's History Network.
Barbara Haber, Curator, Schlesinger Library, stands behind Buckminster Fuller.
Roland and Vanessa Barth, background, left.

HARVARD

Ramona X, Laurie, and Buckminster Fuller converse with an
appreciative audience.

Anne Forman, artist, stands in front of her painting of Laurie James as Margaret Fuller, with Laurie, December 29, 1979.

Anne Forman with Ramona.

Dr. Marcella Maxwell, Chairman, New York Commission on the Status of Women, reading the Mayor's Proclamation declaring Margaret Fuller Day.

Jules Goldin unveiling Anne's painting of Laurie as Margaret Fuller.

The presentation, on stage.

Sandra Mitchell Caron, UUA Moderator who introduced, and Anne Vendig, President, Women's Group, North Shore Unitarian Universalist Society.

LINCOLN CENTER

The Margaret Fuller Ossoli Square, Cambridge, Massachusetts.

The Dedication. At podium, Pat King, Director, Schlesinger Library; seated, Laurie, Mayor Duehay.

MARGARET FULLER SQUARE

In front of Cambridge City Hall. Laurie, Mayor Francis H. Duehay, Councilman Alfred Vellucci, Ramona.

MARGARET FULLER/ EDNA ST. VINCENT MILLAY DAY

Peggy Campbell.

Mt. Battie, Camden, Maine, July 11, 1981. Ramona, Buckminster Fuller, Laurie.

On stage, The Opera House: Alfred Vellucci announcing the naming of the Margaret
Fuller Ossolia Square, with Laurie

The Owl and Turtle Bookstore,
Camden. Buckminster Fuller
signing his book, CRITICAL PATH,
for
Laurie.

Backstage, The Opera House, Buckminster Fuller explaining the universe to Laurie.

MEMORABLE

Edinburgh Bed-and-Breakfast, 1988. Katheryn White, Pat Kaufman, Laurie.

Edinburgh bedroom-for-one accommodating three: Katheryn White (before we got kicked out).

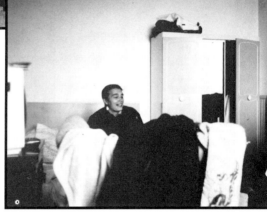

Sensei Joseph Carbonara presenting Sho-Dan, Honorary Black Belt, to Laurie, December, 1990.

MOMENTS

Dedication of the Margaret Fuller Room at Marriott Hotel in Cambridge, October 20, 1987. Left to right, Bill Munck General Manager, Mayor Walter Sullivan, Ramona and Laurie.

Laurie and Ramona protesting the demise of the ERA, June 30, 1982, in front of the statue of Anne Hutchinson and the Massachusetts State Capitol building.

Women's movement gets back to basics

By JEAN COLE
Staff Writer

Some of the most radical members of the feminist movement think that blind devotion to enactment of the Equal Rights Amendment has derailed their cause.

They want to put it back on the track.

As ERA continues to fall short of approval in more and more states despite a 40-month extension for ratification, grassroots feminists are becoming impatient to get back to the "gut issues" that originally brought them together.

"It's boringly myopic — ERA

[...couple]

[...e ERA]
[...nt Su-]
[...e Hyde]

tions for the poor jolted some life back into the women's movement, Kennedy said.

"Like most pathological people, nothing keeps the movement going like a kick in the pants which we just got in the panties," she added, laughing.

Actress Laurie James also is disturbed by what appears to be ERA tunnel vision.

"I think the women's movement is slowing down because of it," she said.

Both James and Barth said attendance at feminist functions for the past two years has fallen off.

The New York actress and artistic director has revived a one-person play on the life of 19th-century women's champion Margaret Fuller in an attempt to renew the consciousness-raising tactics employed by feminists pre-ERA.

"Fuller first brought women together back in the 1830s . . . she called her sessions 'Conversations With Women.' And she can do

Front page article, Boston Herald American, Sunday, July 6, 1980.

The picture on page 12A: Ramona, Laurie, Atty. Florynce Kennedy.

Rosemary Matson with the dove of peace on her head at the United Nations Conference in Copenhagen.

Susan B. Anthony's birthday, 1982, in front of the statue of Anthony, Elizabeth Cady Stanton, and Lucretia Mott in the crypt of the Capitol in Washington D. C. Ramona and Laurie present Maine Representative David Emery with a Margaret Fuller poster as a tribute to National Women's History Week.

The 1980 Mexican tour organizers, Left to Right: Diane Stanley, Cultural Attaché; Jesse Reinburg, Director, Benjamin Franklin Library; Laurie; Carolyn Sammet; and Katie Walsh.

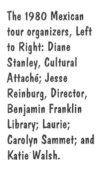

The Boston Junior League Women's Van, an information, referral, and education service. Director Gwen Harper, (Laurie's sister), in the driver's seat, opens the door to greet visitors. Gwen helped to stage the Hasty Pudding performance at Harvard, March 25, 1982.

ON STAGES

Chautauquans riding in Epping, North Dakota parade. Carroll Peterson as Walt Whitman, Kevin Radiker as Henry David Thoreau, George Frein as Herman Melville, and Laurie as Margaret Fuller.

Laurie performing under the Chautauqua tent in Alliance, Nebraska, 1991.

The Thirteenth Street Theater Box Office: Laurie and
Edith O'Hara.

Edith O'Hara, Artistic
Director, The
Thirteenth Street
Theater, New York City.

On stage, The Burbage Theatre, Los Angeles on
Margaret Fuller Day, March 29, 1992. Left to right: Sandra Siegal, Film Producer;
Anne Dunn, Assistant Executive Director, Commission on the Status of Women; Yoon
Hee Kim, Special Advisor to the Mayor; The Reverend Douglas Morgan Strong, Santa
Monica Unitarian Universalist Fellowship; Andy Griggs, Director; Doug Dutton,
Dutton Books; and Ellen Marano, Co-Producer, Siegel/Marano Productions.

Hancock County Auditorium, Ellsworth, Maine, August 31, 1980.

At the first rehearsal it totally worked.

But the rest of *Gibran* was a jumble. Rehearsals were piecemeal because actors didn't show up and dropped out. Sassi never truly developed the depth of the piece. Moments were not carefully constructed. In order to please some actors, he permitted them to repeat the same avant guard actions they'd done in *Paradox.* Dissensions developed.

Sassi tried to hold the group together by giving it the name of The Bazaar Theater, so called because we were to have an abundance of diverse offerings. He said we were going to perform in Tunisia. He made expensive long distance phone calls, faxed papers, and he did obtain an invitation from the Tunisian government and transportation costs from Paris to Tunis for all of us. He and his girl friend frantically tried to raise the balance of the money from American sources, but were late for deadlines. Moreover, Sassi was so eager to accomplish his dream, that he made the irreparable mistake of promising each actor whatever each most wanted. When the actors talked amongst themselves, they discovered empty promises.

As an appeasement, he and his girl friend arranged three nights' performance in the famed Washington Square United Methodist Church, which had a long tradition of supporting the arts and offered their large sanctuary on a cost-reimbursement basis. For performance, the space is a "barn" with impossible accustics. I knew exactly how to work the resounding echo, but none of the actors did, and there was no time for coaching. Most scenes went badly, light cues were missed, sound was blurred. Except for my scene, *Gibran* at Washington Square Church was a disaster. Luckily, the audience was minuscule.

Shortly thereafter, Sassi and his girl friend broke up, as did Bazaar Theater Company. Sassi hired on as a bellhop at a hotel. I know he still dedicates himself to his lifelong dream as theater director, and he searches for some way to do his work.

After two years at the Thirteenth Street Theater, I began to wonder how I could further launch the name of Margaret Fuller nationally.

My daughter, Mary, was living with her Significant Other in Sherman Oaks, the Los Angeles/Hollywood area, starting up a

corporate video business from their home. It was natural to project
the notion that I had credentials to pique the interest of a West Coast
artistic director. Also, my third book on Fuller had been printed and
I could try peddling my series in West Coast bookstores.

First step was to obtain a current listing of Los Angeles theaters
and write about forty letters enclosing my New York press. I received
no answers.

Three weeks later in Los Angeles I sat down with a friend of
Mary's, Howard Rosenstein, director of dramatic programming at
CBS, who had produced in small theaters. He narrowed my list to
about twenty well-located theaters.

You sell your idea in two sentences on the phone to a tape and
hope you are called back. You are not called back. In one case I
connected with a person whose response was: "Oh we get letters like
that all the time. No, the artistic director is not in and he wouldn't
be interested."

After several calls to the Burbage Theater, I was surprised to reach
the artistic director, Ivan Speigel. I nearly fainted when he said he'd
seen my letter and materials. He bluntly said, "I want to tell you right
off, that we can't offer you a living wage."

"I didn't expect that. And I don't need it, since I'm staying with
my daughter while I'm here."

"And you might be very disappointed with the audiences in Los
Angeles. They just don't go to the theater like they do in New York.
It might not be worth your time. This is film city."

"I'll take my chances," I said. "There's got to be some people here
who're interested in Margaret Fuller."

He set up an appointment. Amazingly, his theater, on Pico and
Sawtelle, was about fifteen minutes away from Mary's house. It was
supposed to have a sign but it wasn't visible as I drove through traffic
around a nondescript three-story warehouse-type building squeezed
in between other insignificant looking buildings. Nor did you see the
entrance that was hidden under some kind of California smoggy-dry
greenery. When you got to it, though, the door, locked, was of
welcoming glass and through it you could see a neat, dark, gray lobby
with carpet and ticket table. Where was the office? I trod along the
side of the building down a wide, dreary, alleyway which opened
onto parking space. On the back of the building were two doors, one

of which was open. In a tiny outer room someone was shuffling
papers. I had to wait and then was led into a second small room
jammed with papers, dirt, empty coffee containers, a desk with
broken drawers, beside which were two men, one of whom was thin,
tall, dark, bearded, and the other was heavyset, redheaded, freckled,
clean-shaven. Both were smiling.

The thin one, Ivan Speigel, had been depicted in articles in the
Los Angeles Times as being a volatile, well established leader in the
city's theater millieu. He introduced me to Andy Griggs whose
dancing eyes were congenial. Griggs had run a theater in Santa Cruz,
and was well aware of the significance of Margaret Fuller. In fact, he
was an active UU (as well as his mother) and knew an audience for
my drama could generate from these circles alone. I presented these
men with my books and launched into my pitch, but Speigel quickly
interrupted.

"Would one day a week — Sundays — be okay with you?"

"That's what worked at the Thirteenth Street Theater," I answered.

"We'll give you 25% of ticket sales; that's all we can offer."

"Perfect." I hadn't expected a penny.

Our conversation was constantly broken off because Speigel
accepted phone calls.

"And maybe Andy can get you an additional date or two in
colleges — he teaches at Long Beach City College. That way you can
pick up a few extra dollars."

Could I argue?

Speigel said, "We had a one-woman show about Dorothy Parker
and it ran for over six months."

Dorothy Parker, the fabulous humorist/writer of the 1920s,
naturally would attract audience. Would forgotten Margaret Fuller
last more than a month in a city where the only people I knew were
my daughter's friends?

"I can't go past May 31," I said, "for I'm committed to touring the
summer with The Great Plains Chautauqua Society. And actually
May 17 is out of the question, because I have to be in New York
for my daughter's wedding."

"Tell you what, you can have ten weeks, opening March 15 for
Women's History Month, and that takes us through to May 30, but
we'll omit May 17th, your daughter's wedding day. If anybody wants

tickets on May 17th we'll say we're sold out." They laughed.

So stunned was I with these agreeable words that I agreed, for I was certain audiences for my show would trickle down to four or five persons in four or five weeks and I'd be back home in New York in plenty of time for the wedding.

"Andy will take care of all details"

There were two stages in this large, clean theater, actually one of the best and oldest of the small houses in Los Angeles, in its twenty-third year of operation. Griggs wasn't sure which I'd be assigned; it depended on what shows would be on during my run and how long they lasted. The smallest stage was a black box that seated about fifty on an unstable tier of black wooden boards. This seemed acceptable, but the mainstage space that held almost a hundred was what I craved — a perfect setting with comfortable, inclined theater seats that bordered an oblong floor-level playing area. Here were adequate flats, lights and tech room. The problems included lack of storage space for bulky items; furniture for shows had to be piled at the side of the house in full view of the audience. Luckily, audiences never seemed to notice.

Griggs pointed out that I could "borrow" whatever I needed. (Theater people are so clever at making the same furniture look different for every show!)

But the bigger problem was that the set for the mainstage production would also have to service mine, because there would be no one around who could move the flats. "Sometimes it works out well," Andy explained when I looked worried, "because the backdrop is general enough to blend with your show too, but other times, yes, it presents a problem."

A good sense of humor is of A#1 importance when you work in small theaters.

I began compiling lists as soon as I stepped out of the Burbage Theater. Also, I visited Dutton's Bookstore in Brentwood on a lovely sunny day and found the independent owner Doug Dutton basking in the courtyard. He had wonderful blue eyes, like Paul Newman. The idea flashed. Here was Ralph Waldo Emerson! Sure enough, Dutton was flattered to be compared to Emerson; besides, he wanted to do something different for his regularly scheduled author signings. With great enthusiasm he introduced me to his gracious staff who were titilated to hear that their employer was going to read the part of Emerson in my play, *O Excellent Friend!*, at the bookstore, and we scheduled April 10. I figured this would help to attract Burbage Theater audience during the middle and end of my run.

Back home in New York, I revised publicity releases, and made sure everything California was correct on my computer. Then I contacted Joanna Rose, book buyer in one of the biggest bookstores in the United States, Powell's, in the city where I was born and raised, Portland, Oregon. She and her store were planning "LitEruption," a three-day book fair in March, and I could be on the agenda reading a few pages from my book and signing. No pay/no expenses, but the committee was finding paying dates for participants travelling a distance, and they helped me schedule workshops for dollars at Lake Oswego High School and a talk for drama students at my alma mater, Lewis & Clark College.

Eight weeks in advance of my Burbage Theater opening, I returned to my daughter's Los Angeles/Sherman Oaks home for on-foot promotion. The Burbage people were not organized with volunteers and interns, and were unenthusiatic about promoting my drama in any way other than doing the usual newspaper and magazine listings. When I asked them for their mailing list, they told me they didn't do mailings anymore. I showed them my press release and flyer, and told them that I was contacting Mayor Tom Bradley for a Margaret Fuller Day proclamation. They were taciturn. I did the same promotion that I'd done for the Thirteenth Street Theater, except that I had no intern to help, plus I visited UU churches, bookstores, and a few women's organizations and gave several talks. Also, I started to organize the Margaret Fuller Day panel of speakers. This took innumerable phone calls and personal visits.

I sensed my first two performances could be no better than technical rehearsals. Therefore, I set my Margaret Fuller Day as late as possible, Sunday, March 29, 1992. This ploy gave me two weeks after opening for more promotion which might boost audience numbers on the third week — just when there was possibility of trickle down. Then, so fearful was I about having an audience for the opening performance that I invited all my daughter's friends to a gala after-theater party at her house. The Burbage people said nary a word about any of this.

The large waiting room off the front lobby where I was to display my Fuller exhibit was plain and dreary. But I was instructed that I would have to set up and take down my pictures before and after every performance.   To this day, I can't conceive why photos shouldn't remain up during the run of the show. Did the Burbage people want to exist without hoopla of any kind?

It was an ego-boost early March to fly north to my hometown, Portland, Oregon, to participate in Powell's "LitEruption," to cover the workshops at Lake Oswego High School and to tread the same rolling green grounds I'd trod so long ago at Lewis & Clark College. The theater in which I'd performed was no longer there; it had been replaced with a long, low building with surperb stage and seats. In the large black box which served as a rehearsal hall, I read Chapter I of this book to the small but eager group of aspiring actors and then opened the session to question-and-answer.

In one sense you might call the performance at Long Beach City College, Calforina, a tech. At least it preceded my Burbage Theater opening. Griggs coordinated and arranged with ease and conviviality. Typical of all college experiences, I performed on an abnormally high and large set of platforms so that it was difficult to establish a relationship with the audience, and the lights which came at me from all corners, were bothersome. I like to think some students did get something out of it, though most behaved as though they were on holiday. It did offset expenses.

Luckily, at the last minute, I drew the largest and best space in the two-stage Burbage Theater. Also, it was lucky that the current backdrop for the mainstage production consisted of black flats and curtains. Griggs sensed the style and mood of my play immediately, and suggested a "special" light which the tech guy had to set up every week.

On opening day I arrived at the theater early. The doors were locked. Nervously I waited, getting in and out of my car dozens of times. After a long while, the lighting guy arrived with the key.

You scurry around crazily, figuring you'll forget something. You envision that by the time you get everything done, you're going to be too exhausted for the performance. (And you are.) Shouldn't your main concentration be on your lines and the emotions of your character, not on a spoon, a teapot of water, a chair placed in a position? You know this technician, who claimed to know everything, can never get all cues right on opening.

Did anybody come? There is no hole in the curtain. You can only see one small end section of the audience area as you stand in the wings waiting for the cue. Two middle-aged women are sitting amongst empty seats, talking and leafing through the program. The lights dim to black. You step into place. You hope the adrenalin will rise and not too many members of the audience will cough or arrive late to distract. The lights go up on you.

There are about forty people out there; they are warm, ready to laugh and enjoy. Over half are my daughter's friends. *Push that thought away.* They *paid.*

Oh, why do I do this; why does anyone do this? Will I ever find the satisfaction I need and be able to give up this thing inside me that propels me forward? Stop! Stop! Focus! Get back to Margaret Fuller. I force myself to lose myself into this woman and the changing of her emotions.

All too soon I am repeating the last lines, am feeling the lights dim to that almost blackness, and then I stand up and take my final bow, once again, hearing the applause of the audience, and then exiting.

In the dressing room, reality overtakes, as I sense the drab disarray and loneness of it all. But there is no time for such thoughts. Quickly, I slide into my old pants and T-shirt and anticipate striking props, driving home, taking off makeup, washing hair, and tomorrow, facing the concerns of daily life.

But soon my willowy daughter appears with a hug and kiss and, with a smile that could melt the coldest, she introduces me to a group of three.

"Sandra Siegel is a film producer, Mom."

Sandra Siegel looks young, full of vitality, well dressed. "What a coincidence!" she is exclaiming with warmth. "I've long admired Margaret Fuller and have thought that her story could make a movie." My books would lend credability to their project when they made "pitches," as it is called, to Hollywood producers and stars.

We met in my daughter's home/office with Ellen Marano, the partner, who taught high school in a tough L. A. neighborhood and was expecting a baby in three months. I am always drawn to people who fight for their dreams and, as we talked, I felt we might just make a team. Sandra Siegel had experience in the Hollywood arena and I was the "heavy" when it came to Margaret Fuller.

The partners wanted to option my three books for a year for $1.00, a deal writers often accepted, I was told. When the movie was produced, there'd be good sums of money. I was not to play Margaret Fuller. "We need a star, though after seeing your performance, you are, to us, the *real* Margaret Fuller."

Nor could I write or help write the script — needed was a professional screen writer with credits. I would be consultant, but with no control over decisions. Or I might have a title such as associate producer — which held little appeal to me because I am the first to know I am not an administrator.

In a week or two they sent a contract. I handed it to a theatrical lawyer, Tom Bliss, a friend of Mary's. Everyone, including the lawyer, advised that 95% of options never make it to the screen; it might be smart if I just took the money. But the thought nagged that Margaret Fuller just might be successful as a film and I had better be prepared. Bliss negotiated and I was offered $500. He drew up a sliding option schedule over three years, and upped the money should the movie be made. I paid Bliss $250.

We met with Barbara Gunning of Bob Banner Associates, a top movie company. Siegel and Marano encouraged me to do the talking. Though I barely understood the subtleties of "pitching," it was easy to zero in on whatever aspect of Margaret Fuller proved to be of most interest. Gunning interrupted when I talked about Fuller's achievements; she wanted info about Fuller's love life in Italy. But Gunning liked the project and agreed that she would be executive producer in affiliation with Bob Banner & Associates, who would put up the money, and Sandra Siegal and Ellen Marano would do the work.

A treatment needed to be written — a synopsis which is sent to stars and directors. With commitments, a "package" could be developed and all would fall into place. When we walked out of Gunning's office, Sandra Siegal and Ellen Marano were elated because, they explained, usually producers have to go on two or three dozen "pitches" before an idea sells.

I sat down in front of my computer and wrote a treatment in a couple of days. "It needs juice," Siegal said.

Marano took over. When I read it about six weeks later, Margaret Fuller's mind-set was girl-looks-for-boy, girl-can't-get-boy, girl-realizes-her-mistakes, girl-overcomes, girl-gets-boy. I complained.

The new treatment was faxed to me while I was touring with the Great Plains Chautauqua Society, Inc. In this version Emerson was miraculously *sending a telegram* to Fuller in Europe; I say miraculously because the telegraph had not yet been invented. No account was taken of the fact that it took about six weeks to travel to Italy. Furthermore, Emerson was entering Italy when most Americans had left because of war. In this treatment, Emerson, who in life had difficulty expressing love to his wife, tells Fuller articulately that he can't live without her. In life Fuller never took anyone's advice, but in these pages Fuller asks George Sand why she can't find a man, and when Sand says, "Go to Italy, dear!", Fuller rushes off to the country. Fuller, who could barely earn a living in Italy — and the story pivots from her desperate struggle — is shown in this script to be wearing the latest fashions and living in an expensive hotel in Rome. Flirtatious and sexual scenes abound and Fuller is pictured as having the quintessential high-school mentality, while Emerson is characterized as a milktoast. So unaware of the Italian Revolution were the writers that they did not mention one gun shot or cannonball. Fuller's lover, Ossoli, is never shown as the gallant soldier he was.

When I noted the implausibilities, another improvement came through. When I again complained, I was told, "This is just the treatment. It has to be written with the 'juice' — so it will sell. Believe me, Laurie, these movie moguls are not intellects. They are out for money; they want to see sex in the story. Later, when we get the writer, then we can turn it into something better."

Other people told me, "Hollywood always distorts. What difference does it make. Just think of all the money you'll make!"

The truth and complexities in the lives of Fuller and Emerson offer more dramatics than any writer's imagination can devise.

I was sure no quality actress could be interested in a script which structured characters so vapidly. And no star was. I was told it was sent to all at the top.

A year later the option ran out. Siegal called and said it was her favorite project, but she did not have the money to hold it longer.

Would I please waive the option and allow her to pursue it?

There the project stands.

I am just as happy, for if Fuller and her contemporaries cannot be depicted as they lived and breathed, then I am not interested in a film.

While all this was going on, I continued to perform and promote my show at the Burbage Theater. Foremost was the presentation for Margaret Fuller Day. I got a phone call: Would I be around for an interview from a *Los Angeles Times* reporter?

Into my daughter's living room came a photographer, followed by a quiet, avant guarde, inquisitive history buff named Robert Koehler, who listened intently while I poured out information about Fuller. Of course, I had the dining room table covered with Margaret Fuller pictures and the exquisite Mayor's Proclamation which I had picked up that morning.

On the day of the presentation of the Mayor's proclamation, a full page story appeared in the entertainment section of Sunday's *Los Angeles Times*. The headline read: ACTRESS-AUTHOR DEVOTES HERSELF TO MAKING A NAME FOR 19th CENTURY WRITER AND FEMINIST. There was a terrific picture of me, a good picture of Margaret Fuller, and there was the announcement of Margaret Fuller Day along with the titles of my books, and the date of my reading of *O Excellent Friend!* at Dutton's Bookstore.

I began getting decent-sized audiences.

Meanwhile, Doug Dutton postponed our *O Excellent Friend!* reading to May 1. I was perturbed because the new date was rather late for my purpose of audience cultivation. But there was nothing I could do about it.

I prepared marked scripts and drove to Dutton's for a rehearsal. Dutton was frenetically busy. I was led upstairs to a meeting room by a person who was to read the narration. We waited. When Dutton appeared, we read a page. I must admit he seemed self-conscious, entirely different from his own unique personality which I had figured would naturally filter through. I was about to feed him some Emersonian info when someone opened the door and asked Dutton to take a long distance phone call. We waited. He returned and said it was just not going to be a good time for him. Could we arrange another rehearsal? So we arranged the two hours before the reading on May 1.

April 29, 1992 was an ordinary sunny California day that turned extraordinary.

In the late afternoon we watched on TV as violence broke out across the predominantly black and Hispanic South Central section of Los Angeles, about twenty miles away from my daughter's house. "What's this?....This is happening *right now?*....It can't be!" we interrogated, as we listened to the newscasters. We flowed back and forth amongst the rooms of Mary and Andy's home/office where they were getting out a mailing.

On the screen people were maniacally throwing things, smashing windows. Was this a TV movie?

Soon the picture shifted and we saw several black men storm a truck and pull the white driver out and beat him with some objects so that he lay prone and bloody in the middle of the street beside his truck.

Could this be *live* in *our* city?

Then we heard. The California Superior Court jury in suburban Simi Valley had acquitted the four white Los Angeles police officers on all but one charge stemming from the March 1991 beating of black motorist Rodney G. King. The beating had provoked outrage at police brutality nationwide.

While the sun set we sat stunned in front of the TV. Gangs rampaged, cars were turned over, rocks were hurled, fires were started, looting was rampant. Hour after hour the anarchy escalated.

The next day, the chaos and anger spread throughout downtown Los Angeles. We watched throngs of people including women and children scurry out of stores with arms full of goods. The situation became so out of control that we saw Korean store owners, armed with guns, pacing on their rooftops. Mayor Tom Bradley called a state of emergency. Governor Pete Wilson ordered the National Guard to duty. People were reported being killed.

That afternoon I got a call from Doug Dutton. The mayor had ordered a curfew. People were too frightened to leave their homes. We cancelled our *O Excellent Friend!* reading. Postponement was impossible because Dutton's reading schedule was booked solid for the month. I secretly believe Dutton was relieved for being able to so gracefully slide out of a commitment he found wasn't within his best capability.

At the Burbage Theater shows were cancelled.

By Sunday the city was calming. There was no rioting in the Pico/ Sepulveda area. Since I performed in the afternoon, I was given the go ahead. I got an audience.

As the month of May logged in, my trickle-down audience just didn't occur, and my daughter was to be married at our home in New York on the 17th. I would have to fly home after my Sunday performance and on the next Saturday fly back to Los Angeles for my last two Sundays at the Burbage.

After the wedding, I stayed at my daughter's house alone for she and Andy, the groom, were off on their honeymoon. I finished out my run, collected my final percentage which over the ten-week period totaled to several hundred dollars, and gamboled across the USA again.

I had one week to catch my breath before my next venture — my highly-salaried ten-week Midwest summer tour with the Great Plains Chautauqua Society, Inc. I'd be Margaret Fuller again, but this time under an open-air tent, and audiences could be expected to be in the hundreds.

PUBLISHING EFFLUVIA

The day came when I was no longer willing to wait until some publisher made up his or her mind that what I was writing should be out there.

Your books on Margaret Fuller won't sell.

That's what I was told by an eminent literary agent, who handled the work of a writer/husband of a friend who suggested I send along my manuscript.

This needs cutting.

That's the word from a top banana of a marvellous publishing house specializing in women's history that advertises they want to change the way people think. She'd kept my draft for six months.

We're no longer interested in subjects such as yours.

That's the statement I got from an editor I'd met at a party, who invited me to submit my book because it was just the thing they were looking for.

Naively, I'd thought I was dealing with idealists who wanted quality to fill voids so today's readers could gain broader perspectives.

What they meant was:

(1) We can't make a profit because books on Margaret Fuller won't sell a million copies.

(2) We can't invest the time it would take to work with you through an editing process.

(3) The economy is bad and so the higher echelon won't invest dollars in "risky" books such as yours.

There are so many able writers out there who think their work is substandard because it gets rejected.

I could have shaped my material in at least five different ways. I wanted to work with a sympathetic editor.

Publishers today want the finished product. They don't have or want to take the time to develop an author.

Traditionally, top-drawer houses published quality literature as an obligation to culture and the world. Editors were people of distinction who took pride in creating enduring works of merit.

Now the greatest expertise seems to be in the marketplace. Today if an author wants to reach a wide audience, he/she needs to write in the style of Jackie Collins, Judith Krantz, Robert Ludlum, Stephen King, or be a supercelebrity, a disgruntled child of a supercelebrity, an athlete, a politician, a lawyer, a violent criminal, a sexual deviant, a terminal patient, or extraordinarily outrageous.

These are things they don't tell you in college writing class.

Despite movies, TV, cable, computer games, CD's and distractions in our daily lives, people are still reading and books are in a healthy state. But at a conference, I have been told by the Random House publisher of the adult trade division that twenty-nine books of his division that made it onto *The New York Times* 1993 list of Notable Books lost $698,000 collectively. Also, eight books he published in one year, which won awards from the American Library Association, lost a total of $370,000. These books received rave reviews and much promotional money, but were paid for by two best sellers that made a profit of over a million dollars.

There is very little to motivate you today to take your *time* and to turn out a superior, well-thought-through, artfully developed work.

Since World War II the major conglomerates have taken over the publishing industry. In recent years hundreds of publishing companies have been bought and sold. A handful of firms account for more than half of all sales of adult books. The goals are to produce and promote mega-best sellers. Some of the finest work, including poetry, short stories, first novels, philosophy, history, biography are placed on sluggish publishing schedules.

There's an efficiency trend. Some of the most elite houses have been "realigning," "downsizing," laying off, looking at the future of electronic publishing. Today some of our best editors are unemployed.

If yours is not about what's making headlines, it might take two or more years to get to the marketplace. When you do reach print, more often than not, the publisher will decide not to sink dollars into advertising and promotion. Since your book gets neglected, it doesn't sell and, thus, the decision to reprint is negative because the majority of profit has already been taken. Your book is remaindered. They are onto something new.

There's a pie out there, and everyone gets his piece or is out of business. The printer always takes what is rightfully his; after all, he has overhead. There's the typist, the editor, the layout person, the researcher, the paper supplier, the photographer, the color separator, the copyright fee collector, the proofreader, the publicist, the advertiser, the overnight express delivery person, the postmaster, the trucker, the warehouser, the wholesaler, the distributor, the bookseller.

Your author's game is to get a strong "advance," money the publisher puts up for you to write the book because, unless you have a best seller, you will probably never see another penny. Your next move is to hurry up and get the writing over with, so you can go on to another book and get another advance. Perhaps when you have four or five titles you can begin to make a partial living.

It was a shock to learn that your average author earns about five cents on every book sold. On my calculator that's $50 for every 1000 copies. Only a few authors get the megabucks.

Story after story has reached my ears of how editors cut, revise, distort. Writers compromise, or their work doesn't get published. I'd heard of a major biographer whose major publisher told her that her book would be out in five years. That was over eight years ago, and I'm still waiting to read this definitive work.

We've all heard how some writers receive twenty-eight rejects before their book gets accepted. Let's see, if twenty-eight publishers kept my manuscript for six months each, that's 168 months, or fourteen years before my book would be accepted. Thereafter, the acquiring publisher would take a couple of years for the editing and manufacturing process. So add another two years, which makes sixteen. Taking my age into account, I'd be how old when my book gets to the marketplace? But this is all conjecture, isn't it?

In the years I was marketing my manuscript the new scholarship on women was burgeoning; people were opening eyes, talking about the necessity of putting women's perspective and experience out there. Traditional views of humanity had to be redefined because half the world's population had been marginalized. College administrators and professors were outlining a new field of endeavor and bookstore managers were clearing out bookshelves to make room for the latest, hottest subject, women's studies.

People thirsted to read Fuller's words after my performances. Her work could not be found without prolonged searches in libraries and waiting for inter-library loans. Even then, almost no one cared to plow through Fuller's outdated, erudite style of writing. No easy-reading anthology of her writings was available.

Why shouldn't I think "small" — like Virginia Woolf, Tom Paine, Ralph Waldo Emerson, Walt Whitman, Immanuel Swedenborg, all of whom had bucked the tides of popular demand. Driven idealists, they had published their work themselves.

Others who've joined the small press movement have been T. S. Eliot, Edgar Allan Poe, Carl Sandburg, Stephen Crane, William Cullen Bryant, Anais Nin, Paul Lawrence Dunbar, James Joyce, Ezra Pound, Upton Sinclair, William Blake, James Weldon Johnson, D. H. Lawrence, Edward Arlington Robinson, Marianne Moore, William Faulkner, Mark Twain, Frederick Douglass, the Brontë Sisters, Edna St. Vincent Millay, Emily Dickinson, and Marcel Proust.

Years ago the making of a book meant intense labor via the letterpress printing linotype. Eventually this process was improved with the utilization of camera-ready paste-up mechanicals and high-speed offset. Now, desktop publishing is creating a technological revolution. I can give my computer disk to someone for the design and layout — thus I have control — and go straight to a printer.

I had been reared in the middle of the twentieth century, when bona fide authors would never pay to have work printed. A company that people paid to print and promote work was called the vanity press. In all circles it was scorned and degraded. If a writer made a move to utilize these services, it was considered the height of egotism. It was felt that if a mainstream publisher did not accept your work, then your work was not worthy or professional. You were an amateur. Only amateurs would stoop to this lowest level of degradation.

But I was noticing the independent press. The mergers of the multinational corporations were making the independents the creative grassroots alternative. Some energetic souls were publishing on a shoestring. Some small press books became best sellers, like *The Christmas Box* by Richard Paul Evans, or *Mutant Message Down Under* by Marlow Morgan, or *The Joy of Cooking* by Irma Rombauer. Some small press authors, I learned, had become Pulitzer Prize winners, like Edna St. Vincent Millay.

Looking over my 700 computer-written pages with a new eye, I was overwhelmed with the multitude of decisions that lay before me. Luckily my sister, Gwen Harper, was on hand. She'd shepherded innumerable books as national program director for Camp Fire Girls, Inc. She suggested I plan a pair of smaller books instead of one long book.

I jumped. An entire book was contained in my Foreword, which had taken me a solid year to research and write, an experience that had been soul shaking. For what seemed an age I'd kept librarians busy supplying me with volumes most people had never heard of. Tucking out-of-print inter-library loans into a suitcase, I had flown three thousand miles to join my husband in San Francisco where he had a job for six weeks and where I rarely took leave of our transient quarters so I could read every biography written on Ralph Waldo Emerson.

I was paralyzed to learn how, if Fuller was mentioned at all in these books, she was degraded time and again in her person, work, and relationship with Emerson. I was pained to discover that in book after book Emerson's wife of forty-two years — who outlived him and assuredly held some influence — was delineated barely three times: (1) she married him and rode with him in a carriage to the house he had bought in Concord; (2) *he* was *given* a son; and (3) she died.

In books published during the last century and a half, I noted, the achievements and significance of men whose paths crossed Emerson's were detailed so that they could be traced in history. But women were left out, briefly mentioned, or portrayed in unfavorable view. In biographies written during the 1970s and '80s by men, the Emerson/Fuller story began to be explored and some of the women were mentioned, but the perspective was insensitive. One new and acclaimed scholar compared Emerson's wife to a Salem witch.

More than once I had to stop reading to pace the floor in frustration and anger. The claims women's studies writers were making were true. Women and their work were not valued, were not given the space they deserved. Their daily presence was not seen as important or influential. My hundred-page Forward was worthy of being an entire book. I called it, *Why Margaret Fuller Ossoli Is Forgotten. A True Account— Typical of How Famous Women Have Been Buried in History.*

Then, it took me about two weeks to go through Fuller's books (by this time I owned all of them), to select, edit, and arrange excerpts under subject headings for a companion book entitled *The Wit and Wisdom of Margaret Fuller Ossoli.*

Meanwhile, I was getting quotes from designers and printers. Producing two small paperbacks would cost less than buying a car — and this investment had the potential of returning my money.

How many books to print? What kind of paper? Hard cover or paper? What color cover? How long would it take to print? How does one price? Would anyone review? How to publicize? How to market? What are jobbers, wholesalers, and distributors?

I had to become incorporated as a small press. Advice came from my sons-in-law, Andrew Gross, a financial wizard for Sony Records International, and Robert Schultz, a C.P.A. who had his own business with a partner. I found a lawyer to draw up the papers, and paid with moneys saved from my performances. I didn't know it then, but creating Golden Heritage Press, Inc. was adding another to the list of 6,000 small publishers in America who brought out 30,000 to 40,000 publications per year.

I went wild waiting for my book designer to finish his job —

which I thought must be comparatively easy on a computer. I waited while I attended to ISBN number, bar code, copyright, including sending copies of my best forty pages to an artists' fellowship program sponsored by the New York Foundation for the Arts.

The printer took longer than he'd estimated. I found him about an hour from my home, in the wilds of the North Shore on Long Island. He worked out of a converted barn with gray paint peeling off. Inside, there were long rows of neatly organized floor-to-ceiling shelves of books and tons of machinery. Meandering in and out were young bearded people in jeans and T-shirts. They looked like they knew what they were doing. This printer told me there were over a hundred steps in manufacturing a book.

A big blustery macho character who always seemed rushed, he did take the time to relate stories of customers who never paid him, who "took him" in one way or another. I had no idea whether this was a trustworthy operation, but his plant seemed to turn out books.

This is the way I was cornered into unplanned costs. This printer informed me he'd probably send my book cover to another printer who had better equipment for color work. After about two months, when the text was completed, I received a phone call from the printer of the cover. While I had ordered a short run of 1,000 covers for each title, his minimum run was 2,000. He would do 1,000, but the price would be the same as for 2,000. I was to be stuck with 1,000 extra covers for each book.

There are plenty of horror stories. I've since learned one printer was sent front cover art that was too large and, even though he received replacement art, *he ignored it* and reduced the print so small it looked ridiculous. Another printer never sent the publisher bluelines (proof pages) for approval, and *put the wrong bar code and ISBN number on 5,000 copies.* The publisher had to sue.

I had to go for a substantial loan. I borrowed from a home equity loan newly taken out by Robert Schultz, my son-in-law. For almost two years, I paid back this money with interest with fees from my Margaret Fuller dramatizations and book sales, *plus* on Saturday nights I worked for my son, Mike. As a newspaper distributor, every Saturday he dragged up our basement stairs stacks and stacks of "pennysavers" and supermarket advertising sections. I piled the various sections of newspapers on an old coffee table in front of the

TV, and there I'd sit, collating and bagging. If I worked fast enough, I could earn about fifty dollars in ten hours. This was more than what he paid to the teeny-boppers he usually hired.

When I brought my new set of books home, I felt akin to Henry David Thoreau who'd carried upstairs to his room 706 unsold copies of *A Week on the Concord and Merrimack Rivers*. Thoreau said: "I have now a library of nearly nine hundred volumes, over seven hundred of which I wrote myself. They are something more substantial than fame, as my back knows, which has born them up two flights of stairs."

My books did sell. I never tried for reviews, figuring these small companion books were insignificant compared to what critics received from the major companies. Instead, I sent out announcements to a selected list of contacts, and also I carried my books to every Margaret Fuller presentation. I bought self-publishing manuals and made sure the name of Golden Heritage Press, Inc., was included on various lists in the trade. I had to devise invoices, and work out best ways to ship books, figure postage costs and state taxes, keep files and records.

I signed up for a two-day Publishing University Conference sponsored by Publishers Marketing Association and American Booksellers Association at the Grand Hyatt Hotel in New York City. High powered, business-minded, black-suited, highly-skilled small press publishers were a different breed from the actors and writers groups I was used to.

Was anyone as green as I? I attended two conferences in New York sponsored by COSMEP, an association of independent book publishers, and there met many people who were publishing because of dedication to a cause. I collected all sorts of information packets, took voluminous notes, and had questions answered in workshops.

I learned that in the past thirty years there'd been enormous change. In the mid-1960s the small press was regarded as a useful alternative for social, revolutionary and political minds, as well as for those who explored foment in literature. But over the years subject matter widened and the independents began to profit. In fact, today some complain that the problem with the small press is that it has become The Establishment.   (This parallels the situation of Off-Broadway ventures.)

One day a year later, I collected my mail and glanced at a large brown envelope that had a return address from The New York Foundation for the Arts.   Some kind of advertising, I thought to myself, and set it aside so I could give priority to my more interesting mail. Finally, I opened the brown envelope. Spying a neatly typed letter with some back-up materials, I confirmed that it was another pitch for an arts contribution, and I was ready to throw it into the trash. "We are pleased to inform you that you have been awarded a $6,000 fellowship — "

I blinked.

Was this some sort of magazine promotion?

What *was* this?

I reread the lines.

Then I remembered!

There were no strings attached. This fellowship was designed to advance your career. If you felt you needed a vacation, you could take a vacation. If you needed to pay bills, you could pay bills. Whatever you wanted to do with the money, you could do. Fifty-five hundred dollars were to be paid immediately, and the remaining five hundred were to be paid after a public service project was completed.

I solicited quotes for the cost of a third book, my major biography of Fuller and Emerson, some 500 pages long.

"Why don't you just keep the fellowship money and find a publisher for the book?" suggested Edith O'Hara of the Thirteenth Street Theater.

I just couldn't face the prospect of heartache and time in trying to connect with another publisher.

Priority for the next few months became pulling this manuscript together. Never sure of my own judgment, I wished constantly to have the help of a more knowledgeable editorial eye. But where to find it? As far as Margaret Fuller was concerned, I was the most knowlegeable person around.   My most difficult and unweildly Chapter IV was nearly 300 pages long. Somehow I had to cut and hang it together. For about a month, I spread pages over the living-room sofa, the coffee tables, the floor —they reached onto the dining room table and chairs. I read, read, merged, merged, cut, cut.

Two months after I'd given the manuscript to my designer, I learned he'd barely begun work. Two weeks later he confessed that his marriage had broken apart and he was moving upstate New York to take a new job. He turned my book over to his friend who worked out of a room in his home which he'd set up with a complex of computer equipment.

Words typed in italics on my computer did not come through in italics on his. I must have proofed those 500 pages twenty times, and made dozens of trips to the designer's home. I found pictures of the Transcendentalists, paid for permissions, procured the copyright, the ISBN number, the CIP data, the barcode, and made innumerable decisions.

I had to locate a new book manufacturer, one who could include the paperback covers. At a press in New Jersey I was given a tour of plant operations, so I saw the entire process of book making from printing to binding. I went for a six-color cover, and had to learn about and contact another outfit for color separations. I waited. Approved proofs. And waited. Coerced my son to truck the books home in his van and stack the boxes in the basement. What a thrill to unpack and see those beautiful red covers.

Still, this manufacturing process was only the beginning. Like walking blindfolded, I commissioned my designer to work up a brochure featuring my set of three books, and I did a direct mailing and got a few orders. I spent about a week researching the names of reviewers across the nation. I sent out press releases and complimentary books. I badgered with follow-up phone calls.

Someone mentioned distributors, so I located a list in the library. I read self-publishing manuals, followed directions, and sent off sample books, made phone calls. I was treated like the greenhorn I was, but I began to learn.

Discount policies were like trying to understand Greek. How could distributors and booksellers demand such high percentages? Why didn't they care about the content of a book? How cold seemed the world of business.

I rented a list of a thousand names and sent out brochures. I quickly learned that the costs of direct mail eat up profit.

I sent Gloria Steinem my books — she'd helped me on an earlier project — and asked her to pass them onto the *Ms.* magazine reviewer, and eventually I got a mention.

One day an academic library wholesaler called on the phone and enthusiastically suggested I sign a contract to send them fifty books at discount. I hesitated because actually I had no idea how to negotiate the discount. Finally, she said they could work with 45%. I thought that was outrageous, but agreed — then later learned I'd made a fair deal. Eventually, I also signed deals with another major wholesaler and two small-press wholesalers. Also, book orders began to scatter in from jobbers and wholesalers.

I received some reviews, not as many as I would have liked, and nothing in *The New York Times* — which, of course, I did not expect because they are beseiged with thousands of books which they do not have space to review.

There was a rave from critic Ivy Burrows in a major library journal, *Booklist:* "The book is well written and meticulously researched and provides fascinating insight into the entire transcendentalist movement."

From *The Library Journal* there was Jeris Cassel, from Rutgers University Libraries: "Paralleling, comparing, and contrasting Fuller and Emerson...a collage of the numerous men and women involved....Intended for the lay reader..."

Fairfield University's K. J. Dykeman reviewed for *Choice*, another important library journal: "An exciting introduction to Fuller, Emerson, and their friends...Lacks a critical evaluation of Fuller's philosophy...Does fulfill criterion of 'feminine perspective.' Good bibliography; good index. Recommended for every undergraduate...."

Diane Donovan reviewed favorably in *The Midwest Book Review:* "All three books should be required reading in any women's studies class where historical figures are re-examined in new light."

The critic from *The Small Press Book Review* called my book "a biography of many dimensions," and the writer for *History: Reviews of New Books* said, "Important information about the daily lives and the emotional and intellectual exchanges of the key figures....Professional historians will find in it a profusion of useful details...."

Two small newspaper critics were complimentary. David Horn, Staff writer for *The Pilot-News* in Plymouth, Indiana, summed up: "Scholarly and smooth....A perfect gift for the reader who has everything."

And an anonymous reviewer for *The Citizen Tribune* in Morristown, Tennessee, had thoroughly perceived my thesis: "Fuller and Emerson played a battle of the sexes game that lasted far after her death....Told for the first time with well documented facts and intelligent verve....It is fascinating in its complexities...."

I had an excellent full-page interview in a Long Island paper, *Women's Record.*

All of this gave me press to include with every order I sent out.

By this time I was subscribing to small-press periodicals, and a "jolt in the arm" came when I read these words: "Literary publishing is no longer what it should be: an underground activity....Writing that is too safe, too easily assimilated, or too inoffensive is not likely to be writing that is remembered."

Richard Morris, executive director of the International Association of Independent Publishers, argued that America, unlike Europe, is not weighted down with the burden of centuries of literary tradition.

He continued: "I am not saying that a work must be unusual, or odd, or outrageous to have lasting literary value....Some of the greatest works of literature are ones that contain nothing that is outlandish or shocking, but which are valued for their understatement and elegance. What I am saying is that we have a national literature that has always been ready to incorporate elements that were unacceptable to the refined literary sensibilities of the day. And I believe that we don't see enough of this literary perspective nowadays....I would urge that literary publishers again learn to think of themselves as members of an underground, and to act accordingly. For it is the literary undergrounds that have created the greatest American literature....If we care about literature, it is the writing of the 1990s that should be of greatest concern to us now. And if we want this writing to be remembered, we're going to have to create a new literary underground in which it can thrive."

I could see why Richard Morris was being honored with the 1991

Poor Richard's Award for distinguished service to small presses by the Small Press Center.

The first time I walked into the Small Press Center I felt humbled and empowered. I was walking into one of the oldest private subscription libraries in New York City, founded for members of trade groups in 1820. This is the high-ceilinged landmark building of the General Society of Mechanics & Tradesmen.

I ambled over to a corner which comprised the quarters of the Small Press Center. Two women came out of a small office. I introduced myself and showed them my books. They made me feel like a million dollars. Here was a world that nutured combinations of idealism and entrepreneurship.

The Small Press Center is the brainchild of Whitney North Seymour, Jr., a former United States attorney and state senator who'd created his own enterprise, Lime Rock Press. The Center opened its doors in 1984 and has grown to serve as prototype for a companion organization in Great Britain. Executives hope it to be a part of an international effort.

The Center is funded by grants from foundations, annual contributions, fees from members, and a small amount from the sale of posters and publications. They provide shelf space for small press books, and promotional opportunities such as an annual book fair, a small press directory sent to libraries and bookstores, readings, special exhibits, receptions, book signing parties, and window display space. They offer memberships to serious publishers, but vanity presses aren't accepted.

For two days during the years 1989 through 1993, I was one of 200 earnest presses from the U.S. standing behind a table to showcase my books at the Small Press Book Fair. There are no names here such as Harper & Row, Simon and Schuster, Knopf, Doubleday. The room is filled with Just Us Books, Square One Publishers, Real Comet Press, Sri Rama Publishing, Jackdaw Press, Burning Books, Seal Press, B. Rugged Books, Nightingale Resources, etc.

Poets, novelists, scholars, historians, social activists, artists, and writers of every type are represented. Every variety of topic is covered: fine art, literature, New Age, photography, travel, cooking, children's fiction and nonfiction, thrillers, sports, self-help, the environment.

Some presses are run single-handedly, some are made up of two people who do one or two books a year, others have ten to twenty employees and publish more than twelve books annually. The commonality is caring about books, dedication to publishing.

Among the three thousand visitors who ventured by to view my books the first year was Ina Wishner. We struck up a conversation. She'd seen my performance, was a great admirer of Margaret Fuller. A dark-haired, homey, down-to-earth person with a lovely smile, she is of the kind you feel comfortable with immediately. As we became friends, I learned she was a good painter who'd exhibited and sold her own paintings. She was chair of the poetry section of the Pen and Brush Club. I knew about this club for writers and artists, and I wanted to join. She promised to forward my name, and since then this club has given me a place to connect with other like-minded people on a regular basis.

At the 1990 Small Press Book Fair I read a 15-minute section from my book during the reading session. The director, Karin Taylor, asked me to also read throughout a lunch hour and be aired on the local New York radio station, WNYE. She also set up and promoted a performance of my Margaret Fuller drama in the balcony museum overlooking the main library. The next year Tom Tolnay, the director, asked me to write for their newsletter the front page story on Edna St. Vincent Millay, who was the Small Press Writer of the Year.

I walked into my first bookstore feeling queasy. The manager was nice but said, "We don't like to buy directly from individuals because the bookkeeping is too complicated."

I was stunned.

Wearing out shoe leather, I learned how true this was. Bookstore proprietors do not like to take time to order, stock, return, credit, that is, track one or two books through an individual press that they consider may go out of business or bankrupt. They want to order numerous titles in one planning session through one or two trusted distributors or sales representatives so that records are kept on three or four accounts, all of which makes bookkeeping so much simpler. They want to deal with those who will accept the return of shop worn and unsalable books for credit. They take less risk on quick turn-over

— selling best sellers. The bottom line is, most bookstores do not stock small press books. They couldn't care less about content or commitment to culture.

If a customer asks for your book, sales people will special order if its listed in *Books in Print* or other directories or appears on the store's microfiche system, but all of this takes time. How does the public know your book is available? In general, the public is unaware of the existence of the wide and struggling independent or small-press market.

There are independent bookstores struggling to exist that will buy from individuals and small presses, mostly on consignment, but where they are, one must discover. Their numbers have shrunk by over 50%.

The consignment method of distribution limits you to your hometown or to those cities you can visit from time to time. Consignment means you leave your books at the store without being paid for them, and every month or so you go back to see if there have been any sales — because the manager will probably never contact you or bother to pay you if your books are sold.

I paid visits to bookstores and libraries in whatever city I visited. For three days in Los Angeles my daughter, Mary, drove me around. With a driver, I could visit about twenty-five bookstores per day. Twice, on my way to Los Angeles, I stopped in San Francisco, stayed in a bed-and-breakfast, and hired a driver for two days. In Minneapolis I hired a town car. On Long Island I drove myself because parking is easy. In New York City I took subways and busses because parking is a headache.

Most bookstore managers were busy, would shunt me off. Some said "No" right away; others would politely listen, seem impressed, take my literature. A few did promise to buy — through a distributor. I was surprised when I was treated in a friendly manner. When one manager said she'd give my books a corner display, I was elated. Another went to a cash register, pulled out some cash, and bought my books on the spot.

I mailed off letters and free books and got on local radio- and TV-interview shows in all of those cities. I'm sure I made the distributors some money as orders trickled in.

How true is John B. McHugh's statement in an article for Publishers Marketing Association newsletter: "The cost of self-publishing — that is, the cost of your valuable time when you consider the learning curve invested in producing and promoting your own book — could be invested in a more profitable, more assured opportunity."

He goes on: "The distribution system for trade books is a combination of inefficient and archaic practices that are unfriendly to small press publishers or self-publishers."

It would be smart to commssion a sales representative, but commissioned sales reps whose salaries go into the six figures will not give time to an individual or a press that has only two or three books. They want to represent publishers who list at least twenty to fifty new books every year so they can have large paying orders when they make their calls.

One knows before one starts that it's impossible to break through the barriers set up by the major chain stores. This is the area where money makes a difference because the big publishing houses put up huge amounts to boost sales. But, like Don Quixote, one valiantly makes the heroic attempt. After all, you are confident that your books compete in your subject area, and if you can just convince the powers-that-be of their importance, your books will have a national reach.

It's easy to get the phone numbers of the executive offices. You can even walk into your local chain store branch. If you can convince them you represent a bona fide press, the managers will (pretending to be reluctant) give out the number, but if you ask for a name, they will say, "I don't know the person you should speak to."

Call the number, and after punching in several other numbers, you will get a recorded voice telling you to send in your book. You will not be able to reach a human being or leave a message. If you send your book (which costs you something like $10 per book, depending on the price), you will, months later, receive a letter telling you they cannot accept your book. (They will not return the book.)

I did not give up on Waldenbooks who listed that they bought from independent presses. One day while visiting a friend, Sylvia Koose, in Hyannis, Massachusetts, I walked into a Waldenbooks and the manager said, "Do you want to have a book signing?" He handed me a business card, and then punched his computer. "Call this woman — she coordinates all the signings in Connecticut, Rhode Island, and Massachusetts. Tell her I've ordered all your books."

I nearly dropped dead. *Somewhere there was room for the little person!*

The woman was cordial and friendly, but was losing her job because the corporate office was moving and reorganizing. Would I like to contact the stores in her region myself? She sent me the list.

There were about fourteen Waldenbooks in Connecticut, Rhode Island, and Massachusetts on her list. When I mentioned her name, calling long distance, ten Waldenbooks store managers eagerly set dates. Two of them requested boxes of books which I mailed off.

I figured I had, at last, unbelievably, my toe in the chain-store door. I would soon be in line to knock on the door at the top and prove my books profitable enough for them to carry nationally.

I spent at least a week rounding up lists of schools, libraries, and organizations in the New England areas, and spent about $200 sending out announcements about my book signing tour.

My first signing at Waldenbooks was in a shopping mall. This store had done nothing for my arrival. The cordial manager I'd met earlier was no longer there. The store was now being run by a young man who treated me with great respect, who set up a table at the front entrance, but who obviously was greener than I. For about two hours I stood there, dressed as Margaret Fuller, and talked to numerous people who stopped by, but none of them bought my books. My friend Sylvia arrived full of spirit. We had a lively talk and she bought my book as a gift (she already had a copy for herself), and asked for my autograph. The clerk took her money and I told the manager I would give Waldenbooks 40% discount and send an invoice. When I left the manager took three autographed books for later sales — he'd feature them on the counter. To this day this store has never paid for these books though I have made calls and regularly send invoices. To be at this store cost me at least $100 in travel expenses.

After that I received a call from the Waldenbooks district manager. She was canceling all of my books signings because I was not a publisher that Waldenbooks dealt with. She said they could not get my books through an approved wholesaler and the stores were not allowed to order directly through me. I argued that my books

were available — and had been for years — through a major
wholesaler that they dealt with, Baker & Taylor. But buyers at Baker
& Taylor were informing Waldenbooks that my books were on "back
order" and would take three months to get. This only meant that, at
the moment, my books were not on Baker & Taylor's warehouse
shelves for immediate distribution. I made many phone calls to both
the Waldenbooks district manager and Baker & Taylor. It was a
"catch 22" situation. All the store managers, who'd asked me to mail
my books to them, mailed them back to me.

Some chain stores do welcome and support local authors because
it's presumed you will have friends who will come into the store and
buy your books. I'm on great terms with Tiku Mandeheim, the
manager at the superstore Borders, in Bohemia, Long Island, not far
from where I live, and have had readings and signings there. She
promotes local authors with posters, flyers on counters, and
announcements in newspapers. She says "thanks" to her local
authors every year by staging a party for them. But attempt to
advance to a national level — you get the voice mail on the phone
and the closed door.

Librarians are committed to the small press because special-
interest matter broadens the reach of their collections. When I
walked into libraries and pitched, I received attentive interest, but
acquisitions librarians — who receive thousands of solicitations and
can in no way read every book they buy — depend on reviews in the
library journals. I know many of my book orders from distributors
went to libraries — all due to the fact that I'd received excellent
reviews in library journals.

Acquisitions librarians will automatically purchase the best
sellers. They then fill gaps in whatever special subject-areas their
library holds. Next, readership demand is considered and orders are
placed through distributors.

If you really want to sell to a library, you are advised to have
friends go to that library and ask for your book. Not many authors
have that many friends spread across the United States.

The college market has its own hurdles. Most college bookstores
buy from the lists professors provide. A publisher's job is to convince

professors that your books are needed in the curriculum. You mail them free copies to evaluate. (No wonder you see hundreds of books in the offices of professors.) If what you have is right for them, you will be in business for years to come. Getting lists of the proper persons to target is another three-week job.

Some book dealers never pay. Stores and jobbers go out of business and you are left holding the bag. Most pay three months later; some wholesalers pay a year after receiving your books. Returns will come in and you are supposed to give credit — up to a year later — even after payment has been made. If you don't give credit, they may not order from you again.

Some distributors and bookstores send books back worn from being on shelves for long periods of time. One time a book came back to me with a nasty pencil hole punched in the cover, right on the picture of Margaret Fuller, at the point of her breast.

Someone who attended my performances at the Thirteenth Street Theater bought three books with a check that bounced. I found her name in the telephone book and called her. She said she would send another check. She never did.

But what happened with a group of women who ran a Margaret Fuller Festival was devestating. It hurt to the quick, for I considered these women to be friends when I should have been the cold-hearted business woman.

They ordered one hundred each of my three titles, worth about $4,000. The director of the Festival assured me they would sell. They gave me an autographing session after my performance, and many of my books sold. I received a check for about $200, and later another came for $29. After that, nothing. I received letters from the director mentioning how the woman in charge of the Festival merchandise, was ill with breast cancer. I did not badger. I was confident these women, my friends, would pay as they staged events and as books sold. Two years later I received a note that the Festival was defunct and the director had just discovered my books in an office. She and a friend returned them via UPS. They packed them so poorly that many were damaged. When I did the count, books were missing, books for which I'd never received payment. I figured, with a 40% discount, my press was owed about $2,000. I wrote several times.

The director responded twice, saying she hadn't been in charge and
she wasn't aware of any sales or moneys due. As to the damaged
books, she'd check out her home insurance policy. She never
responded to my third and fourth letters. I finally went to a lawyer
who advised me that it wasn't worth going through the small claims
court — I was sure to win, but how was I to collect. I was deeply
hurt. Frankly, any money I earn from sales goes towards producing
more books.

How could I call it quits now?

It was jubilation to think that I had sold (or given away) all my
books — 1,000 each of three titles.

In the fall and winter of 1991-2 I sank money I'd made into
reprinting. The Long Island printer wasn't around when his
employees were collating the reprint of *Why Margaret Fuller Ossoli
Is Forgotten*. (Yes, I was utilizing the 1,000 extra covers I'd been stuck
with.)

The employees inserted endpapers that were cut too short.

It was my fault, I was told, because I'd supplied the wrong size.

Why didn't they call me when they'd discovered the mistake?

Because the printer hadn't been there.

Luckily, he wasn't there when I'd picked up the finished copies,
so I didn't pay for the last third of the job. Thus, I was able to negotiate
a deal for what I thought was fair under the circumstances.

I had served as my own editor for *Men, Women, and Margaret
Fuller*. Actually, this is not advisable because, as the writer, you get
so close to the material that you really can't see your own errors, no
matter how many times you go over the material. A fresh eye is
needed. I learned this the hard way, for as the first edition was read,
people pointed out to me various mistakes in spelling and grammar.
So my chance to make corrections came with the second edition. But
each page the printer has to re-do costs money. So I invested my
dollars from performances again, about $2,000; I wanted perfection.

When the second printing of *Men, Women, and Margaret Fuller*
came off the presses, I went through each box at home, examining
each copy, as good publishers are told to do. Out of 2,000 there were
defects in all but 140 — that is, if you disregarded the fact that every

one had a badly over-inked word on page 241.

Almost all copies had light pinkish ink smears on the first and last pages.

At least 361 books needed additional glue along one or both endpapers.

One hundred and seventy had dirty endpapers with either white glue spots that did not come off or black ink marks near the bottom or top edges.

Sixty-four had white spots or smears on the cover.

Thirty-three had spots on the dedication page — some were flaws in the paper.

Thirty-one covers were either folded or faultily trimmed.

Twenty-five had defective front endpapers — one side was red, the other side was rough, whitish pink.

Twenty-two had no index pages — they had been left out.

Thirteen had crumpled pages.

Six had a middle section of pages that were too short.

Five were missing back endpapers.

Four had crushed endpapers.

Three had spots or ink markings on the first page.

Two had red-ink fingermarks on inside pages.

Two covers had a blurred picture.

Two covers were crushed.

One had a greenish paper pasted on the back cover which, if removed, would ruin the cover.

One had an extra endpaper inserted.

One book had some pages inserted upside down.

My calls to the manufacturer were not returned; the powers-that-be were "not in." I had to pressure and get nasty. They gave me the "stall" for over a month. Finally, they made good. They sent a truck, picked up the books, made all the corrections by hand, and redelivered the books. The entire process took eight months.

Competing in the jungle of the small-press business is, I suppose, tantamount to stepping into a boxing ring.

The odds are against an individual who goes up against mass-marketing sophistication.

The way I did it — and do it — is always challenging, but there has been no big-time winnings from this horrendous fight which consumes my time and thought.

But there are positives.

Most important, I have helped to broaden the awareness of the name and achievement of Margaret Fuller — and that has been my goal from the beginning.

Second, because my books were out there, I was found and hired at a high salary to tour three summers as Margaret Fuller with the Great Plains Chautauqua Society.

The major benefit in publishing your own work is that you hold control over your product. You have it like you want it — even though you may face struggles with designers and printers. Today, maintaining control over your product is a significant advantage.

Anybody who denigrates anyone who publishes their own work is either blind or ignorant. If you publish your own work, you work harder than anybody in their right mind would do. You expose yourself. You take risks. You put your own money into your product — you invest in yourself. Therefore, you have to believe in the worth of what you are doing. You have to have self-confidence and perservering faith. For me, these qualities have grown largely because a number of people and organizations have been there and offered the encouragement I needed to continue.

RISKING THE EDINBURGH FRINGE

Anybody can do anything at The Edinburgh Fringe Festival —
and do — from serious dramas to who-done-its to zany cabaret acts.
There's nothing like it in the United States — or in any other country
— and that's where the excitement lies for artists from all parts of the
world.

One sixty-five-year-old British actress who invested herself onto
the boards quipped, "I'm up against it because I'm not obscene,
grotesque, or stark naked."

Somebody mentioned the festival which I'd never heard of. I
found the address in the library. Soon, out of my mailbox I pulled
a huge packet of colorful materials describing a wild scene with
hundreds of madcaps, many of whom were American.

This serious craziness began in 1947 when Sir John Falconer, Lord
Provost of the City, Harry Harvey Wood, a senior official of the British
Council, and Rudolf Bing — who later became Director of the
Metropolitan Opera House in New York — had visions that it would
be grand to have an International Festival of Music and Drama in
Edinburgh with the attendant tourist and financial rewards. Gold-
plated talent was brought in from around the world. Lesser-known
companies were ignored so, cleverly, the small fry started promoting

their own audiences, selling their own tickets, and getting their own accolades. The next year more fledgling companies joined in.

Quickly, the word "Fringe" was coined,* and eventually, there evolved the Fringe Society, which published a program and a daily listing of events, and managed an information service, central box office, and a club. By 1974 there were 115 small theaters selling more tickets than the offical Festival. The local newspaper, *The Scotsman*, established Fringe First Awards to encourage new and innovative work, after which came the Perrier Award for excellence. The Fringe became so big that it subsisted on about $150,000, funded with about $25,000 from Edinburgh District Council grants.

The Festival packet had been lying around my house for several days when my husband questioned it. "Well, you better go over there and see what it's all about."

I was thunderstruck.

"You should take a look at it and, if it's right for you, you should find a theater for yourself and make arrangements for next year."

"I — I — " We had no money to spend on "extracurriculars."

"I just got $1,700 I didn't expect and you can have it. It's enough to cover your fare and expenses, and maybe to put a downpayment on a theater." He put the check into my hand and turned to leave the room.

"I can't anyway. The Festival starts in two days."

"It goes on for three weeks."

I'd made plans for the next three weeks.

"You can take off *a week*, can't you? Your passport is still good."

Within a few days I was on a plane headed for the absolute unknown, "the Athens of the North," the land of Mary, Queen of Scots, Sir Walter Scott, Robert Burns, James Boswell, Robert Louis Stevenson, and I was very much in love with my husband.

I felt strangely adventurous, grandly independent, but where would I stay? According to the travel agent, every room had been taken during Festival season. Many people slept on the street, I'd

---

*In1960 the revue called *Beyond the Fringe*, starring Peter Cook, Dudley Moore, Alan Bennett and Jonathan Miller, was a hit at the Festival, and was launched on a worldwide tour.

read, so perhaps I was to have a "total" experience.

In the Fringe Program Guide there were listed more than 900 shows which took in more than £430,000 in theaters, store fronts, churches, elementary schools, colleges, institutes, museums, parks, trucks, you-name-it. Shows ran from 9:00 A.M. and continued every hour on the hour of every day until 3:00 A.M.

I cared nothing about the famed military tattoo with its Scottish regimental pipes and drums and Highland dancing. I wouldn't attend the festivals of jazz or film, or the exhibits, or the forty-odd expensive international mainstage performances from around the world, which included:

The Caucasian Chalk Circle by Brecht, presented by the Berliner Ensemble

Michael Kohlhaas presented by the Cameri Theater, Tel Aviv, Israel

Mary Stuart by Friedrich Schiller, a Festival production in association with the Scottish Theater Company, directed by Frank Dunlop, the Festival director

The Woman Warrior, presented by the Shanghai Kunju Theater from the Peoples' Republic of China

Descent of the Brutes by Hideki Noda, presented by Yume No Yuminsha Company from Japan.

These surely had the largest budgets, most lavish sets, superb writers, marvellous directors and actors. But who cared about seeing star-studded commercialized smashes? I wanted to survey the enterprising *un*established. I tried to figure out a route whereby I could walk from one theater to another in order to attend the most in the least time.

I arrived on a sunny day in this convivial, Gothic city dominated by a gray medieval castle and statues. Edinburgh, usually known for its reason, moderation, and austerity, was covered chaotically with posters, flags, flowers. Scottish bagpipers in colorful regalia were fifing at thoroughfares. Performing artists, young and old, were standing on corners, hustling flyers to passersby. "See our show! See our show! Guaranteed you'll like it!" The energy of it all!

There were actors in Groucho Marx masks carrying rubber chickens on sticks, mimes enacting a book burning, a young woman, pillow in stomach, being wheeled about on a hospital bed — all screaming *look at us.*

The cobblestone streets were teaming with tourists of all countries, sizes, classes, sexes, races, religions. People were bumping into each other, greeting each other, apologizing, asking directions, scurrying off, laughing, buying souvenirs, making plans to see a show and figuring where to eat dinner. I carefully eyed the many T-shirted backpackers to determine if they were sleeping in parks.

At the harried Tourist and Information Center set up especially to help coordinate the Festival influx, I, with suitcase in hand, impatiently waited on a long, slow line, amidst people who did not speak the same language. Standing here was going to take a minimum of two hours. Everyone wanted the same thing: a bed.

Flyers and brochures of every kind and color were on window ledges, on floors, in people's hands, and I amused myself by trying to decide which of the seductively publicized shows I most wanted to attend. Some flyers were slick and professional; others were crudely written and printed with weird black drawings. Many were humorous and provocative, others blatantly sexual and violent.

As I finally approached the head of the line, the man behind the counter turned away the people in front of me. When I stepped forward, he shook his head dubiously, but poked through lists, grabbed a phone, dialed a number. The last room available in Edinburgh that night was in some type of guest home at a rather incredible price, but I took it. "Come back again tomorrow," I was told, "maybe we'll have something less expensive."

Day Two, the same long line, and it took me another two or three hours to collect my belongings and catch a cab. This room was at least permanent, in somebody's home, and I was only about a twenty-minute bus ride away from the main streets of the city.

The remainer of Day Two and all of Day Three were absolute heaven. I marched from venue to venue. They had names like Canongate Lodge, Traverse Theater, Torn Curtain Theater Company, the Open Eye, Mandela Theater, Oxford Theater Group, Headoverheels Company, Questors Theater, the Loaves & Fish Theater Company, the Guilded Balloon Theater Company. I saw as many productions as I could, all day and evening.

Every niche was called a theater, but every one was make-shift. Some were hidden, down alleyways, or upstairs, or down long halls inside a dignified stone building. Others jutted into the street so pedestrians had to walk around them. Inside, some were too oblong and narrow, some too cavernous, some cut audience view with posts. The best had black curtains hung as backdrops, with tiers of benches brought in. Others had strangely raised platforms, too high or too low, with hard-backed chairs set up on flat cement, seating as few as ten or twenty or as many as a hundred. Some floors were entirely flat, the playing and seating area arranged in the round. Most had lighting systems, but some were plain schoolrooms with no lighting, no curtains, nothing for special effects. Still others were church pulpits and actors performed in front of stained glass windows, the audience sitting in pews.

I scrutinized. Is this a good location? How many does this seat? Is the theater run well? Would the venue impresario want my Margaret Fuller? Have they been long in business? Could I get an audience here? Was I as good as what I was seeing on stage?

I loved this crazy scene.

But an echo rebounded everywhere I went: "You don't go to the Fringe expecting a profit." "It's a losing battle — especially for first-time players." "Within the first week many productions take nosedives."

I conjured the image of the noble six hundred riding to their deaths in Tennyson's famed *The Charge of the Light Brigade.*

Many people complained that the The Fringe was "middle-aged." It had lost its spontaneity. It was too large. Too impersonal. Too traffic-congested. It cost too much. Too radical. Too much competition; the pressure too intense. Always, there were political wrangles, not to mention cash crises.

Criticism was directed against the Fringe Society, the Festival director and the Lord Provost. They were always going to meetings and getting their pictures in the paper, forging cultural links between Scotland and other countries. Forums for a Fairer Fringe had been organized and issues were constantly debated such as the press's vested interests or problems of property owners who rented flats and venue spaces at exorbitant rates. Fire laws jeopardized certain experimental theatrical elements. Then there was theft. Imposters pretending to be members of the press were caught getting free theater tickets. A new Local Government Act forbidding local authorities from "promoting" homosexuality was satirized and belittled. Glasgow was suddenly competing; with its own festival it aimed to serve as cultural heart of Scotland.

Yet each year the Fringe seems to have broken attendance records. Career-minded individuals and groups continue to bolster dreams with dollars never to be recouped.

To me, it was people making theater happen against all odds. It was artists daring to express beliefs, crying out for innovation. It was grabbing onto the first rung of a ladder. Though there was a lunatic fringe, the spirit equated equal opportunity and entrepreneurship — actors investing in themselves. It represented the joy of theater.

Whatever shocked was the standard — taboos, exploitations. You were normal if you made a statement against government, the environment, the class system, prejudice, the bomb, human cruelty, poverty, homophobia, etcetera.

The one-person show was hailed with open arms. Women's issues were treated liberally. Historical figures were rampant. Therefore, my Margaret Fuller might be uniquely visible.

By Day Four I had a list of my ten "Preferred Theaters." I crossed several managers off my list because they stalled. Most said it was too early to make decisions for next year; one said he might not continue his venue. Finally, I narrowed my names to two theaters with administrators who could book me into desireable time slots at reasonable cost.

By Day Five I had made my decision.

It was a quaint theater that had been in business about twenty years. It seated about seventy-five, was located on a traffic-congested street, just beyond a gray-stoned facade which looked like a mini-castle. Audiences had to troop through a cobblestone courtyard that had a picturesque cafe where people could sit outdoors sipping beer or tea and dippling chips or shortbread.

I confirmed the deal with the Scottish manager who was kind, attractive, interested in history and women's issues. I offered a hefty down payment, but he insisted the check be sent later. Then I scurried to the Fringe office and told them to put my name on next year's list. Not one person had as yet signed up.

Next, I hiked over to the most historic St. Mark's Unitarian Church on Castle Terrace (one of only two Unitarian churches in the world identified with a saint's name), and introduced myself to the Reverend Andrew Hill. I suggested I give a talk about Margaret Fuller in the church the next year, perhaps we could have a reception, etcetera. It turned out he was beseiged all year long with offers from people like me.

I went to the University of Edinburgh, the Women's Club and the Graduate's Association, and suggested similar ideas. People hemmed and hawed. I was told that the University was closed during the summer except for a skeleton faculty. Most of the permanent residents of Edinburgh purposely left town during Festival season. I learned, too, that the majority of residents, known for their chilly manner and withdrawal from vulgar associations such as the arts, vigorously resented the city's support of the Festival. Some people I met took my name and address and mumbled, "See what can be done." Out of the telephone book's yellow pages, I xeroxed lists of bookstores, libraries, colleges, and churches in Edinburgh.

Day Six I was on a plane, heading home, elated, mission accomplished.

In September I sent my venue manager a check, as per instructions. By December, I'd written to both of his addresses in Scotland and London. Phone calls. No answer. Finally, a letter. He was terribly sorry, but the owners of the building he had rented for the past twenty years had decided they were not going to make it available for the Fringe this next year because they were going to renovate it for use as a school. Therefore, my manager had decided against running a venue. He returned my money.

Blank. Numb. That was the state of my mind for another month. Then I started receiving routine materials from the Fringe office. They were planning a meeting in London so that companies and venue managers could get to know one another and set up schedules. In no way could I afford to go to London for a half-day meeting.

A month later, the unexpected occured when, as a member of the Dramatists Guild, Inc., I attended Women's Committee meetings and got into a conversation with Katheryn White, a writer of heart-warming comedies about unusual people, and Pat Kaufman, a writer of off-beat comedies. I had not seen or read their work, but Pat had a comedy, *$$Plenty Money$$,* about the societal impact of money, featuring "He" so bored with wealth that "She" resorted to whips, ropes, and honey. She wanted to produce it in Edinburgh, and Katheryn volunteered to direct it!

Pat knew the manager of the American venue, the American Festival Theater. I'd seen one of their shows in Edinburgh. Plays such as *The Grapes of Wrath* and *Our Town* were staged; the audience was good on the night I'd attended. It was one of the best venues on the Fringe, clean, large, well equipped, situated in the Royal Scots Club which had an impressive brown-panelled lobby with bar, and it was within walking distance of the center of Edinburgh. The producer had spent over ten years establishing it. It had a fine reputation, and plays there often received good newspaper reviews.

After a number of phone calls and meetings in Pat's spacious Greenwich Village loft (of which Katheryn and I were envious) or in Katheryn's upper West Side five-room apartment or in Harold Easton's New York University office, all was arranged. Since this venue was expensive, we would share the time slot, that is, Pat and I would alternate performances at 6:00 P.M. every night for the entire three weeks. We would have a half-hour before and after each performance to set up and take down props. We could hire, inexpensively, one of Hal's technicians who would be familiar with the lightboard. Hal would sell our tickets at his box office, and we could hang a poster outside the theater and place our flyers in the lobby. Hal would arrange an inexpensive guest home for us near the theater and supply a list of publicity contacts and deadline schedules. I could set up a Margaret Fuller exhibit in the lobby before my performance (if I took it down afterwards), and Hal's ticket seller would sell my books. And he'd help us by asking his young interns to peddle our flyers along with his on the streets of Edinburgh. What could be more perfect?

We were a trio. Pat Kaufman was short, petite, fun-loving; she had short-clipped reddish-blond hair and wore snappy clothes. A divorcee, she lived alone and was attending the musical-theater program at New York University. She had a daughter who was going to be married just before our Edinburgh trip.

Katheryn White was tall, black haired, white skinned. On first sight she was as sophisticated and mysterious as Batwoman, but as unpretentious and open as Murphy Brown. Separated from her husband who had been a director in community theater, she worked full time in the photo research department of Time/Life publications, and supported and cared for her twelve-year-old son. With a background in theater, she had acted, directed, taught, and was one of the editors of *Women & Performance, A Journal of Feminist Theory,* an international quarterly magazine headquartered at New York University whose purpose was to celebrate women's experimental work in theater. In true Fringe spirit, we three needed a name. I figured the words "New York" would impress in the overseas Scottish scene, so we wound up calling ourselves the New York Outgoing Theater Company or, as Pat suggested NYOT, and paid the Festival fee so we would receive mailings and have our schedule printed in the hefty program guide.

Publicity is the key to the fierce race and it consists of sending press kits to newspapers, radio, and TV. When in Edinburgh, you are supposed to post flyers on any wall space you can find and, if you can't find any, you tack or paste over somebody else's. Whenever you are not performing, you are supposed to stand on street corners and hand out flyers.

But the major goal is to get good reviews right away, especially in the most distinguished newspaper, *The Scotsman,* because you need to attract audiences as well as agents who might sign you for a European tour, a film, or whatever. You want complimentary words you can blow up and display in front of the theater, quotes you can show to somebody, like an agent. After that, word-of-mouth will spread like wildfire.

From the reviewers' perspective, the Festival presents a three-week nightmare. All the critics receive stacks of press kits from individuals and companies around the world during the spring and again in mid-June. Collectively they do want to cover every show on the Fringe, but they physically can't — even though extra help is hired by most publications. Many exciting press kits lie unopened in piles in corners.

The first shows reviewers pay attention to are last year's winners and those organized by well-known theater companies which have proven themselves year after year. What are they presenting this season? What is "fashionable"? What does the public want to read about?

The second groups to command critical attention are the big names coming to the Festival for the first time, creating high public excitement. Next in line are those aspirants who are "heard" to be excellent, those who advertise the innovative outrageous, such as performing nude or painting their bodies. Bold political statements on man's inhumanity to man, or the downtrodden, will get a response. Presenting classical material, Shakespeare or a story from the Bible, in an innovative manner is likely to draw reviews.

After that, it's a scramble.

Ours fit best into that last "scramble" category. Still, if our publicity was sharp, we stood a chance. Also, we were coming in under the auspices of an established American company. After all, the journalists and the city fathers know that people like us are the backbone of the Fringe Festival, annually bringing in tourist dollars.

My product had previously been tried, tested, and publicized, so all I needed was to slant it properly. It wasn't hard; Margaret Fuller had travelled through Edinburgh, had stayed at a hotel on Princes Street, had visited the Castle, and watched the Highland dancers. One of her best lines shows how she and her contemporaries viewed progress: "Sir Walter Scott's statue stands with his *back* towards the *new* railroad terminal."

It took a couple of weeks to pull together about thirty press kits backed up with copies of my American press. Pat turned out short, simple but spiffy pages which obviously would catch eyes.

We sent them off, and I got the bookstore lists I'd xeroxed from the telephone book the year before. Wouldn't a bookstore like to display my books in their windows during the Festival? In return I would publicize their store at my theater as selling my books. I got one response — one was all I needed — the James Thin Bookstore.

I wrote to Andrew Hill, minister of St. Mark's Unitarian Church, who eventually promised I could give a ten-minute talk on Margaret Fuller at the end of one of his Sunday sermons. I wrote to libraries and colleges. One library, Musselburgh, some miles out in East Lothian district, scheduled my author's presentation.

Pat and Katheryn were advertising for an actor to play "He" in her play. Pat had decided to be the "She." In pursuit of honing her skill as a playwright she had studied acting with Gene Frankel and at the New School, and performed in several plays in Santa Fe. Still, she was relatively inexperienced as an actress and hearing that she was casting herself gave me cause to worry about the outcome. The Edinburgh Fringe was a place to experiment — filled with college students on a lark and in rebellion; youngsters whose proud, hardworking daddies gave them the money; misfits who happened into a theater group and had nothing better to do; untrained hopefuls.

I expressed my concern to Pat and Katheryn. But their advertisment had attracted response, and they set auditions, found an actor, scheduled rehearsals, and I heard all was going well.

All too soon Katheryn and I were on a plane. Pat, who'd had to attend to her daughter's wedding, and her actor were following in a day or two.

Then we were knocking on the door of our bed-and-breakfast, climbing stairs, settling into a tiny, grungy room for three, laughing because we had the biggest room and the only private bath in the place, speculating on the breakfast we'd be served.

Very soon we heard a knock on our door. It was the owner of the house. "I guess Hal told you. You can only stay here a week, because we are booked with another group for the second two weeks of the Festival."

"What? No, Hal did not tell us."

"Well, he intended to, I'm sure."

"This was all arranged months ago. We paid the total fee for this room."

"Sorry. I think Hal has another place for you to stay. Check it out with him."

Our first day, when we should have been out on the streets

hustling audiences by handing out flyers, Katheryn and I walked the three cobblestone blocks down a steep hill to the Royal Scots Club, carrying suitcases of props and Margaret Fuller books and exhibit, trying to find Hal.

Yes, it was a shame but these things happen, not his fault. But Hal had just the B & B for us, all paid for, not to worry, on the other side of Princes Street. He would even pay for our cab when we had to move, plus tips.

The theater looked in great shape, as I remembered it from the year before, with Hal's shows advertised on posters outside: *Our Town* by Thornton Wilder, *Scenes from American Life* by A. R. Gurney, *Bus Stop* by William Inge, *The Early Girl* by Caroline Kava. The displays were all in good taste, moderate in comparison to other garish poster-plastered venues.

The mainstage was a large square black platform raised about two feet off the floor, jutting out to the audience. The seats were plain chairs painted black, on a raised black tier, so sight lines were good. We found our backstage spaces, a bit cluttered and cramped, but not bad, left our suitcases of costumes and props in special spots, and scheduled our technical rehearsals with Hal's lighting person.

Later that day Pat arrived woebegone because she and Ed, her actor, had landed somewhere where they'd had to rent a car and drive all night long. Ed was staying at a nearby campground; he had rented a bike so he could ride back and forth cheaply.

"Did you learn your lines yet?" Katheryn asked her.

"No."

"Technical rehearsal is set for tomorrow morning at 10:00, and we're scheduled to open the next night."

"Well, I have to get some sleep or I won't be good for anything." Pat slept the clock around.

In Edinburgh there was no time for learning lines or sleeping. You had to be selling your product. The city was already wall-to-wall flyers. Every fence, doorway, post, fire hydrant, and telephone pole was brightly ornamented. We were in competition with all kinds of dramas featuring women, including three on Sylvia Plath, four women performing Hamlet, and Peter Stack doing a Marilyn Monroe when dead.

But I could hardly worry about Pat's production; my job was to find a printer who could blow up my master flyer so I could hang a large sign in front of the Royal Scots Club, and then to xerox a thousand flyers, and post them. With Scotch tape in hand, I hung up my flyers and left piles on appropriate tables and window ledges.

The James Thin Bookstore turned out to be one of the best-established bookstores in Edinburgh. Mr. Thin hardly remembered me, but reread his letter to me which I proffered — and said coldly, "I can only display your books for a week — unless you get exceptional reviews."

"Well, I will get good reviews," I said, handing him a large sign I'd prepared. "I will advertise at the Royal Scots Club that my books can be bought here in your store." He took my sign and about ten books of each title, and brusquely turned away.

At other bookstores I convinced managers to post my sign and carry my books. I called the Musselburgh Library and confirmed the date for an author's talk, and went to St. Mark's church, where I also posted a large sign.

The Festival "send-off" was Fringe Sunday, a day-long celebration in Holyrood Park in which we performers were to advertise our shows by "hawking" excerpts of our productions. One art student created crayoned drawings to raise extra cash, a seven year-old impersonated Michael Jackson, somebody dressed and elevated himself on stilts to become a fifteen-foot rabbit carrying a carrot. There was a Canadian reinacting Macbeth's death scene. There were guitarists, fire eaters, jugglers, mimes, bowler-hatted men cycling, children flying kites, face painters, African drummers. There were pipe bands, steel bands, jazz bands, street organs, giant hot-air balloons, inflatable balls, buskers, and more. This type of display was not for our trio.

At the media party I crowded into a huge hall filled with people. Drinks were served on side tables but you couldn't elbow your way to them. Armed with flyers and my past newspaper clippings, I tried to locate the press representatives who were there because that was the purpose of this party sponsored by the Fringe Society, to give performers the opportunity to meet the press, and vice versa. Artists who'd been to Edinburgh before could recognize the press, but I was soon able to spot them because they were the persons who were being surrounded and badgered.

"Hi! I'm Laurie James, the one who's doing Margaret Fuller."

"Who?"

The noise level got louder and louder.

One or two had read about me, which made me feel I had reached base one. An Associated Press reporter who was doing a story got interested in the early American journalist, Margaret Fuller, and kept me talking for fifteen minutes. He was going to publish my statements in his article, but when it would be published he had no idea.

"Can you do a review?" So many shook their heads, No.

Somebody was giving on-the-spot radio interviews. I edged my way up to him and spoke for about three minutes.

"Can you do a story?" "Can you...?" "Can you...?"

Imagine my astonishment when someone identifying himself as the BBC said, "Yes, you're on my list for a news spot on BBC-Scotland, a show called "Reporting Scotland," maybe Thursday night. I want you to give me a call. Here's my card."

Few performers were invited to be on the BBC.

Pat and Katheryn were spending every moment rehearsing, on the stage, in our room, in our B & B dining room, and I was waiting nervously for a call from the BBC. That's not easy when you're staying at a rooming house that has only one hall phone.

Walking towards the Fringe office the next day, I noticed that many of the flyers I'd posted were no longer up. I replaced them. Who has the energy to go around every day, checking out flyers? Most artists were in a group situation and all the members shared the task. An individual was certainly at a disadvantage. From thereon in I gave flyers to everyone I passed on the street and to everyone I sat next to in restaurants.

Pat had brought along a suitcase of T-shirts with the words *$$Plenty Money$$* printed on top of a large, green dollar bill. Her plan was to sell them at the theater. But other than wearing her T-shirts, she, Kitty and Ed were not hustling. They told me rehearsals were going badly.

During my technical rehearsal, which was going well because the lighting guy obviously knew what he was doing, I paid little attention when three dark-haired men wandered in and quietly but aggressively looked around. The next day I saw a tasteful new sign posted in front of the theater: *Sideways Glance...Garbo in Edinburgh,* produced by Arte Livre Company of Brazil. The next day I saw copies of the sign plastered all over the city.

For my opening performance I had about ten or fifteen people in the theater which seated about seventy-five. Don't worry, everyone told me, that was average for most shows on the Fringe. In fact, a writer in a Fringe paper claimed his group played to "no audience at all for a week."

In that entire first week, *four* people *paid* to see my show. Not to be ashamed. After all, I had not yet been reviewed and I did get good applause.

Every day as I left the theater, I could hardly get past the audience that was lined up for Hal's show. They crowded the lobby with the bar. Smiling, well-heeled, good-natured, lively folk, good paying customers.

Sideways Glance...Garbo in Edinburgh opened. This production had the time slot immediately following mine. The company shared the dressing room with me — the only dressing room — and their lead actor came in just as I was leaving to go on stage. By the time I returned, their six members, two of whom were women, were busily applying makeup and pulling on costumes. We did not communicate much because they spoke Portuguese. To my amazement the handsome male lead actor transformed himself into the sizzling Greta Garbo with rouge, long eyelashes, wig, long, shimmering, gray satin dress, and elbow-length gloves. Their first night they attracted about two or three audience members.

$$Plenty Money$$ opened. I did not attend because I knew my roommates were not ready. All things pass, and this opening passed too. They got through it with only one faux pas. They had about five people in their audience. They asked me to attend the next night, for I would be one more person there, so that night I made up an audience of four.

By now, Pat seemed to hate Ed and she didn't show much admiration for Katheryn either. Evidently, they'd all had an unpleasant shouting match on the streets. Pat did know her lines and she was good in the part. She talked about the possibility of finding another actor to replace Ed. Katheryn claimed she had not had a chance to utilize her best directorial skills.

Even so, Pat's peppy press attracted three newspapers, all of whom published her picture, and she had two reviewers the first week. But the reviews were disappointing, and in time honored theatrical fashion, Pat found good words within the article to accentuate and blow up ads. She and Ed spoke to each other only on stage. The atmosphere was frosty.

In an attempt to cheer, I dropped comments like: "Never mind. We didn't come here to get good reviews or to make money. We came to have fun...to learn...it's the process that counts." "I've had lots of failures. Nobody promised us a rose garden." "More important is being a part of the Fringe, sharing it with friends." "It's better being at the bottom of the heap where you can remain yourself, where what counts is the stimulation of the *work*, not the commercialism." "And anyway you *do* have a credit, your play *was* produced at Edinburgh." She did agree with all this.

It was like I hardly existed on the Fringe. No critics showed up to review my show. I did not get my picture in the paper. My audiences started to dwindle to five and six. I kept waiting for that call from the BBC. Hal's shows continued to fill the Royal Scots theater, and I spent more and more time in the lobby where my Margaret Fuller exhibit was propped, sipping wine and striking up conversations with people who might be interested in my show. After all, if they came to Hal's show, surely they'd want to see mine. (They didn't.)

The critic that you "draw in the lottery" is vital to a production's success. Since I noticed that many of the critics in Edinburgh had literary rather than theater backgrounds, I thought I'd have a chance. I also noticed that many of the professional productions seemed to be judged on the same level as university productions.

Coming into play were the "stringer" critics, those temporarily brought onto the scene by the newspapers whose regulars can't go to all the shows. Some were students. Two of the popular Fringe papers were university publications and these young journalists, without a wealth of experience or perspective, could help to damn a show fairly quickly.

Audiences picked up for *Sideways Glance...Garbo in Edinburgh*. The name Garbo triggered interest and people started talking because it was performed in Portuguese, a language almost no one at the Fringe could understand — what a daring risk and novelty. I figured it was no use sitting through it. The actors seemed energetic and undeterred; they all pushed word-of-mouth, and the exotic lead actor/co-author, Roberto Cordovani, commanded curious stares everywhere he went. He was tall, heavyset, exuberant, erratic and exciting. In the play he was a nightclub performer who identifies with Garbo, who portrays Garbo, and who in time comes to think of himself as Garbo, even going so far as to make love to a man as though he were Garbo. Sexual ambiguity was the avenue the authors intended to explore as well as myth and reality in concepts of self.

This ambitious group had waited three weeks prior to the Festival before deciding to come, so of course they were severely handicapped by not being listed in the official program. But with their sights set, the woman producer and co-author, Alejandra Guibert, found a cancelled time slot in the American Festival Theater venue, and she hand-delivered press kits to editors. All company members continued showering the city with flyers.

On the first Sunday, I delivered my ten-minute pulpit talk at St. Mark's Church. That came off very well, and Andrew Hill kindly introduced me to some of the leading UUs at the regular coffee-and-cookies afterwards. I got to know them individually by attending every Sunday service. Almost none had heard of Margaret Fuller, and everyone showed enthusiasm to learn more — but what happened? I saw in total about six at my performances. I believe I did sell one book to one of them. Of course, I donated one copy of each title to the church library.

At Musselburgh Library in East Lothian the librarians were gracious, but had warned me this was off the beaten track, and I might not get the response I probably hoped for. I drew about twenty-five interested people, none of whom came to my show. The librarians were the only ones to buy a book.

Boldly I approached the National Library of Scotland. The Acquisitions Librarian was marvellously welcoming and impressed with my books. She bought them.

When our first week came to a close, our trio had to move living quarters. So, on another morning when we should have been hustling, we packed our suitcases, hailed a cab and were driven to the other side of town, about two miles from the theater, in an area with rows of attached houses with tiny yards of blooming flowers and black-iron fences with gates. The quietness catapulted my mind into a respectable suburbia atmosphere rather than the noisy theatricalism I craved. However, nothing could be changed to feed my personal appetite and, as we entered the rather small clapboard building and crammed ourselves into the hallway, we were informed by our hostess right away that this B & B was filled every year by dancers and show people, and they had a spare room now only because there'd been a cancellation at the last minute.

Our hostess rushed us to our room as though she wanted to get this obligation over with fast and then immediately made herself unavailable to us. The room was what we would consider a double for small children where we would install bunk beds because it would be too crowded any other way. Well, *three single adult beds* had been pushed in, leaving about one foot of space between the two outside beds and the walls. To get into the middle bed, you had to climb onto the end of it and make your way over the blankets up to the headboard. There was no closet, chest of drawers, or chair.

Pat, Katheryn and I looked at each other, all of us thinking the same thing. We each selected a bed and put our suitcases in the only space available — at the foot of each bed.

We checked out the long, narrow bathroom down the hall, decent enough, but it had a big sign posted over the shower: NO SHOWERS BEFORE 9:00 A.M. OR AFTER 10:00 P.M.

The dining room was a dismal square room, adequate for four, but into this space was squeezed a round table for six and three tables for two. The chairs were back-to-back. On the door hung a sign: BREAKFAST SERVED BETWEEN 7:00 and 8:00 A.M. ONLY. With no restaurants nearby, we'd have to eat lunch and dinner somewhere downtown.

The bus, a block or two away, took about twenty minutes to Princes Street, and from there it was a five-block walk to our theater. The bus ran less frequently when we would most need it, after 9:00 P.M. The two miles to the theater could be walked — it was not unpleasant if it wasn't raining and if you didn't have to carry anything. It was safe at night. The black night, the stars, the moon, and the lights cast an aura over Edinburgh castle that is quite fairy-like and romantic.

After two weeks of performances, Ed disappeared into the wide unknown on his bike, leaving Pat stranded. She decided to go off on a day's sight seeing bus tour. "I came all the way to Edinburgh," she said. "I might as well enjoy something while I'm here." She did not find another actor to replace Ed.

Our cubbyhole being too cramped to enjoy the camaraderie we'd earlier shared, we daily went our separate ways, and saw each other sleeping late at night. Katheryn's job as director was essentially over. She was off seeing the shows, and peddling her magazine, *Women & Performance*.

The first night in our new quarters I arrived late and remembered NO SHOWERS AFTER 10:00 P.M. What was I to do? I felt grimy after being on the streets all day and performing. My makeup was still half on — smearing it off with cold cream never does the trick. Well, I would go to bed grimy.

In the morning I had to dress, grimy, because BREAKFAST SERVED BETWEEN 7:00 AND 8:00 A.M. and NO SHOWERS BEFORE 9:00 A.M..

At 9:00 A.M. I undressed again and slipped into my bathrobe and grabbed a towel. There, in the hallway, were two other bathrobed people. Steaming forth from the bathroom was the sound of somebody's hot shower. "I'm next!" the first person on line said. "And I'm next!" the second person said.

It was 10:00 A.M. by the time I got a cold shower because the hot water had been used up, and it was noon before I got into town.

Pat closed her show and, like Katheryn, concentrated on being an observer of other shows.

But things are shaky in Edinburgh and it's not uncommon to arrive at a theater box office, tickets in hand, and to be told, "Cancelled, sorry."

Some of the problems that are not uncommon: Plays reported to be folded when they were actually in performance; theaters shut down by fire inspectors; actors disappearing with costumes; actors experiencing voice loss or broken legs. Frequently, you saw newspaper articles that called for emergency-replacement actors.

Even mainstream events had their share of disaster. That year it had been Italy's leading musical-comedy performers Peppe and Concetta Barra who pulled out just before their premiere at the Leith Theater. Frantic efforts had to be made to find the several hundred people who had already paid for seats at the four performances. The reason for the cancellation was given as insuperable administrative difficulties in Italy.

On the Fringe, I tried to see the Lavonne Mueller one-act, *The Only Woman General,* but was told "Sorry." This play stirred quite a bit of interest due to the reputation of this award-winning American playwright, and because the leading character is about a female recruit who climbs the regular army ladder, reaches the highest military post, and travels in a space capsule.

The attractive and most personable American actress, Eileen Wilkinson, was so sure of the worth of the project that she ventured four months' work and her own money — into the thousands — to bring it in, and even worked as a venue manager in order to offset expenses. With an early review in *The Scotsman* lambasting the play, with her director gone after the first week, with her playwright not showing up as promised, with her lead actor giving her frightful problems, and with two people showing up in the audience one night, she closed it in the second week, stating, "I've had it up to here."

But on that same day the play was chosen by a major newspaper as "Pick of the Fringe." ("How it happened is amazing," she said, "since no reviewer from that newspaper ever saw it.") When she received more good reviews, she re-opened it, but when only a handful of people showed up, she closed again, a bad experience she vowed never to repeat.

Pat told me I could use her time slot on the stage, gratis. But my show was already publicized in the listings, and not doing well in the time slot I had. Still, people kept telling me that as long as I got an audience of six I was averaging what most shows attracted on the Fringe.

Hearing excellent comments about *Sideways Glance...Garbo in Edinburgh,* I was still hoping that, with reviews and a spot on the BBC, audiences for my show would pick up. Every day I tried to phone the people at the BBC, but they were never in. I was also phoning the newspapers every day trying to bring in the reviewers.

Of course I was told, don't bug them. If you pressure, they will *never* come to your show. But my calls weren't getting through anyway.

One night I returned to our B & B and went to bed grimy, only to awake grimy. No way was I going to waste the whole morning trying to get a shower. I slipped under warm water at 7:15 A.M. At 7:45 A.M. I made my clean, shiny appearance in the tiny breakfast room.

Almost immediately there came booming a voice: "Did you take a shower?"

It was the host, whom I'd never seen. *"Did you take a shower?!"*

I mumbled yes, because I was so gr—

"She took a shower!" He stuck his head through the open serving shelf and said to somebody cooking behind it.

"She took a shower," said the cook, dropping a pan that made a great clatter.

"SHE TOOK A SHOWER!" repeated our host.

There was flurry of activity and confusion, as our host scurried from the room.

Everyone in the dining room looked at me.

"Well," I said feeling as though I'd commited murder in the first degree, "I needed a shower."

A quietness descended as everyone picked up their forks and ate scrambled eggs silently.

Soon the hostess pushed her way to my table. *"YOU TOOK A SHOWER?"*

"Yes, I — "

"IF YOU CAN'T OBEY THE RULES, YOU'LL HAVE TO BE ASKED TO LEAVE."

I explained my situation.

"I DON'T CARE," said the hostess. *"YOU HAVE TO FOLLOW THE RULES."*

"I - I don't know if I can," I began, ready to explain.

"THEN LEAVE."

Within an hour she was knocking on our door, handing us the remaining money for the two weeks that Hal had paid for the room. *"I WANT YOU OUT OF HERE TOMORROW."*

Privately, she approached Katheryn. "Your friend has to leave but you can stay. You're a fine person and you follow the rules."

We called Hal. He laughed. "Well, yes, the Scots have rules like that. I don't know why. It's an old-standing tradition. Most of them — especially the ones who cater to show-business people — don't really stick to those rules because they *do* understand. But I guess these people abide by the old."

We told Hal we thought we could find another room in the neighborhood because we had seen "Vacancy" signs in windows. Sure enough, we three walked about two blocks around the corner and knocked on a door. When a kind-looking, middle-aged woman said she could put us up, our first question was, "Do you have rules about taking showers?"

We dragged our suitcases and selves into a larger, more acceptable space.

By now superb reviews were coming out for *Sideways Glance...Garbo in Edinburgh*. I had to take the time to see it. It was a visually structured script, and Roberto Cordovani played Garbo with the most mesmerizing grace and beauty. You did not need to know Portuguese to understand it. Their business picked up substantially. Their rise to acclaim was phenomenal.

Now Katheryn and I started going around together because I wanted to see some of the same shows she did and we were able to attend with press passes. Neither one of us had time to be interested in the international mainstream, tantalizing as the shows sounded.

Katheryn suggested I write an article about the Fringe for her issue of *Women & Performance*. Going to shows interfered with hustling but I was beginning to feel that hustling paid less dividends than I'd get from a theater magazine. Besides, I still gave out flyers to everyone I passed on the street, and after every show we interviewed some of the most interesting women on the Fringe.

Sue Lenier was a British feminist who'd returned a second year with a new black comedy, *Eden Song*, about a fallen Eden where men have forgotten how to reproduce, where women behaved like animals, and where deadly mating games were played.

Lenier promoted by handing out flyers with the words SEX WAR THEATER. Her theater was usually half-filled.

Lenier was trying to gradually carve a reputation. Each year she expected to lose money, but she anticipated that press and public would come to know her work. She was going to use her reviews to apply for grants and playwrights' residencies in theaters. "In England you can get a playwright's residency — they pay very little," she said, "but enough to live on. This is what I want, so I can spend all my time writing."

What women get out of the Fringe experience varies from person to person. University students and groups use it as a testing ground. With solid university support, they generally do not need to invest money beyond living expenses. They find the best, least expensive quarters and manage to achieve goals with the least frustration.

Vanessa Dodge, from Imperial College, chose to direct the well known tragi-comedy, *Dusa, Fish, Stas and Vi*, by British playwright Pam Gems. Produced successfully ten years earlier at the Fringe, it concerns four diverse women living together, sharing the commonality of human compassion. Dodge chose this play because she wanted to give talented university women a chance to perform and experience the Fringe. For the past six years her group, Theater West End Productions, had the same superb location on Princes Street. With a strong script, knowledge of the play, and good publicity she got good audiences. Profits went to the university for next year's start-up expenses. Her goal was typical of her age group — to graduate.

It was great fun to bump into playwright Sara Plath, one of our colleagues at the Dramatists Guild who'd been undecided about the Fringe when we'd set our plans. She and her partner, choreographer Wendy Taucher, also from the United States, had written and were producing a theater-dance work, *Reasons for the Beginning of Delight*, which concerned an anxious, passive, inarticulate, young woman, played by two dancers and an actress, who, while seeking a job, travels a soul journey and achieves self-worth. Since doors were closed to them in New York, Plath and Taucher felt they'd find better response in Europe. They could return to the States with credits and reviews. They'd sunk $25,000, partly sponsorship, partly their own hard-earned money, and were going to be in debt for months to come. They paid salaries and expenses to their ensemble, an almost unheard of Fringe arrangement. Their publicity materials were excellent and they promoted by having their members dance in the streets and hand out complimentary tickets. They got good reviews.

"With good reviews I hope to get a tour," said zesty white-haired Faith Kent, who lived outside London, and who had reached that point in life when people plan leisurely cruises.

Not being content with one one-woman show at the Fringe, she mounted two, *Just Like A Woman* and *The Dark Lady Reads the Sonnets*. This crippled her financially, and how she was to pay back her loan, she said, "God only knows." But performing and sharing material she'd devised from women's poetry and prose, both past and present, was work rooted in her heart. Every day she was out on the streets in a "Faith Kent T-shirt," along with all the other Fringe promoters, many of whom were forty years younger than she.

There is no commitment quite so deep as that of playwright/ director Shimako Murai. Her subject matter and the intensity of her production harrowed the souls of those who saw it.

Murai missed being in Hiroshima when the bomb fell because she had entered Toyko Woman's Christian University a few months before. Many of her friends died or were exposed to radiation, only to die later. The disaster numbed her and, years later, she videotaped the stories of survivors. Because of the personal agony and horror of recall, she did not release the video to the public. However, she wished in some way to keep the memory of the awful day alive, especially for the younger generation. *Woman of Hiroshima* was a monologue, the feelings of a girl orphaned by the bomb, which was played with intense emotion by student actress Chieko Kurihara.

Murai, who had been awarded a prize from the Japanese Ministry of Cultural Affairs, and the Maui Peace Prize, was married, but she had made a vow not to have children, not to repeat the mistake her parents made by conceiving her in a time when her country was at war and her family was in dire poverty. The world is not safe enough to bring children into it, she told us. "In Japan it is up to women to protest against war, because the men do nothing. Women have the wisdom."

Weekly, *The Scotsman* announced the Fringe First awards. On the front page one day Roberto Cordovani, of Garbo fame, stood in the winner's circle. But the next day the newspaper announced that he was unqualified to win because, according to rules, Arte Livre of Brazil had previewed too often in the U. K. Red-faced, the authorities created a new awards category: Outstanding Performance, so Cordovani did get the recognition he deserved and needed.

The next week the Fringe First went to *Woman of Hiroshima.*

Finally, I connected with BBC-Scotland. A time and day was scheduled to videotape in the theater. I was to do my Margaret Fuller equality speech. I stood in one spot on the center of the stage. They set up the equipment about four feet away from me. I felt totally surrounded as everyone focused on me. I was directed to begin my speech.

"Cut." The director, very British, stopped me. "A favor, please, look over that way, will you?"

I started my speech again.

"Cut. Equipment problem. One moment, please."

I waited.

"Take it up where you left off."

One must unearth every sense in the body to conjure the images needed to give expression to the material, even when you have delivered that speech five hundred times. Four feet away from you, all around you, men are moving, pushing a camera this way and that, turning switches and dials, angling lights. On the stage you relate to your audience; in front of cameras you must relate to vacant, unresponsive air beyond the technicians and their fiddling. Constantly, your best visualization vaporizes as you must slightly turn a shoulder or point your chin, or some technician takes care of some technical problem. Or the corner of your eye catches a light so that your sensibilities are stifled. Your energies numb at the very moment you need to summon them.

The director finally says, "Good! That's a take!"

Your instinct tells you it was bad. There's a sense of helplessness, incompleteness. The sustaining forces that make sense of the drama are just not there.

It took about an hour to do a five-minute segment. The edited bit that was shown had an announcer who introduced and talked about the Fringe, and there were close-ups of my books. Katheryn saw it and said it was fine. I never saw it because it was aired during one of my performances. I was promised a copy of the tape. I phoned for it several times, but could never reach any person who knew anything about it. I wrote after I returned to the USA; I called. I never got my tape.

The third and last week of the Fringe dawned — my play was still attracting a handful of people, but I had not been reviewed. I began to go to newspaper offices, for I finally figured everyone else must be doing it, even though we were told not to. At the office of *The Scotsman* I could not get beyond the downstairs guard.

I found an editor of another paper at his desk. He said: "If you are doing poorly, you should sit down with a journalist over a pint of beer and mention how tough things are."

My problem is I do not like beer.

Besides, doesn't it seem out of place for a woman to casually open a conversation with a male critic at a bar?

Anyhow, how does one recognize these journalists?

I begged my plight to editors and then I did get reviewed. My reviews came out within the last few days of the Festival, too late to attract significant audiences. The reviews were good, not raves, but there were quotes I could have used.

Monique van Heek of Festival City Radio was my one woman reviewer and she gave me a star rating, saying that Margaret Fuller was "portrayed with great dignity" and it was "overall, a good performance."

A critic of stature, Charles Osborne of *The Daily Telegraph*, wrote that my portrayal did not "rise above a church hall level of performance." (I feel empathy for him if he's never had the fortune to attend one of many inspirational church hall programs.) "However," he ended, "I don't regret the time I spent in the company of this Boston blue stocking whose reverence for plain living and high thinking is leavened with good humour and whose account of being rowed out on Walden Pond by the 23 year-old Thoreau is sensitively written and affectionately delivered."

The most respected reviewer, Ian Spring of *The Scotsman*, wrote:

"Margaret Fuller is revealed as a brave and perspicacious woman who strove against the hypocrisy of the time but...could not fully escape from herself."

For women artists, a problem is, in the lottery of critics, drawing a male who lacks sensibility towards the female perspective.

If my character had been Ralph Waldo Emerson or Henry David Thoreau, both conflicted men, would he have written that either "could not fully escape from himself"?

In six words Ian Spring made Margaret Fuller a victim of herself. She was another person audiences would not want to spend time knowing about. He ended by stating that the trouble with my drama was that it "doesn't really tell you much about how Miss Fuller lived — although it tells you a great deal about what she thought."

Specifically, my drama tells how "Miss" Fuller lived as a teacher, a leader of "Conversations," an editor, a scholar, a journalist, a foreign and war correspondent, a director of a hospital.

Spring revealed that he has little understanding of the plight of a female intellectual giant who lived at a time when the barriers for women were more constrained than in any other period in history. He followed the stereotypical patriarchal pattern that has for over a century and a half kept Margaret Fuller from her rightful place in history.

It would be easy to react with *c'est la vie*. But it is vital to speak out. Women must bring forth their viewpoints in order to open eyes and broaden the one-sided perceptions prevailing throughout the world.

I had kept my show running the entire three weeks, which some people thought a worthy accomplishment. It was time to travel back to the United States. Pat had left a few days earlier. Collecting my mainly unsold books from the bookstores, props, exhibit, and clothes, I said my thanks and goodbyes, and Katheryn and I boarded the plane.

Katheryn returned to the Fringe four years later with *Sojourner,* and *Alien Doctors,* original plays that received splendid reviews.

Pat had several of her clever plays produced in small theaters in New York; *$$Plenty Money$$* was printed in a magazine, *Confrontation,* published by Long Island University.

Would I ever return to the Fringe?

It's tempting.

If I had the money it takes, I suppose I wouldn't hesitate.

Perhaps what I'd really prefer is more of the Fringe spirit to come to the United States.*

---

*As this book goes to print, there are Fringe Festivals in Seattle, Washington, and San Francisco, California. The New York International Fringe Festival, presented by The Present Theatre Company, is to be offered for the first time, and Laurie James is "on board" with a new play. These festivals are independent and organized with guidelines that are different from those in Edinburgh.

I'M A CHAUTAUQUAN

"The difference between a scholar and an actor," claims Charles Pace, "is that one performs at 8 A.M. and the other performs at 8 P.M."

I am *chautauqua* — with seven scholars, a road manager, a tent master, and a truck driver.

Chautauqua is an Indian word meaning "moccasins bound together."

Nine of us travel in two rented vans, each of us taking turns driving.

The truck driver navigates the Chautauqua truck which carries the 50 x 90 foot tent, the five hundred folding chairs, the lights, the sound system, the platform stage with curtains, prop table and chairs, photographic Chautauqua exhibit, luggage, costumes, ironing board and iron, trunks of books, plus our extracurriculars such as a Harley Davidson, a bicycle, weights and barbells, video camera and equipment, computers and printers, golf clubs, coolers, etcetera.

The golden rules of the traffic-free Great Plains roads: When you get the chance to use a bathroom, use it. When you find a fine restaurant, eat a fine meal.

The search is on as soon as we hit town...where is the best restaurant...the laundromat...the post office...the movie theater...the library...the swimming pool/aerobics class/running-walking track/ golf course. With these essentials spotted, we are happy.

Passing under our lofty Chautauqua banner wavering in a light wind above a street and going by posters hung in windows, our motley crew of characters — motley because we are dressed in jeans and wrinkled T's with hair and beards windblown (every man in our group except one, Nathaniel Hawthorne, maintains a beard) — lifts heads out of books or awakens from catnaps to gaze out the van's windows, seeing the one movie theater is closed, the bowling alley is closed, several store fronts are vacant on the four-block-long Main Street, which boasts a ladies'-wear store, a barber shop, a beauty parlor, a drug store, a gift shop, and a bar which more than likely has a misspelled neon sign: "Coctails."

Of course, the community has to *want* Chautauqua, has to compete to get it, has to offer commitment, and pay a fee.

Everett says, "We can always go to the places where we'll attract eight hundred people per night. But our aim is also to go into sparcely populated areas. We owe it to them!"

Our Chautuaqua attracts from 100-800 people every night in every town.

When I arrive amongst scholars in 1991, I am ecstatic — here are true friends because they travel with tons of books! My husband, seeing me pack a valise full of heavy books, says with horror, "You're not going to take *those*, are you?" He's smart enough to plan sans suitcase — he keeps clothes on both coasts. Ramona would call my habit "Compulsive container-ism...An occupational hazard— mother of 5!" My guilt is alleviated as I contentedly watch George Frein, Kevin Radaker and Charles Pace heft *steamer trunks* of books in and out of motel rooms.

One day I am called on the phone. "This is Everett Albers, executive director of the North Dakota Humanities Council."

He's seen my books on Margaret Fuller at Powell's Bookstore while at an administrative meeting in Portland, Oregon. He's contacted the humanities councils from whom I'd received grants, and finally located my phone number. Did I know what Chautauqua was?

Chautauqua originated during the 1870's on the shores of a New York lake resembling a bag tied in the middle — another meaning of the word.

An outgrowth of the camp meeting and lyceum movements, Chautauqua is a community coming together where people are stimulated by knowledgeable leaders to discuss deep thoughts and dangerous ideas.   First, Chautauqua was a training retreat for Methodist Sunday School teachers. It quickly escalated into a multi-denominational institution for adult education. It spread throughout the United States and into several foreign countries. It died out during the 1920s as radio, movies, cars, and upward mobility eased into the American horizon.

Years ago Chautauquas headlined long lists of talent, among them: Clarence Darrow; Mark Twain; Will Rogers; Theodore Roosevelt; James Garfield; Rutherford Hayes; William McKinley; William Howard Taft; William Jennings Bryan; Warren G. Harding; Henry Ward Beecher; Billy Sunday; Roger Ingersoll; Wendell Phillips; Artemus Ward; Lincoln Steffens; Dr. Frederick Cook; Commander Peary; Lew Wallace; James Whitcomb Riley; Carl Sandburg; Conrad Nagle; William Allen White; Susan B. Anthony; Jane Addams; Carrie Nation; Ida M. Tarbell; Louella O. Parsons; Alice Nielsen; Madame Julia Claussen; Edgar Bergan; and Charlie McCarthy.

There were politicians, orators, musicians, Shakespearean actors, play readers, even child talent, plus others whose names are no longer remembered.

For all our qualms when we scholars know we could have performed better, these are the after-the-show comments we hear time and time again:

"This is an unforgettable night."

"I've learned more than I've ever learned in class."

"I never could understand poetry or history, but the way you people do it, I can understand."

"Chautauqua inspires me — I want to go into women's history — and I'm taking correspondence courses because no college around here offers women's history."

"This was so strong that I had dreams last night that were sort of horrendous about my own life."

"You scholars left your homes just to come here and do this for us. It is really a shot in the arm."

"I don't know what I'll do tomorrow night when you're gone. Everything will seem so dull!"

Everett Albers' idea was to revitalize the lecture circuits.

Albers is a guy with energy, imagination, and the kind of common sense and humor that comes from having attended a one-room schoolhouse forty miles north of Bismarck, North Dakota. Ask him how he got from school to director of the Humanities Council, and he'll say, "Library. The library mailed books to the school and I was the lucky kid who grew up without TV, so I read every book the library sent."

His vision encompasses scholars of the humanities who portray historical figures talking about their lives and work and answering questions from the audience, first as their characters might have responded a hundred years ago, and then as the scholars they are today so that there is the added dimension of twentieth-century perspective — all performed on a simple platform in a tent.

Chautauqua involves a ten-week, ten-town, summer tour, in five states known for their extreme flatness, molten heat, withering drought, dusty wind, and flashing electric storms — Oklahoma, Kansas, Nebraska, South Dakota, and North Dakota. The program is funded with major grants from the National Endowment on the Humanities and coordinated by the North Dakota Humanities Council, and selected state affiliates,

The theme of the 1991 Great Plains Chautauqua Society, of which Albers is president, is the "American Renaissance," and the chosen characters are Margaret Fuller, Henry David Thoreau, Walt Whitman, Herman Melville, Louisa May Alcott, Frederick Douglass, and Nathaniel Hawthorne.

Am I interested?

Mere actors are not what is wanted because scholars have to give workshops, write articles, fend questions, and socialize on a one-to-one basis. Albers feels that my books and drama qualify me.

I have to apply immediately. I have to write an essay on my character, fill out various forms, and send in a video of myself in costume as Margaret Fuller opening an envelope on camera, answering whatever questions lie therein.

This job *pays*.

Albers got started in the mid-'70s by organizing a small tent which he sent around to summer fairs. He supplied it with audio visuals and printed literature about North Dakota's environment and a philosopher, Ben King from the University of North Dakota, who talked about public issues such as irrigation and population loss.

But more people were drawn to the penny arcade than into the little brown tent. Once a friend of King's dropped by to say hello. Albers quickly pulled down the sides of the tent and refused to allow the young man to leave until King had gone through his entire discourse about Ortega y Gasset and hunting.

At Devil's Lake Albers feared there'd be no audience when an evaluator from the National Endowment on the Humanities was going to visit. But luck was with him, *he thought*, because there were about a hundred mothers with their babies standing about for a beautiful-baby contest. He strutted like the best of producers but, when the contest ended, the mothers gathered up their cherubs and melted away. Alber's audience consisted of empty chairs.

In the beginning, Albers selected characters more or less by the luck of the draw, but they had to be generic to North Dakota: Waheenee, a Buffalo Bird Woman of the Hidatsa Nation; Turkey Track Bill, a drifting, ne'er-do-well mythical cowboy who roamed the plains at the end of the nineteenth century; Nancy Underwood, a composite character based on the diaries and letters of early Plains schoolteachers.

By 1991 scholars are carefully selected. Our chief Chautauquan George Frein, who portrays Herman Melville, is a doctor of philosophy and religion from the University of North Dakota in Grand Forks.

At one reception Frein introduces us to the community: "This is Anne Bail Howard from the University of Nevada, Reno, who plays Louisa May Alcott. She is a movie buff and remembers every movie she's ever seen, and can tell the plot line of each, as she's so pleasingly demonstrated to me many an evening over a draught of Irish whiskey."

Howard, who's been awarded Most Honored Teacher, had read

all of Louisa May Alcott's books by the time she was eleven. She'd wanted to write her dissertation on Alcott, but was told Alcott was insignificant because she wrote for children.

Frein continues his introductions: "Doug Watson from Oklahoma Baptist University, Shawnee, the portrayer of Nathaniel Hawthorne, who disappears a half day every Chautauqua week searching out the town's golf course and who has just achieved his world record here on your golf course."

Watson is a senior professor of English and literature, a Fulbright recipient, who'd taught Hawthorne works for years. He's too young for the Hawthorne he chooses to play, so he finds silver spray for his hair and adopts a slouch.

"Charles Pace from Purdue University, in Lafayette, Indiana, who plays Frederick Douglass. Be careful — he brought along his video equipment and tapes everything in sight, and he's getting ready to edit and sell his videos in small towns such as yours."

Pace is a professor of African/American studies, a Ph.D candidate in American studies-anthropology. He so admired Frederick Douglass that he'd studied, written, and performed a one-man show which he'd toured throughout the U.S. and Africa with a state department grant.

"Kevin Radaker from Anderson University in Anderson, Indiana, who does Henry David Thoreau. We're glad to have him with us and we thank his new wife who was kind enough to let him grow a beard in order to come to Chautauqua."

Radaker is an English department chairman. During his teens he had long hair and was inspired by Thoreau's words: "If a man does not keep pace with his companions, perhaps it is because he hears a different drummer." He landed the part of Thoreau in a high school play, *The Night Thoreau Spent in Jail*. His dissertation was on Thoreau.

"Carrol Peterson from Doane College in Crete, Nebraska, who plays Walt Whitman, didn't ask his wife if he could grow a beard because he's had one for fifteen years."

Peterson is a professor of American literature who's traveled with Chautauqua four years, formerly portraying Tom Paine. Like Frein, Peterson had vast knowledge of the nineteenth century, and has the advantage of looking like Whitman in his later years.

"Laurie James — the only one of us who is not affiliated with academic nonsense; she is an independant scholar from Dix Hills, New York, who does Margaret Fuller. She came to Chautauqua, I think, in order to sell her books, and this is why you can find her sitting every night under the tent behind the book sales table and it may account for one reason her Margaret Fuller books sell better than Herman Melville's *Moby Dick*."

My books were selling nicely in Chautauqua.

"Eagle Glassheim, our road manager, who's been with us six years. You can always spot him because he's sewn two big purple patches on the back of his khaki shorts — yes, right *there* and *there*. These past two years he's brought along his computer and turns accounts into the Humanities Council printed out nicely, which is something the Humanities people have never quite gotten over."

Eagle will be graduating from Dartmouth in one more year.

"Mark Frein, my son, who has also been with us six years as tent master, and who claims that most Chautauqua stories are oral tradition and ought not to reach print."

Mark is also graduating from Dartmouth.

"Bob, our truck driver, who honors you today by wearing formal attire. You'll notice a very unusual phenomenon — he's wearing a shirt with sleeves."

Almost always the audience asks how we came to Chautuaqua, how we chose or got involved with our characters, how long it has taken us, and how we researched.

Frankly, our study is ongoing. The books we lug focus on our characters. We are constantly validating and advancing our knowledge.

Someone in the audience asks what is the most shocking thing we've discovered about our characters. My colleagues begin by mentioning some bias or dispiteous action. *What will I say? What is the one thing every person wants to know about but is afraid to ask?* When it's my turn, I answer: "Margaret Fuller's ugly hairstyle." It brings down the house.

Once when Carrol Peterson takes off his wide-brimmed Walt Whitman hat, someone asks: "I want to know if Walt Whitman would have approved of your taking off your hat?"

Carrol swiftly puts on his hat and becomes Walt Whitman: "No, I wouldn't approve." Then he takes off the hat: "But now I'm me and I don't have to do what Whitman would do."

Some of our best questions come from children. An eight-year-old asked Watson who's been scowling as Nathaniel Hawthorne (concerned with despair and depravity): "Why are you so *sad*?"

After Charles Pace's performance as Frederick Douglass, a little boy earnestly asks, "When did you die?"

At a children's workshop, Louisa Alcott (Anne Bail Howard) says she grew up eating bread, fruit, beans, and porridge. Her audience of youngsters doesn't know what porridge is. One girl says it sounds like pizza to her. Louisa responds: "Pizza, what's that? Is it like apple pie? Sounds foreign to me."

At my adult workshop a woman thinks I play Fuller with too much of a "nice smile. Why don't you show how frustrated and tragic a figure Fuller was?" She doesn't understand that I am conducting a workshop on Fuller, not portraying her. So that night, during my presentation, I add a Margaret Fuller quote to my dialogue: "I love best to be a woman but womanhood at present is too straightly bound to give me scope." Afterwards, she says she knew the minute I stepped on stage that I was Fuller.

The great majority of people tell me they have never heard of Margaret Fuller. A young woman approaches me after my adult workshop and tells me she doesn't believe in everything Fuller said, but then, she doesn't agree with everything anyone said.

In most towns I get the message that most people are strongly anti-feminist. At one large reception I walk past a group and hear a woman's harsh voice directed at me — *"woman's libber!"*

Another young man tells me, "I just don't like Margaret Fuller." I ask him why; he cannot express why.

Several people ask me at different times, "Wasn't Margaret Fuller arrogant to say, 'Now I know everyone in America and I can find no intellect comparable to my own.'" Why would — or could — a woman say that? At one after-show reception, as I walk in, a group of women tell me all the men have agreed they hate Margaret Fuller. These women say they are quite aware of their husbands' negative attitudes and they get around them by never asking if they can do something; they just go ahead and do it.

Two college-age women at another reception explain to me that they don't want to be known as feminists because all feminists hate men.   I suggest they if probe a little further, they'll discover that feminists are as diverse in their outlook as individuals are in any group, and that Margaret Fuller and many others in the women's movement have sought close, loving relationships with men.

In Ada, Oklahoma, several women tell me "confidentially" — they would not ever tell the other scholars but they respond to Margaret Fuller more than to any other character.'

One woman tells me she had never before met someone who did research. She feels she's walking a blind alley in doing her "thing," researching the Bible. I offer her probably the only support she ever gets.

Once after a children's workshop a whimsical twelve-year-old girl approaches me with some scribbled notebook pages. "Have you time to read my story? My teacher doesn't have time and my parents tell me they can't help me, so I am wondering if you could?" I sit down and spend over half an hour showing her how to smooth sentences and correct grammar.

At another children's workshop in a one-room school (to which I drive fifty miles) there is no audience except the woman with the key to the door and her adult friend and grown son. No one came because the town had been under a tornado warning. We sit down at the old-fashioned desks and I launch into my workshop dialogue whereupon the son begins, in hesitant stutters, to speak about the problems he's had growing up. He spills out his awareness of his inability to focus. He admits he'd be interested in Chautauqua if only he could understand what we were talking about. I say, "We all grow at different points in our lives. Chautauqua is in a tent and if you get restless you can just walk out and come back in when something interests you. Why don't you try it and see if you like it?" That night he comes alone. He stands apart and listens intently. Afterwards, I ask him how he likes it. He likes it.

In Kansas, a father from Cushing, Oklahoma brings his fifteen year-old son because "they need guys to carry things." Steven Handlon carries things, watches our show, and declares he wants to travel with us. For a month he camps out in his own pup tent set up just beyond ours, and he rides in the truck alongside Bob, our truck driver. We bring him to our receptions so he can have some free food. He comes to every performance and joins one of the Student Institutes.

So successful was the first Chautauqua Assembly that met for a two-week session in August 1874 that more than five hundred representatives from the Baptist, Congregational, Presbyterian and Methodist churches came. The second-year program headlined President Ulysses S. Grant. National newspaper recognition followed.

After the great industrial and commercial expansion following the Civil War, there was a new thirst for knowledge. But universities were admitting wealthy white men only. Most women weren't prepared for college, nor were blacks. Chautauqua offered a popular level of adult learning, and it was not relegated to class, gender, age, or color.

Chautauqua started because the Reverend John Heyl Vincent, had never attended college. He once rode horseback from one parish to another, visiting small communities that did not have a minister. Serving as secretary of the Methodist Episcopal Sunday School Union, he realized that Sunday School teachers needed training.

He met an Akron, Ohio, industrialist and inventor, Lewis Miller, also an enthusiastic Sunday School worker, who suggested a training session be held in a summer-vacation-camp-meeting atmosphere.

By 1876 Vincent and Miller lined up twenty days which included boating, fishing, swimming and outdoor games. Lake Chautauqua became a permanent community with its own post office, homes, classrooms, recital halls, lake port, and tabernacle.*

Ladies used to come dressed in their best. Today it's pants and T-shirts. Ladies carried fans. Today businesses provide heavy cardboard fans with stapled ice-cream-stick handles. The old-time plank seats were hard and splintery and people brought newspaper and cushions to sit on them. Today fold-up chairs are quite

---

*Some Victorian buildings survive; you can visit today's summer-long Chautauqua Institution in Chautauqua, New York, which carries on the tradition with elaborately scheduled, top-level events. The Chautauqua Institution is not connected with The Great Plains Chautauqua Society, Inc.

comfortable. Yesteryear grandmothers left rocking chairs under the tent all week. Today fold-ups are left out all night; they seldom disappear — though it has been observed that at midnight foxes play hide-and-go-seek amongst them. Long ago popcorn machines and hot roasted peanuts were staples, and today these still are preferred snacks.

One elder from Blue Rapids remembered a watering tank for horses filled with big cakes of ice that had tin cups tied around the rim. Everyone dipped in for a drink. Today we recycle soda cans.

In the "golden years" there grew up three distinct Chautauquas: (1) the tents which traveled from town to town with their talent; (2) the circuits, which provided permanent buildings or tents and whose managers booked in "packaged" talent from agents who kept their clientele touring ten or eleven months out of the year; and (3) the independents who owned and operated a site, oftentimes an elaborate resort with boat houses and steamboats. In those days Chautauquas attracted up to forty million Americans in a single season.

The community organized a committee, usually businessmen, that contacted a Chautuaqua company. After dates were set, a contract was signed and a sizeable amount of upfront money had to be allocated. The committee immediately launched a ticket-selling drive and asked for donations.

The Ellison White Chautauqua that toured Montana and parts west of the Rocky Mountains as well as Canada, Australia, and New Zealand, hired pretty college girls as advance agents to sign up the local businessmen. In Australia the businessmen looked at the girls instead of their contracts. After signing, they commented to each other, "I hear you signed up with the 'She-Got-Ya' too!"

In the 1970s and '80s money was raised through raffles and games. In the Old Fashioned Bed Race, humanities scholars (or local celebrities) rode down Main Street in beds on wheels. Another popular attraction was to sit a humanities scholar on a bench under a target. If the paying participant hit the target with a gun, the scholar fell into a bucket of water.

In another game everyone in town bet on numbers painted on the top of a table surrounded by chicken wire. At a specific time a chicken was dropped onto the table, and the first number on which the chicken left a mark designated the winner. (Somebody said this was a chicken-shit operation.)

In 1980 Albers exported Chautauqua to Sheridan, Wyoming for a single shot. To his previous roster he added: Teddy Roosevelt; Meriwether Lewis, of Lewis and Clark fame; Aurelia Paez Jordan, a fictional Wyoming ranch woman; and a popular radio personality known as Garrison Keiller, who told humorous monologues and ghost stories.

A year later Albers got his first national grant and named his organization the Mountain/Plains Chautauqua Society. He used a Teddy Roosevelt quote as a logo: "Chautauqua is the most American thing in America." He had a board of directors and he conducted a national search for applicants.

But he'd expanded too quickly without careful planning and coordination with the states. The twelve week tour was too long, the scholars were overtaxed, and because the program was not grounded firmly in text, the scholars improvised with dialogue that did not edify.

Still, one bright moonlit night at the Lewiston, Montana, fairgrounds, Clay Jenkinson was brilliantly received as Meriweather Lewis by five hundred patrons, including ranchers and cowboys, most of whom couldn't care less about the humanities. The follow-up discussion was so marvellous that the regional Chautauqua group re-affirmed their joy in the value of the tour.

By 1984 Albers realized that the theatrical and scholarly experiences were different. After an emotional drama, audience members needed time to digest what they had seen before they were ready to discuss. In his humanities program Albers wanted the audience to ask questions immediately.

His 1984 theme was "Jefferson's Agrarian Dream and the Great Plains Experience," featuring the Rhodes Scholar Clay Jenkinson portraying Thomas Jefferson as moderator. Now Albers commissioned scholars to write essays and bibliographies of their characters and published a thirty-two-page newspaper-like tabloid. It was attractive but the ink came off on fingers.

"The Chautauqua Reader is something you can use again," the

moderator announced to the audience. "You can wrap fish in it —
but read it first!"

Reading has always been a major part of "Mother Chautauqua."
In 1884 Vincent inaugurated the Chautauqua Literary and Scientific
Circle — a four year, college level, home-study course that awarded
diplomas. Books with precious red and gold bindings on every
phase of human inquiry were sent out from the headquarters in New
York. By 1891, there were over 180,000 C.L.S.C. members, located
as far afield as the British Isles, Africa, and Japan.

Albers' 1985 theme was "Writers on the Plains," which included
the characters of William Allen White, Willa Cather, Mari Sandoz,
Sinclair Lewis, and Hamlin Garland. The 1986-87 theme was "Over
the Edge: Traveller's on the Plains," with Meriwether Lewis, Elizabeth
Bacon Custer, Robert Louis Stevenson, and Father Pierre Jean
DeSmet (played by our group leader, George Frein).
The scholar who played Robert Louis Stevenson that summer
almost got arrested. While rehearsing his lines in a park, a woman
looked out her window and immediately called the police to report
a "mental" who was wandering about talking to himself. When an
officer drove up and asked his name, the scholar said, "I'm Robert
Louis Stevenson."
That year another person from the National Endowment on the
Humanities came to visit. Anxiously, the Chautauquans offered him
beer in their motel rooms and entertained him with a riverboat ride.
He finally admitted he was not an evaluator, merely an observer. He
cheered Chautauqua, which proved historic text could be made
popular! He took this news back to the NEH — and more funding
came through.
The 1988-89 theme was "American Visions," featuring our
George Frein doing Henry Adams as the moderator. Clay Jenkinson
portrayed Thomas Jefferson again, and Alexander Hamilton, Abigail
Adams and Elizabeth Cady Stanton were also included.
This was a year when Susan Lockwood, playing Abigail Adams
"stopped the show" when she admonished her husband, John, to
"Remember the Ladies!" Her historic quote was answered from a
passing cattle truck with a profound "MOOOOO."

In '90, when Tom Paine came on board, Chautauqua was a first-class act.

Our typical week's schedule is: Wednesday, travel in our vans, which includes packing, unpacking and settling into the motel room. Thursday, pitch the tent with community volunteers, an event usually including a supper or ice-cream social.

Midmorning Friday, a press conference is held under the tent; we are in costume. At about 7:00 P.M. the entertainment begins, with a half hour of local performers, followed by George Frein as Herman Melville offering a monologue of sea stories, *Moby Dick*, *Red Jacket*, *Billy Bud*, or *Typee*, after which Melville takes questions from the audience. Then he calls the "American Renaissance" characters onto the platform.

What question will he ask?

We haven't the slightest idea.

Perhaps it'll be simple such as, "How did your career develop during your life?"

But more often Melville relishes in asking something more complex, such as "What did socialism mean to the intellectual in your day and how do you position yourself into that American experiment?"

We pass the microphone around, taking turns answering as though our characters are speaking, delighting the audience by disagreeing with each other.

Soon Melville moderates questions from the audience. Often he rephrases what someone says in ways that titillate and clarify, thereby giving us time to formulate an intelligent answer.

Finally, he introduces us as the individuals we are and invites further questions of a more personal nature.

Each scholar is responsible for one forty-minute monologue during the week or, sometimes, two of us are scheduled to dialogue together, such as Margaret Fuller and Frederick Douglass. Those of us not "on stage" are in T-shirts and shorts, sitting and mingling with the audience, or helping to sell books at the book table.

Dutch Treat breakfasts, to which the public is invited, are scheduled in local restaurants — everyone paying for their own bacon and eggs. Thus, at 7:00 A.M. with coffee in hand, we scholars hold a mini-seminar.

During the week we each preside over an adult workshop and a children's workshop. This is in keeping with the early independent Chautauquas wherein college-age directors were hired to organize games, parades, or talent shows with prizes for the youngsters.

Also, in Chautauqua tradition, we attend receptions so there is more community give-and-take. These include light teas, Sunday brunches, extravagant barbecues and dinners, or catered gourmet buffets; sometimes in community halls, backyards with swimming pools, lush living rooms, churches, university rooms, or country clubs; hosted by families or groups, or interested community folk who worked on the committee or put up money, or by the state humanities council or foundation people who are saying "thanks" or are raising money. Dignitaries are introduced and honored, and George Frein pays court — we stand and wave friendly hands.

In addition, Frein as Melville and Peterson as Whitman generally capture the realism of the Civil War with a late evening poetry reading in a local bar or club.

Further, one or all of us do a "special" — we cover a local radio or TV interview, or a luncheon at the Rotary or women's club or at a senior center or nursing home. In our second year a Teacher's Institute is funded; a group of about thirty teachers from the five Great Plains states arrives for the week and we offer workshops and one-on-one at tent raising, or at picnics or at chance meetings on streets or near our motel. In our third year the Bismarck Student Institute is added; twenty honors students throughout North Dakota are brought in for a week to earn semester credit. Once we lead a four-hour "how-to" session for ten people who are to participate in a "Living History" program developed by the Kansas Humanities Council.

On Tuesday, the last night of our week, George Frein tells the audience at the end of the show, "Now we come to the best part. We are looking for strong women, good looking men, and smart children. If you fit into one of these categories, will you please, at the appointed signal, stand and do what Doug does."

Doug Watson, with fold-up chair in hand, snaps it shut.

Frein continues: "And if you will also fold up your neighbor's chair — but be sure your neighbor is out of the chair before you fold it up — and take it to the Chautauqua truck. Also, if you can please help us dismantle the tent, you will see how much fun it is."

With the light from headlights of parked cars, the tent comes speedily down and is packed away in about forty-five minutes. The night's darkness descends while only the harsh headlights and the brightness of the stars illuminate our efforts.

"What time should we be ready to go tomorrow?" we buzz amongst ourselves.

"We'll load our baggage onto the truck at 8:00 A.M., and we'll be on the road by 9:00 A.M."

It's always taken a hardy person to survive a season or two of Chautauqua. The old-time lyceum lecturers learned to orate with one eye on the audience and the other on the clock, for they were frequently booked ten different nights in ten different states. In the days of automobiles, as soon as they finished, they'd jump into a car with its motor running. Connections were usually bad and there was no leeway for missed trains. Baggage was often lost or delayed. "Get there!" was the admonition of mother employer. Frequently, they'd get there just in time to step onto the platform. If late, the venue manager held the audience with a community sing. The story goes that when William Jennings Bryan was caught in a railroad tie-up, the audience was kept waiting until 1:00 A.M., then he spoke for two hours.

If you worked for one of the major Chautauquas, the Redpath de Luxe Circuit for instance, "getting there" was a mite easier. Talent, musicians, stage directors, managers, superintendents, advance men, junior workers, and crew boys were sent in seven Pullmans — the Redpath Special. Then, eight seventy-foot, steel baggage cars transported a half million pounds of tents, stages, chairs, and electrical equipment.

With circuits, a leap-frog game was played out. A company would have nine tents to keep the program going in seven different towns for seven days. The tent crew had two days to tear down, travel, and set up again in the next place.

It is the tent raisings I find hardest. Ours is not any pup tent — it's a blue and white striped *circus* tent that towers over three hundred people. What *am* I doing, at my age! Camp Fire Girl that I used to be, I always hated camping.

From the very first, though, Anne Bail Howard pitches in with great zest and spirit. "I want to see just how to do it," she chimes enthusiastically. Then I hear how in 1988 Sally Wagner (Elizabeth Cady Stanton) brought affirmative action to tent raising when she and Eagle Glassheim recruited women onlookers to help pound stakes.

At the beginning of the season, we go to the park in old clothes and *wash* the tent. Actually, this is not too hard. The local fire department brings a fire truck and hoses. The men unload the heavy canvas bags containing the tent pieces and drag them onto the grass. With much tugging we spread them out and the fireman wet them down with hoses, while somebody sprinkles on Mr. Clean. Picking up long-handled brushes, we, barefooted, fan out atop the canvas in assembly-line fashion and scrub away.

Then, about five people position themselves at one end of a piece of canvas, grab it in unison, lift it as high as possible, and the firemen hose it, forcing the soap to cascade down. *Then,* to my utter amazement, these five lift the canvas *over their heads* and begin to *walk under it,* creating a moving wall for the firemen to hose. Needless to say, those who do this come out the other end absolutely bedraggled, while the canvas begins to dry in the sun.

At tent raisings, we gather in the late afternoon at the open end of the Chautauqua truck parked close to the tent site. The local committee arranges for community help, and sometimes we get fifty people, other times fifteen. One time we have local weight lifters. Another time there are about twelve fifteen-year-olds from a boys' home. They look tough, but prove to be hard-working, well-behaved lads who attend — and enjoy — our nightly presentation. What a brilliant idea to get them involved in humanity programs!

Many times there are up to a hundred observers who drive to our site and set up lawn chairs, even take out cameras to record the raising of a tent. Frequently, there'll be folk in wheelchairs or on crutches, or persons handicapped in one way or another.

These towns are largely white, with very little ethnic or cultural mix. Strange, for an urbanite like me, to see so few African-Americans, though in one town there is a person from India, the coordinator, and in another an Asian coordinator, and on one college campus there is an international house where we meet a group of foreign students.

George Frein welcomes the community, and begins by saying that we scholars, used to libraries and classrooms, are unused to hard work, so the volunteers are not to expect too much from us. (Frein is the one who works the hardest.)

"Last week" — he seems completely serious — "we had the Girl Scouts to help out, and they put up the tent in record time — one hour and fifteen minutes. So, let's see if we can beat their record!"

Straightaway Bob, the truck driver, appears from inside the truck pushing out the canvas bags while smiling strong men latch onto them and carry them to the grassy ground — hoping a snake doesn't appear while pulling out the blue and white striped canvas. The helpers kneel down and begin to lace the pieces together with attached cords, while others pull the long end ropes straight out from the sides.

"Everybody grab a rope!" Mark, the tent master, yells.

Everyone stretches as hard as possible, pulling the canvas taunt.

"Move it a little this way," Mark calls out. "Two feet more over there! Okay. Drop the ropes!"

Stakes and sledgehammers are brought out, one for each rope, and the men — and women — begin pounding. Next, red, white and blue poles are brought out, one placed at each stake. Two yellow ropes get thrown on the ground at each pole. Then, the pulleys are attached. Bringing things out of the truck is the kind of job at which I excel.

Next, each pole has to be inserted through a hole at the tent roof edge, and a yellow rope is tossed over the pole's point. Each rope is tied to a stake, and I learn how to make the special knot, under which is looped the other yellow rope. At Mark's signal we lift the poles vertically, precariously lifting the sides of the tent.

Then, three huge poles are taken out of the truck.

"I need at least five on each pole," Mark shouts.

Several grab and hold it horizontally, facing the tent.

"When I say 'Go,' go under the tent to the middle, insert the poles, and lift up the tent."

This is the most dramatic moment, and it takes a rush of energy.

"Go!"

With the power of community effort, up raises the tent's roof.

There is a community clapping of hands. A flush of excitement.

All else is anticlimactic, but of vital importance. The poles are straightened, the pulleys set in, the ropes tightened. The canvas sides of the tent are attached, rolled up, and tied to the top. The miniChristmas lights are strung along the inside top. The four heavy platforms for the stage are carried in and set up on two-by-fours for support. The aluminum poles for the background curtains are set in heavy iron plates and balanced properly so they won't collapse. The blue curtains are gathered along the upper and lower poles, for firmness and attractiveness. The rug is lifted onto the stage, two chairs and a table are brought out, and a small step placed at one end of the stage for easy access. Lights are hung on the heavy poles holding up the tent, and the sound system's microphones and amplifiers are plugged in.

Also, a smaller brown tent has to be pitched which houses the local committee's concession stand, as well as the Chautauqua book table for our authors' works, sold at cost.

The main tent secured, about three hundred chairs are unloaded off the truck and positioned in the tent. Sometimes the community helpers form an old-fashioned "bucket brigade," passing each chair from person to person until it reaches those who space them out in rows. (I am *very* good at this job, too; in fact, Anne Howard and I designate ourselves the "Chair Ladies.")

In about an hour and a half all is done, and the first thing that happens is that pleased and proud people sit down in the fold-ups, talking and laughing, introducing themselves, anticipating the week ahead.

Maybe there'll be a picnic lunch, or brown-bag dinner, hot dog barbecue, or ice cream social. Other times there's a come-as-you-are reception or buffet at somebody's home.

Make no mistake, tent raising is tough, often done under a scorching sun above 90 degree heat. We wear hats and drink plenty of water supplied at the truck in a cooler with paper cups, and are admonished that, while we are expected to show the community that we scholars are just garden-variety people, we are not to overstrain.

Elkhart, Kansas, my fourth tent-raising, is extremely hot and dusty. We are in a treeless area not far from a grain elevator. Bringing out the yellow ropes, I feel dizzy. Soon ground is tipping. I go back

to the truck. Wipe the sweat off my forehead with my sleeve. I grab
for the side of the truck. I can't feel the ground under my feet. Sink
down into a handy chair, grasping my head in my hands. Somebody
says, "Are you feeling all right?" The committee coordinator drives
me to my motel room.

It is suggested that I'm dehydrated. I am given water and told to
rest.

In Central City, Nebraska, my sixth tent-raising, all is fine until the
basement party afterwards. A gracious hostess has set out lovely
choices of drinks and hors d'oeuvres. Wine-lover that I am, I help
myself to a second tiny glass. Within minutes, dizziness and nausea.
In the kitchen I collapse.

Because once you dehydrate it can easily happen again, Eagle
Glassheim asks me, just as the next tent raising is about to begin, don't
I want to scout the water and paper cups because he had "forgotten"
to do it.

Why isn't Chautauqua held in air-conditioned auditoriums?

Clay Jenkinson (who played Thomas Jefferson) stated that the
tent is the heart of Chautauqua: "Chautauqua represents a kind of
nostalgia we share for a time in American life when the pace was a
bit slower, when there was less glitter and more substance, when we
talked about things carefully, when people gathered to celebrate
community, when we were less isolated in our artifically-climated
homes, when television was less important."*

It's the ambience, the excitement a tent can cause in a small town,
the informality of the open-air, the thrill of glimpsing a live performer
standing behind the curtain preparing to step onto "the boards." It's
watching the wind disarray a costume, seeing "the star" dealing with
the unexpected or answering a difficult question, walking up to a
celebrity on his "off night" when he's munching a hot dog, and
starting a conversation.

George Frein thinks you just can't rent better space. An airy tent
is anybody's space; it doesn't belong to another institution such as a
school or library. Here, you can walk in and out at will; no one is

*Quoted from the 1984 Chautauqua Reader.

threatened. The format brings together those from different political and social backgrounds. (In one location John Birchers didn't miss a program for one solid week.) Here neighbors astonish each other with their extraordinary depth of thought.

Under a tent scholars can feel comfortable when making fools of themselves and have experiences that couldn't be had indoors, such as: When you are delivering your most powerful speech, effective only if you stand still and make no gesture, a fly ambushes your nose and mouth.

Once a giant mosquito joined the act, biting Carrol Peterson's leg while he was performing. The blood started spotting through his pants. Further and further the red oozed, and the audience was drawn into estimating how far down it would streak. Peterson was totally baffled by the sea of faces snickering instead of attending to his words.

In our third year the mosquitoes in some communities are so bad that, though the tent area is freshly sprayed every night, part of the audience stays home. For the brave who choose to attend, Radaker offers Henry David Thoreau's solution: "Mix pinetree sap with molasses — mosquitoes can't bite through that gunk."

Outdoors there are challenges like babies crying. A child wiggles a chair, or has the idea to walk up to the front row, lift an empty chair, carry it down the aisle, and set it outside the tent. Or somebody's dog chases a rabbit.

Once George Frien, as the seafarer Herman Melville, encounters a three-year-old who wanders onto the stage. Without breaking character, he interrupts his sentence and says to her, "You're the prettiest mate I ever saw." And he picks her up and hands her to her mother.

The following memories are from Elsie Miller Wendt: "In 1909 we went to Chautuauqa in Clapp's Grove east of Elmwood. We went in a two-seat carriage with a top. Dad had to let the horses walk. The dust on the road was 6-8 inches thick that year. Carrie Nation was speaking. She was very much against alcoholic beverages and tobacco and said that people who chew tobacco are dirtier than hogs! One old 'sot' sat in the front row. He got so mad at Carrie that the more she spoke, the more he chewed. Then he spit on the ground with much gusto! One spring, Stove Creek flooded Clapp's Grove. After that, Chautauqua was held in the park by the schoolhouse. Then the boys had no more reason to swing across the creek hanging onto tree limbs. They usually fell in and got soaked, but that was part of Chautauqua fun!"

In Wayne, Nebraska, we are in a lovely park next to a man-made stream, home to a gaggle of geese. One night the geese decide to party — HONK, HONK, HONK! With no indication of irritation, Howard, on stage as Louisa May Alcott, says, "And so that year, I felt like a goose that laid a golden egg."

In Minot, North Dakota, our tent site is in a park just beyond a stock-car race track, and on the night Kevin Radaker (Henry David Thoreau) and I have a dialogue, the race is in full throttle. The entire evening we shout nostalgic, softhearted lines against background sound effects of eh-eH eH....... ROUGHHHHHHH.

In Mitchell, South Dakota, we set up next to the community swimming pool, in full operation until 9 P.M. at which time a horrendous voice over a loud speaker blurts: "Clear the pool immediately — Make sure you take all your belongings with you — The pool will be open tomorrow at 10 A.M. and every day except Sunday when it will be open at 12 noon."

In Marysville, Kansas, we are in a park through which a railroad runs. Radaker is into his Henry David Thoreau monologue, when the mile-long freight train whistles, drowning out every word. He waits, then out of the depths of his immense knowledge, he brings forth lines Thoreau wrote years ago: "The *railroad* — I will not have its hissing and its steam put out my eyes. We do not ride upon the railroad; the railroad rides upon us. It is carrying our pastoral life away."

He gets a round of warm applause.

George Frein often tells the audience this railroad story. Opie Read, a Chautauqua author and lecturer, was sitting in front of his hotel when a passerby asked, "Do you know where the Chautauqua tent is?"

Answer: "Have you a railroad in this town?"

"Yes, sir."

"Have you two railroads?"

"Yes, sir."

"Well," drawled Opie, "find the place where they cross and you'll find the Chautauqua tent."

Where was the first Great Plains Chautauqua located? On picnic grounds owned by the Kansas Pacific Railroad at Bismarck Grove, near Topeka, Kansas.

Where did it move to four years later? A block west of the railroad depot, in Ottawa, Kansas, for a thirty-one-year stay. It became a major Chautauqua, containing a 5,000 seat tabernacle, a dining hall, the Hall of Philosophy, Normal Hall, a women's building, a boys' building, the Willard Memorial Hall, and three hundred tents for campers.

Where was the Nebraska Lone Pine Assembly located? Where the railroad stopped in undesirable sand hills at Crete — but good water came from springs and about 5,000 people camped there.

Where was the sixty-acre Lake Madison Chautauqua Association? In South Dakota, right where the Chicago, Milwaukee and St. Paul Railroad passed. They had a 2,500 seat auditorium and stables for two hundred horses.

In Oklahoma it is always said, "If you don't like the weather, wait five minutes."

As in the old days, we encounter huge thunder/lightning/wind/rain storms. Sometimes the storms come up in the early afternoon and disappear within an hour or two, so all is fine for the evening in the tent. Sometimes the rain starts during the performance. Eagle, Mark, and Bob scurry about unrolling the sides of the tent, and we perform cozily within. With poles they push up the corners of the canvas roof, squishing off the pockets of water. How I admire Carrol Peterson as he raises his voice above the cracking thunder and lightning. By the time the last question is answered, the storm abates and the audience, without a drop on their heads, dodges puddles to cars.

In Hays, Kansas, we are gifted with three and a half inches of stormy, blackened rain. Mark and his wife Nicole, (who became tent co-master in the third year), and Frein and Pace cannot run fast enough to spike up the sagging canvas of the tent. The next morning we worry about mosquitoes. "We have no spray machine," the humanities coordinator tells us, "because it never rains here."

In 1980, in Wyoming, the wrath of the Midwest gods caused the tent to have to be totally replaced. Years before, in July 1913, in Frankfort, Kansas, the driving rain, wind and hail lashed through the city park and collapsed the tent, blowing over the piano and soaking the music, forcing everyone into the Weis Opera House. In 1928 the truck with the tent was mired on a muddy road near Waterville, so the first night's program was performed in the high-school auditorium.

Wicked weather caused low attendance in 1908 in Blue Rapids. Temptestuous heavens delayed farm work for two weeks — thus, during Chautauqua week, the farmers were in the fields, not the tent.

In Yankton, South Dakota, we are located in a beautiful, grassy park alongside the scenic Missouri River where a statue of a sea captain stands watch next to an intriguing historic house that serves as a museum, wherein our reception is held. While we sip punch, rain becomes balls of hail, trees lean towards the ground, and I see a ten-foot arm of a tree fly past the window. In about ten minutes the twister is gone past.

Can we chance to perform in the tent?

It is impossible to outguess Zeus.

A small opera house, closed for several months, is a little musty. The show starts later than usual; our audience is small.

That night, while our tent masters sleep, Zeus shows no mercy and raises 98-mph winds, pushes trailer houses off foundations, takes a roof off an airport hangar, bends flag poles, uproots trees, sprews garbage, and unleashes clotheslines.

In the morning our canvas is discovered down by the river.

Luckily, Yankton has tentmakers who can repair within a week while we play the opera house.

In Chandler, Oklahoma, we are barely unpacked when the motel manager informs us we are in a tornado watch but not to worry because, in the past twelve years, she's only used her "cellar" twice.

"Come over so you'll know where it is," she says as she beckons me behind a building towards a slanted door jutting out of the dirt, like in *The Wizard of Oz*.

"Turn on channel 9 for the reports," she says.

Back in my room I hear the announcer say, "We're in a storm watch but no tornado is in sight."

Five minutes later a siren blasts.

Eighteen of us including four nine-year-olds climb into that dusty, underground, cement, 6' x 12' x 6' cellar equipped with two decrepit chairs, an old wooden bench and a wobbly cot. About ten people sit. Three candles on a ledge emit light. There are two small vents in the ceiling. The air starts getting bad. There are some jokes. The motel manager, who has a walkie-talkie, remembers tornados that killed children and adults. The rain starts to pelt down; the walkie-talkie announces hail. We hear thunder. After forty-five minutes, someone pushes open the door; it is raining, but safe.

1993 is the banner year for incessant, catastrophic water. The Mississippi River and its tributaries climb banks, assault stressed levees, and flood hundreds of people out of their homes. President Clinton declares disaster areas and pushes Congress to approve more than three billion in federal aid. North Dakota, which averages ten to fifteen inches per year, gets twenty-two inches within six weeks. Ev Albers' basement gets its share. Thousands of acres of crops are damaged. In Epping we are beseiged every July day with downpours, sometimes hail. In North Platte, Nebraska, Pace is into his monologue when the spheres turn black and Frein gives the pre-arranged signal: "We now have to ask each person in the audience to take up his chair and move into the Buffalo Bill barn museum."

In Marysville, Kansas, we are forced to unlock the closed-for-the-summer high-school auditorium. There, in this unfamiliar site, Henry David Thoreau searches for a glass to use as a prop during performance. The only thing he finds is a styrofoam cup. So he drinks from that. Afterwards, someone comes up to him: "Don't you realize the environmentally-conscious Thoreau would *never* use styrofoam?"

It's traditional that a lot of hoopla goes along with Chautauqua. In 1914 in Marysville, Kansas, there was a parade with 835 church and school members marching. This drew hundreds to the city. The largest parade was at Broken Bow, Nebraska, with 1,012 marchers. That's when a youthful Bible class wrapped themselves in a large ribbon, and the primary department of the Christian Church Sunday

School rode on a decorated hayrack pulled by a team of horses.

During World War I, circuit Chautauquas brought out all the trappings of a patriotic road show, with military bands and wounded soldiers, drummer boys pushing a homemade cannon, girls dressed as Red Cross nurses. President Woodrow Wilson claimed Chautauqua was a major contributor to the war effort.

In our Chautauqua the hoopla begins with the selling of trendy T-shirts and hats with the attractive logo in full color. I know I've achieved fame when there I am — my picture amidst the other scholars — on red Chautauqua balloons. I send a few home to the small children in our family. "There she is!" they cry, jubilantly blowing and watching my head bloat. "There she goes!" they yell, letting the air burst out so the balloons shoot about the room.

In Pierre, South Dakota we scholars are told we are to be transported, in costume, in horse and buggy, to the press conference at the capitol building. We all gather in the motel lobby and follow our escort, the humanities woman. She gets into her car; we get into our vans. Within two blocks of the capital building, we park, get out, then wait. Sure enough, three horse-drawn carriages with drivers in historic cowboy garb are coming down the street. Anne Howard and I climb aboard a black, open-air, two-seater, easiest to manage with our long, billowy skirts. It has one tiny step and, if you grab ahold something, you can lift yourself up onto the floorboard which supports a comfortable-looking seat covered with soft cream-colored sheepswool. Once the horses start trotting, I desperately clasp the hand rail, wondering how women went anywhere during the nineteenth century. We joggle two blocks to the capital steps where we have our pictures taken. Inside the rotunda, we are interviewed by the local newspaperman. When we finish, we look around for our buggies and horses. They have disappeared. To return to our cars, we walk.

Every night that week, we are driven to the tent in that stylish buggy to make a grand entrance — even though our motel is within walking distance. (After the show, we walk home.)

In Sidney, Nebraska we are given a police escort into town. The police open their sirens and our vans parade nonstop through red lights down Main Street, about ten blocks. A few locals gaze up at us, sheilding their eyes from the bleaching sun. For the most part the streets are devoid of pedestrians.

At the Shelter House, a large barn-like building in a park next to the tent site, the Boy Scout color guard presents the flag, then there are military bugle signals that were heard at Old Fort Sidney a century ago, short speeches by the mayor, county commissioners and humanities committee members. Frein introduces us scholars. There are songs, piano playing, and inside the Shelter House an Army Mess is served which consists of a meal similar to that offered military personnel a century ago — beans with ham and cornbread served on tin plates by the Ladies Divsion of the Chamber of Commerce.

In Seminole, Oklahoma, we arrive as Gusher Days Festival is to commence. This three-day event celebrates the town's oil boom legacy. For the annual parade, a flatbed truck is ready with banner, chairs, desk, hay with quilts. Costumed, we join children who are dressed as Henry David Thoreau and Herman Melville, and four girls who represent Alcott's "little women." Howard as Alcott is given an oversized homemade paper book with the words "Little Women" written on it, Radaker as Thoreau is given the same with "Walden" written on it, and Frein as Melville is given one with "Mobey Dick" written on it. Obviously, spelling is not this committee's strongest point. We wave to the crowd as we ride through town and down Main Street, about three blocks. Going as slow as we can, it takes about fifteen minutes.

In Epping, North Dakota — a frontier town boasting a population of ninety-five — we observe award-winning buildings, lovingly preserved as museums for thirty-five years by a seventy-year-old curator/artist, Elmer Halvorson. Here we climb aboard a shaky, flatbed float with a sandwich board advertising Chautauqua and we join a twelve-year-old boy dressed like Uncle Sam. Flanked by an old steam-powered oil rig, cowboys on horses, and a Viet Nam war veterans color guard, we ride down Main Street, one block long and, just like in the "old days," unpaved. And then the entire parade circles through the back dirt roads and returns for a second tour along Main, as "Uncle Sam" tosses bags of candy to the kids cheering from the sidewalk.

In Hazen, North Dakota, the local committee consisting of wiry, muscular young men, challenge us scholars to a softball game. Mark informs us that accepting their challenge will be great publicity.

Afterwards, Ev Albers comes back to the motel with a knee skinned so badly he can't walk for a day. Kevin Radaker (a former football player) complains about muscles he's never known.

The following year in an area famous for football, Seminole, Oklahoma, we are challenged to softball by "The Shockers," a team of fourteen-year-old girls who rate in the top ten in the nation. Right away Radaker christens us scholars "The Living Dead." We lose, of course, by one run.

Not that we scholars do not try to keep fit. Charles Pace hefts his barbells and weights into his motel room every week, and every day, in hat and jogging shorts, lopes off into rural, tree-lined streets. Shelly, George Frein's wife, does the same, and Radaker is gradually upscaling a walking routine into a jogging routine. Frein walks, Peterson bicycles, Watson golfs, Howard joins local aerobics classes, and I exercise to Jane Fonda tapes in my room and swim when I can find a pool.

We seldom make headlines in the large newspapers, but we almost always dominate the front pages of the hometown papers. There're good stories with headlines such as, "Tent Show, Country Band, Train Rides, Fireworks Set," "Community Pitches in to Raise Tent," "Chautauqua Lets Audience Question 19th Century Authors," "Chautauqua Returns To Huron," "Sidney Gets Opportunity to Greet Chautauqua Crew at Ceremony," "Chautauqua Begins to Build Momentum."

Often, we're interviewed on the local radio station. Othertimes, there are pre-arranged telephone conferences. More than once an interviewer says, "Chatanoo ga." Another repeats "Chataugua " so many times it is embarassing.

It's the people we meet that I like best. In Central City, Nebraska, the woman who drives me to and from my workshop drops me off at the beautiful fitness center so I can have a swim and after she returns home she worries for an hour about how I will get back to my motel — I planned to walk; it is only about a mile away. But she happens to pass George Frein in the van, stops him, and suggests that he pick me up since I don't have access to a car. People in New York City would never be so concerned.

In Huron, South Dakota, I lose my traveller's checks. Putting them down on a drugstore counter, I pick up the local newspaper, ask if there is anything about Chautauqua in it, absent-mindedly put it down on top of my traveller's checks, pay for my purchases with cash, and leave.

In my motel room that night I receive a call from the clerk. She has my traveller's checks and has tracked me down.

After a breakfast with eighty people in Tulsa, Oklahoma, Howard is approached by an elderly woman who carries a stack of Alcott's books. This woman says her life is about to close and she wants to give her treasured books to someone who would appreciate them. She does not offer her name; she just wants Howard to have the books.

Living in motel rooms I like least. (Howard was the best at making a home out of a motel room.) Chautuaqua has a cap on what can be spent on accommodations. The cap is low, even by Midwest standards. This policy seems not to be different from early circuit days when Chautauquans described their quarters as "unspeakable."

For the most part, the rooms we stay in are dark and shabby square boxes with one window which opens onto the road, so you always keep the curtains drawn for privacy (further darkening the room). A faucet might drip, or the TV sound can't be turned above a certain level, or a drawer might fall off its track, or the bed sags in the middle, or the one and only mirror is yellowed and cracked, or there aren't enough electric outlets for computers, clocks, and coffee pots. In one, despite closing the shower curtain, you spill an inch of water on the floor. Never are towels larger than the hand size. Walls are so thin you can hear footsteps overhead, laughing next door. Carpets are moldy. Some rooms are so small I can hardly do my exercises. Some motels don't supply a chest of drawers, nor a desk to write on. In another we get rotten-fish odors. Many hours we stay in our "boxes" studying and working, and after a while the walls close in and the air conditioning stifles.

So we joke. When we arrive at one motel, Bob, our burly truck driver, comes booming out of his room within five minutes. "Have you got any quarters I can borrow? I got a vibrating bed, but it costs twenty-five cents, and I've already used up all my quarters!"

In Plattsmouth, Nebraska, there is no motel at all, so we are stationed in the nursing home with a wing of one-bedroom apartments.

As soon as we arrive, the tall, thin matron spots our bearded, larger-than-life truck driver, Bob, who has done absolutely nothing but carry in his suitcases. Sizing him up, she rants at him for ten minutes: "There is no smoking here, no loud talking, no drinking. If you come in drunk late at night, I'll have you thrown out of here, so help me, I will, by persons who are stronger than you."

The next day Bob, a lamb despite his outrageous comments about bars and women, sits crosslegged on grass under a tree across the street and looks miserable.

The nursing home is clean as a whistle but, since the rooms are unfurnished, the staff has scurried about and found spare cardtables and folding chairs and has wheeled in hospital beds. My narrow hospital bed is nicely made up with appropriate plastic pads — in case I have an accident, I figure.

There are rules to follow, like be in at 6 P.M. or the doors are locked. We are given keys and security badges to wear. We have no telephones in our rooms; we use the pay phone downstairs. Without telephone calling cards, dialing long distance is virtually impossible.

The telephone system in motels changes from town to town, and it is nerve-racking making long distance calls — some motels fail to post directions. In one there is only one telephone line and we can hear each other's conversations; in another, the line is always jammed and we are constantly cut off. Many times we do not receive messages or we receive the wrong messages or our callers are told that we are not registered at that motel.

The other difficulty is in finding nutritious, low-calorie meals. This seems to have been a major problem for turn-of-the-century Chautauquans, too, who claimed they needed "cast-iron stomachs."

Today, small Midwest towns typically have three restaurants: Pizza Hut, Hardee's, and a local cafe whose cook never drains grease. Chefs are good at all things deep fried. In this vast farm country it is surprising to learn that no one has ever heard of vegetables. In Oklahoma the breakfast menu consists of six different ways to serve biscuits and gravy.

In some towns there are no restaurants nor markets within walking distance, so I am jubilant one week to find myself lodged directly across the street from a supermarket with a superior delicatessen and a good salad bar, though it is difficult to select your dinner at a supermarket if you don't have a microwave. Several of us carry along coolers, but the one I buy requires ice every eight hours. Sometimes we try to have dinner at the tent where the local committee often sells hot dogs, lemonade, maybe popcorn, sometimes homemade pies.

We all look forward to wonderful home-cooked food at receptions and the after-show parties the local committees throw, though we never know if we'll be offered cheese and crackers or an entire meal. At the 5:00 P.M. affairs we can pretty much count on fruit cookies. One day I wind up eating only pizza and ice cream.

Once, I eat "dirt cake." During an extracurricular seminar in Alliance, Nebraska, a ten-minute break is called and we scholars are told we are being given a gift in the next room. It is a cake with crumbled Oreo cookies for dirt, decorated with "jubybeans" for worms, and topped with artificial flowers. Only we scholars are so treated because there isn't enough to pass to everyone.

There are also parties in homes away off on dirt roads, or next to Walden-Ponds-sans-trees. One is held at a fabulous old tumble-down dance hall used during the '20s and '30s. During the announcements, one person says, "This dance hall was shut down because the teenagers caused trouble," and a middle-aged woman next to me says under her breath, "It was not! We never gave any trouble."

In our third summer we have a night reception in a fabulous stable with six horses, bales of hay strategically placed, tiny fake mice set in appropriate corners, lighted trees that give a fairy-like Shakespearean feeling, a barnyard pathway with fence and gates trimmed with miniChristmas-tree lights and including two fountains with nymphlike statues, a one-hole golfcourse, a creek, and statues of pigs, piglets, alligators, and baboons.

Nights, sometimes, we hold our own parties under the Chautauqua tent after the community has vanished. Mark and Eagle bring in three large pizzas and a cooler full of beer and soft drinks. We sit on the edge of the platform and in the front row. We tear up the cardboard pizza boxes and use the pieces for plates (our Chautuaqua ritual), and make jokes and talk about the events of the day and criticize ourselves.

We laugh over the fact our Nathaniel Hawthorne speaks with a
Texas accent; talk about "Chautauquaholics," people who come back
year after year, and how great it is to get to know them; affirm we must
cut our monologues and dialogues, keeping them to forty minutes so
there'll be enough time for questions; remember how once I stood
in a patch of gnats during my adult workshop.

Or we mention our sea-captain-Margaret Fuller repartee: Herman
Melville (George Frein) vows to the audience he'll never be brutally
flogged on shipboard as other sailors were. When I, as Margaret
Fuller, come on stage, he quotes her most famous line advocating
women's equality: "Let women be sea captains, if they will!"   He
scornfully mocks: "Women as *sea captains?!* Hump! Sea captains,
indeed!" So I retaliate: "If women were sea captains, perhaps fewer
sailors would be flogged."

Anne Bail Howard and I brainstorm on how to keep the hooks
on high-button shoes from catching on skirt hems. (We covered
them with Scotch tape.) We pity nineteenth-century women who had
to wear tightly laced corsets even in summer. And how were their
long dresses kept clean when they had to walk on muddy roads? We
commiserate on how we couldn't have our costumes cleaned until
the end of the summer as no dry cleaner could have our elaborate
dresses ready in twenty-four hours.

Or we talk about our families and personal lives.

Ev Albers makes a special point to see we are not overscheduled.
Even so, in ten weeks we do not have one day off, unless you count
travelling on Wednesdays. We do have "hours off" and no
responsibilities on Thursdays — except laundry — until about five
or six o'clock when we raise the tent. (How do you get clothes clean
in a town like Chandler, Oklahoma, where there is no laundromat?
You know you're in a small town when you can't buy toothpaste at
four o'clock on Saturday afternoon because the drugstore is closed.)

The local committee often wants to show us their very special
community, and this cuts into free time.   Once, George Frein
remembers, the scholars had to tour a meat-packing plant. "I never
saw so many four-fingered people in all my life."

One group, in their enthusiasm to show us the Old Jules Sandoz
Trail, guides us about in several cars for a distance of ninety miles.
(Trekking about isn't exactly what we look forward to as we do

enough travelling on Wednesdays.) We stop at museums, historic markers, schoolhouses, and listen to talks, wait in lines to buy lunch, souvenirs, for bathrooms, etcetera. The best stop is yet to come at 4:30 P.M. when our Chautauqua moderator and monologuist apologize that we must head back to make it in time for the night's presentation. I know the committee is hurt.

People often comment that being a Chautauquan is a good way to vacation and see the country. Well, in Hays, Kansas, we give workshops in a fort which Custer made historic. During the summer of 1991 Anne Bail Howard and I do manage to have three-quarters of a day to drive through Deadwood, South Dakota, to see the Crazy Horse mountain carving and Mount Rushmore. Our van group does stop for half an hour at one scenic point in the Theodore Roosevelt National Park in the Badlands of North Dakota. In Alliance, Nebraska, it takes ten minutes to get to farmland featuring Carhenge, a group of old cars planted trunkend down in the ground and spray-painted to replicate Stonehenge. We see cyclists, tattoos, leather, and the sidewalk souvenir shops in Sturgis, South Dakota, the week before the famous motorcycle rendezvous, but we are gone before the thousands pull into town. At midnight, after the show, several of us drive into the Kansas grasslands and gaze at the vast diamondlike array of stars in the silent black heavens.

In 1992 Shelly Frein (George's wife) and I take off three-quarters of a day to drive through Arkansas' Ozark mountain country and to tour a cave. In 1993 George Frein arranges a stop in Salina, Kansas, at the Land Institute, a nonprofit experimental laboratory and museum run by beloved Wes Jackson and his family of students, who are devoted to alternatives in agriculture, energy, waste-management, and shelter.*

In North Platte, Nebraska, our tent is situated on the serene acreage of the Buffalo Bill Ranch State Historical Park where we see wild buffalo — Peterson notices they have the tang of an old factory.

And in Mitchell, South Dakota, the local host drives me along Firesteel Creek to the archaeological site of a prehistoric Indian

---

*It is Jackson's radical idea to develop a grain field seeded with a mixture of plants that will lie under the same live vegetative cover year after year, like a pasture, to reduce toxic chemicals and pollution.

village where we walk through a replica of a lodge which housed Plains Indian farmers a thousand years ago.

Moments are what we have for sight-seeing.

Our spouses and/or friends are encouraged to visit and travel along with us. The first year Frein, Radaker, Pace, and Mark Frein, all singles, have visitors whom they marry by the second and third years. Thus, Frein travels with his attractive bride, Shelly, who is soon to start work on her dissertation at Harvard, and Radaker is visited frequently by his lovely wife, Linda, an accountant. By the third year he and Linda are expecting a baby, and Mark and Nicole are our new tent-master husband-and-wife team. Also, in the third year, Pace announces that he'd taken wedding vows three days prior to Chautauqua. "How do you like married life?" we tease him. "I don't see there's much difference being married than being single," he jokes. Soon his bride, Yolantha, shows up and we celebrate with a dinner.

In the tradition of the "old" Chautauquas, every night under the tent there is a half-hour pre-show entertainment. The line-up used to include musical groups such as the Ladies' Regimental Orchestra, the Eleanor Olson Concert Company, Our Old Home Singers, the Philippino Singers, the Massey Five, Child's Hawaiian Singers, Ethiopian Serenaders, Negro choral groups. Or there were magicians, xylophonists, bagpipists, banjoists, accordionists, harpists, orchestras, bands, glee clubs, singers, yodelers, whistlers, acrobats, jugglers, bell ringers, tableau performers, puppetiers, monologuists, mimics, etcetera.

Today the list is similar: gospel singers, women's choruses, an elementary school choir, country western singers, barbershop quartets, Dixieland bands, guitar players, a harmonica-playing father, piano players, violinists, Indian ceremonial dancers, square dancers, ballerinas, etcetera.

Reading about the "old" days, one realizes entertainers were not always of the greatest ability, but they were all costumed and colorful. The same can be said about today's pre-shows, which are just as varied, sometimes good, but often tiresome and downright painful. Locally planned, they help to draw audiences, and give aspirants a marvellous opportunity to perform in a professional setting.

I especially remember one remarkable six-year-old boy dressed in a red and white striped vest, straw hat, white pants and shirt, who is such a showman he magnetizes the audience with songs for twenty-five minutes.

Another astounding woman must have fifty bells on a table on the stage which she rings into beautiful music.

A man in Goodland, Kansas makes extraordinary music out of an ordinary wood saw.

In Sidney, Nebraska, the Fort Sidney Colonels sing a medley of songs dedicated to us scholars.

In Seminole, Oklahoma a theater group dramatizes the heart-rending surrender of the great Chief Joseph of the Nez Perce tribe.

Once, before my monologue, a drama group holds center stage for an hour with a melodrama entitled, "Curse You, Otis Crumy or A Rip in Old Potter."

Each community also organizes their own "fringe" fun, such as old-fashioned box socials, auctions for box lunches, family picnics, pot luck dinners, nineteenth-century teas, tours of local historical establishments, local lectures, autograph parties for local writers, sing-alongs, hymn fests, nature walks, horse-drawn-wagon rides, train rides, museum open houses, walking tours to historic areas, heirloom and freedom quilting bees and exhibits, doll exhibits, art shows, skits and play readings, western bands and country musicals, benefit dances, lotteries to win something special like a Chautauqua china plate, fireworks, mixed doubles tennis tournaments, ballroom dancing, band concerts, grant-writing workshops, mobile testing units for hearing, glaucoma, vision and diabetes. In Marysville, Kansas, the post office conducts a special stamp cancellation in honor of the Great Plains Chautauqua on the Fourth of July.

Lecturers on the old Chautauqua circuit often gave their speeches over and over again. Russell H. Conwell gave his more than 6,000 times. "Old Reliable" William Jennings Bryan gave his Christian oration, "The Prince of Peace," more than 3,000 times. (It was said he had a mouth so big he could whisper in his ear.)

In the "old" Chautuaquas you had to have an uplifting message. You stirred people to greater political and social awareness. Thomas Mott Osborn spoke movingly of the need for prison reform. Maude

Ballington Booth urged more assistance for ex-convicts. Jacob Riis reminded Midwesterners of "How the Other Half Lives." Harvey Wiley called for better consumer legislation. Emmeline Pankhurst promoted women's suffrage. Jane Addams spoke of the need for settlement houses.

There couldn't be anything "off color," anything that would offend any religious or political view. If drinking or smoking were mentioned, it was condemned. Chautauqua had an unwritten moral code. Young ladies were to remain chaste. There is one story where a bureau sent a male representative out to to see if a young lady was "a good girl." When she fell for this man's "line," she lost her job.

The moral code of the day denigrated women who entered the theater, so those who performed in Chautauqua were not considered actresses. They were readers or elocutionists; they read entire plays or books in monologue form, or recited poems or stories. This was called "platform art."

Our forty-minute monologues and dialogues take some planning every week. Howard outlines what she's to say on index cards, studies them, and then improvises in front of the audience. Frein writes out complete sentences on yellow pads and remembers most of them. Watson re-reads Hawthorne's stories and readily brings forth the necessary words to narrate them. Radaker painstakingly memorizes long sections of Thoreau's writing, and Pace and I are so familiar with our one-person shows that we "cut and paste" appropriate portions to serve every occasion.

When we are assigned dialogues, each of us will plan to talk for about five minutes straight in about four separate segments. The two of us meet in the motel room and map out material that brings forward our characters' commonalities and diversities, thus building a conversation that stimulates audience questions. Sometimes we'll select topics for each five-minute section, such as "Childhood," "Work," "Travel," "Insights." Or we'll select an overall theme such as "Turning Points." We aim for a beginning and an ending, including a dramatic climax. We pinpoint cues so we each know when to take the limelight.

Pace and I often select an imaginary location and situation, such as backstage while our characters are waiting to go on stage to lecture. Our meeting is hypothetical since Fuller and Douglass never actually came face to face but, as actors, this does not bother us. Howard, however, feels a problem when Louisa May Alcott dialogues with Margaret Fuller, because Alcott was about eighteen when Fuller died and was too young to have formulated her ideas. She had only seen Fuller once or twice during her childhood. Howard feels that Alcott has little to say to Fuller and her end of the conversation is constrained and artificial. I can sympathize with this view, but I can also temporarily suspend historic time, and feel the audience is able to do the same. In contrast, Fuller and Henry David Thoreau have many opposing ideas to discuss since Fuller had edited (and rejected) his work on the *Dial* magazine. A conversation between Fuller and Hawthorne also works well because their relationship was complex and they can interact on many topics, plus Doug Watson and I found we could play up the sharp comments Fuller and Hawthorne made to friends about each other.

We are encouraged to change our monologues and dialogues every week. The value of this, as explained, is so we scholars won't get tired of our material. As an actor, I privately moan and groan about this concept.

An actor is trained to gain control by thoroughly testing out and knowing the material. He or she "tunes" delivery to a fine excellence. The art is to repeat it night after night with the same vitality and spontaneity.

To humanities people, the presentation is merely a stepping stone to the more important half — the question-and-answer session. To them what matters are the ideas that inspire thoughtful questions from the audience.

On the road, with the various pressures, there is little time to dig out and prepare new material every week so, in Chautauqua, we are encouraged to ad lib, to paraphrase, in fact, to improvise with new material that has never been tested. My colleagues cheer what is seen as the epitome of achievement, to present to the audience that which has never before been brought out.

While Pace and I have to extend our improvisational skills, the college professors have to work on dramatic-acting techniques. Frein as Melville, and Watson as Hawthorne, learn it's much more powerful to open their dialogues in Hawthorne's parlor with a table, a bottle of brandy, and two glasses. Hawthorne despairs because his wife Sophia won't allow them to smoke cigars, but he can at least offer Melville a glass of brandy.

Peterson as Whitman and Radaker as Thoreau find the perfect opening for their dialogue. Melville starts with the usual introduction when Thoreau enters and asks where Whitman is: "It's not like him to be late...Now I might lose my one and only opportunity to meet this great man...Well, since he's not here, I'll just take a moment to do something extremely important — I saw this wonderful wild-flower on my way here, and I just want to take another look at it. I'll be right back!" Thoreau exits and Whitman comes rushing down center aisle: "Sorry, I'm late — Where's Henry?" Melville explains. Whitman enthusiastically catalogues the many positive attributes of Thoreau, who soon returns. Melville introduces them and takes his leave. Left together, Henry and Walt sit down and then there is that kind of long awkward silence when no one can find anything to say. They bite their lips, they drink water, they look at the floor. Finally Walt criticizes Henry's work, whereupon Henry criticizes Walt's work. This is a stunning opening. The audience is with them all the way.

Personally, I face the greatest challenge when answering questions, such as: What happened to Transcendentalism and what is its place today?

If Fuller lived today, what would she be happiest about concerning the women's rights movement?

Would Fuller think a woman could be president of the United States? If Fuller lived today, what position in government would she like to have?

Did Fuller ever aspire to political office?

How did she view Marx?

Do you feel she was judgmental?

What were Fuller's thoughts on prostitution?

Did she ever subscribe to organized religion?

Would Fuller feel religion and government could be combined?

Would Fuller think women should go into combat?

What were the issues people were concerned about in the early nineteenth century?

How would you define literature?

What do you presume Fuller would have thought about the impact of her work?

There's an art to answering on-the-spot questions, which the college professors have perfected. They are able to fend the most exasperating, vague, and inarticulate questions. Often they "skirt" them, or proffer intellectual jargon with incredible common sense and good humor. They joke about this technique and encourage me to acquire the capability.

Once a young woman asks Henry David Thoreau, who wears white shirt and black pants with suspenders, why is he so well groomed, that is, isn't he supposed to be "woodsy"? Thoreau thinks for a moment and answers, "May I answer that question this way: Nature is my bride, and she does not object."

Radaker as Thoreau gets many questions such as, when he was living in the woods, didn't he take his laundry home for his mother to do. One audience member comments that he had visited Walden Pond and found his family could not camp there because there were no flush toilets, therefore, did Thoreau have a flush toilet at Walden Pond. Radaker thinks for a moment, then answers, "In my book, *Walden*, I write I have watered many a plant."

Once Watson as Hawthorne is asked what was he doing for twelve years when he stayed in seclusion in a house in Salem. He answers, "Waiting to see if there is a good enough reason for going out."

Sometimes we are asked questions our characters can in no way answer because our characters were not alive during the time period referred to. For instance, Melville is asked how he responded to the Freudian interpretation given to *Moby Dick*. Frein answers, "I don't know what you're talking about." But Frein does answer the question when he takes off his Melville role and becomes the twentieth-century scholar.

Often we are asked why wasn't Ralph Waldo Emerson chosen to be included in our character line-up. George Frein usually answers, "He didn't make the 'cut,'" which always gets a laugh.

He goes on to explain there is a limit as to the number of characters that can be selected for the Chautauqua budget and time. Even though Emerson is the major Transcendentalist, his work is too abstract, hard to "put across." Henry David Thoreau is a more articulate character, one who will draw forth questions. But, though Emerson is not physically present, he is here in spirit, because we constantly bring him to life through our references to him.

For adult workshops George Frein discusses *Billy Bud* or *Moby Dick.* Radaker examines *Walden,* Peterson analyzes *Leaves of Grass.* Howard talks about *Little Women* and Alcott's stories, and Pace as Frederick Douglass preaches a sermon in a local church on Sunday morning.

My adult workshop concerns Margaret Fuller's article, "The Great Lawsuit, Man vs. Men, Woman vs. Women," which she wrote for the *Dial* and was the basis for her most significant work, *Woman in the Nineteenth Century*.

I give a short introduction describing conditions and circumstances for women in the early 1800s. Then, I read my own edited version of her essay, and open the floor to discussion. There are many questions about Fuller's life but, since anyone can read about that, I encourage participants to respond personally and emotionally rather than intellectually. One women after another brings up the very same issues that Margaret Fuller brought forward a hundred and fifty years ago.

Carrol Peterson and I lunch at a nursing home. Though some of these elders remember the Chautauquas of the 1920s, they are not interested when Peterson or I talk on the mike. Why should they want to hear about a program they can never go to unless a daughter or son or friend obtains the permission and makes the transport arrangements?

Doug Watson and I are assigned to a crowded senior center for lunch. When we enter, the brusque woman in charge screams at the seniors, who are sitting at long tables eating a meal that looks less inviting than what is served in an elementary school.

"The Chautauquans are here! Now be quiet and listen to them! You can play your cards later."

Watson and I take about five minutes to talk about Chautauqua. Then our hostess marches us to one of the long tables where two places have been reserved with paper napkins on which she'd pencilled the word "guest." Tossing them aside, she commands,

"Now you sit here. I'm not giving extra privileges to guests. When it's time, you go up in line and get your food, and after you've eaten, you pick up your dishes and put them away."

With a harsh sigh so all can hear, she announces, "My sister came to visit me today, and she had a massive stroke."

A groan emanates from the seniors.

"I'm off to the hospital. If I'm pushing you, you know why. Are there any illnesses today?"

No one answers.

"Are there any birthdays?"

No one answers.

"Well, if not, then I'll leave."

She leaves.

We appear in costume for the children's workshops. Melville tells sea stories, Alcott narrates her children's stories as does Nathaniel Hawthorne. Henry David Thoreau takes youngsters on a nature hike. Walt Whitman gets boys and girls to write poetry using word games. Frederick Douglass vividly briefs on African-American culture.

I become the schoolmarm, Margaret Fuller, teaching in Bronson Alcott's Temple School in Boston. (Bronson Alcott was Louisa May Alcott's father.)

I seat the children in a semicircle and describe the typical one-room school in1836, noting that it is a *privilege* for children to go to school when schools are often too distant to walk to. I refer to rote memorization and recitation, and mention the differences in track-ing, how qualified boys enter Harvard, but how girls are given no formal schooling after the age of fourteen. I touch on how blacks are denied education, how poor children work in factories, and how colleges, even their libraries, are closed to girls.

Next, I lead a conversation on Conscience that Bronson Alcott conducted with his students. The conversation exists today exactly as it occured in 1836 because Margaret Fuller, as Alcott's assistant, recorded it. At the end, I pass out xeroxed pamphlets of it so that the children can compare their responses with what students said over a hundred and fifty years ago.

In Ada, Oklahoma, I am shaking inside after my first workshop. Fourteen twentieth-century children answered almost exactly as did the children from the nineteenth-century!

In a cavernous Shelter House in Yankton, South Dakota, there is a terrible echo which makes it difficult for me to be heard and develop group cohesion. I feel my session is falling apart. But afterwards two teachers compliment me on the participation I generated. The noise increased, they say, because the children were talking to each other about the ideas.

In Wayne, Nebraska, fifty children and adults are squeezed into a charming one-room schoolhouse, complete with bell tower, wood stove, dunce hat, and texts over a hundred years old. The windows cannot be raised, so on a hot afternoon it becomes extremely close, but the enthusiasm is rampant.

An adult comes up to me and says, "What a pity the children don't get this kind of teaching in school today. You see, the children *can* learn in this way. They *can* think on their own."

These workshops *must* continue to be given, I decide. So, after my third summer with Chautauqua, I write a descriptive book, *Outrageous Questions, Legacy of Bronson Alcott and America's One-Room Schools.** Hopefully, adults working with children will read it and continue to ask children the same questions Bronson Alcott asked.

Years ago, when Ev Albers was first organizing Chautauqua, a fellow South Dakotan who refused to pay taxes, asked if the program was funded with federal money.

Albers figured it out. Each person paid about two cents of their tax dollar for this humanities program.

The South Dakotan said, "I'd pay two cents any time for a program like this. I'll send the government two cents!"

Outrageous Questions, Legacy of Bronson Alcott and America's One-Room Schools, by Laurie James. New York, Golden Heritage Press, Inc., 1994.

CHOICES AND CHANGES

I did suffer burnout.

The solution: Stop.

Begin something else.

Think of Margaret Fuller as little as possible.

I used to begin work on Margaret Fuller weeks before a performance. Now, when a date comes my way, I don't begin to concentrate until three or four days earlier. For about forty-five minutes once or twice a day, I'll go through lines as fast as possible without exerting any effort. Perfect with the words, that's what I must be. Where the emotion is, what gestures to make, where I move from moment to moment — I know all that. I pray I can be spontaneous when I step on stage, to focus with the enthusiasm and energy that comes with first efforts.

I've come such a long ways since I'd first "sinned" by lying to launch my Margaret Fuller drama, so rabid was I to get on stage. My atonement — I hope — is that I've struggled to do my best and that I've accomplished something of what I'd wanted.

Yet I stand in the crosswinds that call for renewal and redefinition. That is the underside of achievement. Fulfillment brings about the stimulus of discontent. I embrace discontent. It is a sign of viability and progress. It opens the way for new levels of achievement.

But now is the time to re-read not only my current yearnings, but also the suggestions of choice that lie before me.

How can I leave Margaret Fuller? It took me so long to acquire the knowledge and skill, and it seems only right that I continue to share her in whatever ways I can...to help spread the large consciousness of her vision.

But powerful forces inside me begin to work .

Ramona was still sending me "flotsam jetsam bits & snips." She was at her two shrines, sink and stove, freezing her squash at 7 A.M. "How I long for Rapid Transit Lines."

We'd gone through a period where I'd write I had research to do in Boston libraries, and she'd write back, "NO, NO, No, HUSTLE!!!"

I'd write: "I've been working every day thinking I'd get this book done, and it is not done. By now, curses on it. But I'm committed; it's like a sick child, I can't abandon it, worse fate."

She'd respond: "Elizabeth Cady Stanton slowed Susan B. down by having babies. YOU slow me down by book obsession."

Now she was expressing that our twenty-year age gap was making a difference. She was: "Really not motivated for my 3 age-75-80 projects I have in head....At 55, Laurie (ole wives tale) women get 2nd breath. I dont wanna whine re my energy but it wanes plus my motivation."

She wanted to "heave and close up and out" her Margaret Fuller Center. Too much of a sweat...."I drone about keeping up with my 50-plus year old godmother (you) - the 20 year pace. Laurie I now become a boring bourgeose [sic.] worry wart & hate myself. MFF [Margaret Fuller Foundation] has been worth it as a launching base for grants.....Your MFF Laurie is eternal and we have such inroads & potentials but I'm IN IT over my head & I want OUT of the thick of it. A normal septuagenarian desire - I Hate to be normal but thats where my body & psyche are....You, my deah, are both mainstream AND cutting edge - avant guarde [sic.] & I admire it so much! I am periphery (everywhere) I belong no where really like MF! So on to our SOLO-DUO strategy deah Laurie. MFF is YOURS."

We remained friends, "tart as apples," as she commented. "We are each grooved in our faraway grooves for now. Amen."

In due time she wrote a play, *Anne Hutchinson — Divine Rebel*, and pressured Governor Michael S. Dukakis to pardon Anne

Hutchinson 350 years after her 1638 banishment from Massachusetts. She found a Maine actress, Ann Foskett, to play the part, and they toured it to Bowdoin College in Brunswick, and several other locations. She tried to get Anne Hutchinson honored on a U. S. postage stamp.

Ramona wrote: "I never say die...it is a geriatric tic and I must get over. I'm getting tuffer." You could compare her to the old saying, "When you're over the hill, you start to pick up speed."

Whenever I talked about being exhausted, she'd say: "I'm 80 and you're just a baby," or "But YOU...Jesus 20 yrs makes such a difference."

She signed her letters "Great Grandma Ramona," and noted that the Maine "Deer Hunters go bang bang - They didn't get me - I'm destined to stay alive."

She talked about changing her image from Mother Theresa to Mother Jones! "I wonder if we'll ever be like normal ole folk I doubt it nor you."

People gave Ramona "kudos" all the time *as a minister's wife* but she was writing: "Why, Laurie, can't I settle at my age for these accolades that I do have by the bushel basket? A rhetorical question - no answer."

One day I received from her an old Kings Chapel return postcard: "A cruel 3 months for Joe ends with his death, Oct 20." Her husband had had four throat operations for cancer as well as angina attacks. "Joe's books to theological school - Papers by truck to Harvard." He eventually had a room named after him in the Unitarian Universalist guest house on Beacon Hill.

Then she had back and leg pains. "Alone I moan and groan."

"DIRGE (Courtesy of Edna St. Vincent Millay) Laurie, my blood pressure IS hi (never before). My excesses are showing! Psyche & body!...Normal ageist misgivings."

"But," she wrote, "I don't shake, I don't slur - I don't overtalk. I know what pushin' 78 sins to avoid."

Her psyche was telling her she still had "young hustling energy," but her body was sending the message that she'd better be "cheering squad from afar."

There were many goals we hadn't accomplished that she'd like to launch: Like pressuring Harvard to give Margaret Fuller a posthumous degree. Staging a media event next to the John Harvard statue in Harvard Yard and next to the Margaret Fuller statue in the Harvard Square subway — "God, what press!!" Having Claire Booth Luce speak at one of my performances.* Donating my Margaret Fuller costume so she could display it in the Margaret Fuller Center.

Then the Reagan Administration cut the budgets of arts endowments.   Humanities councils held their breaths, waiting for the inevitable specifics to be announced. A successful filmmaker, who wanted to work with me on the Margaret Fuller story, called me in tears because her grant application for a film on the Jane Addams story had been slashed.

Though, as Ramona said, "It will continue, IF we make it happen," her "bombshell flashes" came in a half-hearted way: "Boston is still OURS for Susan B. and M. F. exhibit all of August!! However WHO WILL DO - Can you & I — ? Hate not to use. We both have normal abiguities....Laurie, You deah have made me feel so important I'm getting uppity."

One time she sent a quote from Emerson: "The reward of a thing well done is to have done it," with her hand written note: "You've done it, deah, lots."

Her ambiguous words brought me back to those seasons when I faced the negatives:

Go home and get married.

Unless you learn to sweep the kitchen floor, you can't be a good actress.

You are doing too many different things. You must focus on one thing.

You can't take criticism. You'll never be able to take direction from a director.

---

* Claire Booth Luce was first female U. S. ambassador to Italy — one hundred and three years after Margaret Fuller had written from Italy, "Another century, and I might ask to be made Ambassador myself...but woman's day has not yet come."

You can't adapt — you aren't flexible.

You don't know enough about people and the world.

You always say the wrong things to people.

You have no common sense.

You are stupid.

You're a snob.

You're fat.

You haven't got the right clothes.

You'd better get some rest.

Look at your face — terrible.

No one can live with anyone who is as perfect as you.

You can't say that line that way.

You don't understand the scene.

You have to do more than that on the stage.

You'll wear yourself out - you'll burn out.

You're lucky you don't have to make money.

If you'd listened to me —

Nobody cares about what you're doing.

You don't make any money or even cover expenses.

You can't get anywhere without a large organization behind you.

You don't know what you're doing and you'll see.

You're not professional.

You're another frustrated, foolish, old woman.

As long as you work with so-and-so, I cannot help you.

The theater is a rotten business. You'll see you won't like it when you get into it.

The theater isn't art; it's big business.

You don't have an agent.

You are spending all your time on publicity and promotion and you better spend some time on your acting.

Your children won't grow up to be well balanced if you don't stay home and take care of them.

Your family comes first; you haven't time for anything else.

Why don't you enjoy yourself instead of having those false dreams.

It's too hard, not worth it.

At this age — no one wants you — don't bother. You're ridiculous.

If you listen, you freeze.
You have to soar beyond.
You must satisfy yourself.
It is satisfying to know I committed to a challenge of my choice and overcame the negatives and failures.
It is satifying to trace the line of my own growth. How I'd broken through the verbal abuse...through the attitudes that had conditioned

my vulnerability. How I'd gained a depth of understanding of history and of our women's roots which had influenced what I was and am. How I'd journeyed to master the spoken and printed word. How each attempt and each success had bolstered my self-confidence, and how I humbly learned "it takes a village" — communities and audiences — to truly build the product of my choice.

You could hardly find the name of Margaret Fuller in libraries when I started. Now there are several biographies published — including my own books. No longer do you have to travel to Harvard's rare book library to read Fuller's letters in quill-pen scratchings — they are organized in clear-cut type and annotated in six volumes. There are reprints of her books and collections of her hard-to-find *Dial* and *Tribune* literary criticisms and articles. Scholars have issued analytical interpretations and she is included in authoritative listings. Students write their theses on her. Instead of people saying to me, "Margaret *who?*", I often get the reaction, "Oh yes, Margaret Fuller!"

Though surely many forces have combined to swell this resurgence of interest, how can I not feel that I did play a significant part? Ralph Waldo Emerson was right when he said one person can throw a stone into a river and it will radiate outward in influential circles. Margaret Fuller is beginning to have her rightful place in history.

Choose another unknown woman?

Not that I will ever "finish" Margaret Fuller.

Some people, like Margaret Fuller, just have so many layers that the discovery process becomes your renascence. One adventure into Fuller leads to the next, and each will be more fascinating than the last.

Commence a conversation about her. Allow others to ask you questions, as audiences have asked me. If you don't know the answer, you will have cause for celebration — because you will have to go somewhere or do something to find out. And that will take you on a merry chase.

Or — even riskier — start reading Fuller's book, *Woman in the Nineteenth Century*. Stop at her first reference you know nothing about, and go look it up. And do the same for the second reference, and so on. You will be enriched. There are endless paths through which she can guide your wanderings and thirsts.

I've searched for three years and haven't found another Margaret Fuller.

One thing I know, you have to hold on to your visions and dreams. You have to grab the confidence. One way I gained it was by reading about women of achievement.

Then when you "get to Harvard," you can share and give what you have to others.

Remember, to many people what you do is not worthwhile. They won't care about it.

Forge ahead because you want to, not because you think you're to earn money or power. Money and power can be secondary considerations.

You should do what you want to do.

As Ramona would say, "Life's shitwork should be shared."

We continually remake and adjust decisions. There is constant struggle to balance contradictory pulses. The excitement is the change yet-to-be.

You don't know if you'll succeed, but you have to run the Olympic event.

We all change; we do get older, that happens, probably for the best.

As Ramona would paraphrase Shakespeare, "The Past is Prologue."*

We tend to resist change, but we should look at it as our deserved reward. It is a breaking through. An improvement. It brings a new challenge, a new expectation.

Time moves, winds blow, waves ebb and flow. We do get to another place. We do mature, learn, become more accomplished, deepen.

"Success" is how you look at it. Success is your consciousness of experience, your involvement in the action you *need* to be involved in. Success is taking the risk of doing what you want to do, to help create a promise of a better world — or *something* better — and maybe that something is you.

---

*The Tempest, Act II, Scene I, "What's past is prologue."

As Ramona would say, "Failure is impossible, if you keep up chutspah."

"THRUST on!"

APPENDIX

PERFORMANCE SCHEDULE
OF
"MEN, WOMEN, AND MARGARET FULLER"

(Originally entitled *Still Beat Noble Hearts*, the title was changed in 1988 to *Men, Women, and Margaret Fuller*. This listing includes lectures and talks about Margaret Fuller and a few stagings of *O Excellent Friend!*, a three-character play written and performed by Laurie James which focuses on the relationship of Margaret Fuller and Ralph Waldo Emerson.)

1971   June 8   West Islip Library, West Islip, NY

        Nov. 5   Rose Villa Senior Citizen Center, Milwaukie, OR

        Dec. 7   Brandeis Meeting, Great Neck Public Library, NY

1972   May 31   West Islip Library, Islip, NY

        June 8   Gladstone Library, Gladstone, OR

1973   Nov. 9   Women's Studies Class, Dowling College, NY

1974   April 16   Wantagh Public Library, Wantagh, NY – Part I
Sponsored by Wantagh Community Arts Program
Partially funded by New York State Council on
the Arts

May 6   Community Free School, E. Setauket, NY

May 14   Wantagh Public Library, Wantagh, NY - Part II
Sponsored by Wantagh Community Arts Program
Partially funded by New York State Council on
the Arts

1977   May 4   Wantagh Public Library, Wantagh, NY - Part II
Sponsored by Wantagh Community Arts Program
Partially funded by New York State Council on
the Arts

May 8   New York State Conference for Women,
Albany, NY
New York State Education Department

Sept. 14   South Shore NOW, Bellport, NY

Sept. 16   NOW State Meeting, Kings Grant Inn, Plainview, NY

Oct. 3   C. W. Post College, Hillwood Commons Lecture
Hall, Greenvale, NY
Sponsored by Women's Center

Oct. 26   Queens NOW (All The Queens Women),
Flushing, NY

Dec. 9   East End Arts & Humanities Council, East End
Arts Center, Riverhead, NY

Dec. 11   Unitarian Universalist Fellowship, Setauket, NY

1978   March 2   Little Theater, Roosevelt Hall, Farmingdale
College Women's Conference, State University
of New York at Farmingdale, NY

March 12   Sienna Women's Center, The Molloy Forum, Molloy College, Rockville Center, NY

March 18   Eastern Central Theater Conference, White Plains Hotel, White Plains, NY

March 27   Half Hollow Hills Library, Dix Hills, NY

June 11   Old Bethpage Village Restoration, Nassau County Museum, Old Bethpage, NY

July 20   Saratoga Arts Festival, Saratoga, NY, New York State Education Dept.

Sept. 19   Wantagh Senior Citizens, Lido Beach, NY
            Sponsored by Wantagh CAP

Sept. 29   East Meadow Library, East Meadow, NY
            Co-sponsored by Nassau County Office of Cultural Development and Wantagh CAP

Oct. 22   Peninsula Public Library, Lawrence, NY
            Co-sponsored by Nassau County Office of Cultural Development and Wantagh CAP

Nov. 10   Westbury Library, Westbury, NY
            Co-sponsored by Nassau County Office of Cultural Development and Wantagh CAP

Nov. 20   Oyster Bay Chapter of Daughters of American Revolution, Raynham Hall, Oyster Bay, NY

Nov. 28   Hempstead Library, Hempstead, NY
            Co-sponsored by Nassau County Office of Cultural Development and Wantagh CAP

Nov. 30   Great Neck Library, Great Neck, NY
            Co-sponsored by Nassau County Office of Cultural Development and Wantagh CAP

Dec. 15   Wantagh High School, Wantagh, NY
            Sponsored by Wantagh CAP

1979 Feb. 14   Susan B. Anthony Day Celebration, South Senior High School, Great Neck, NY

Feb. 15   Susan B. Anthony Day Celebration, North Senior High School, Great Neck, NY

March 5   Brighton Senior Citizens; Mayor's Voluntary Action Center, Brighton, NY

March 28 Carle Place High School, Carle Place, NY

April 1   North Shore Unitarian Universalist Society, Plandome, NY
Sponsored by Women's Group

May 5   Unitarian Universalist Women's Federation Biennial Convention; National 4-H Center, Washington, D. C.

May 23   Baldwin High School, Baldwin, NY

May 27   Morristown Unitarian Universalist Fellowship, Morristown, NJ

June 1   Calhoun High School, Bellmore, NY

June 27   Unitarian Universalist General Assembly (Conference) Michigan State University, E. Lansing, MI

July 19   Margaret Fuller Day proclaimed by Mayor Frank Duehay, Harvard University, Longfellow Hall, Radcliffe College, Cambridge, MA
Sponsored by ArtiCulture & others

Nov. 12   American Association of Retired Persons, Maspeth, NY

Dec. 7   Unitarian Universalist LIAC Dinner, Freeport, NY

Dec. 29   Margaret Fuller Day proclaimed by Mayor Ed Koch

Lincoln Center Library & Museum of
Performing Arts, New York, NY, Bruno Walter
Auditorium, Reception by North Shore Unitarian
Society, Inc. Women's Group
Sponsored by the Margaret Fuller Foundation

1980   Jan. 12   Palo Alto UU District Delegate Meeting
Palo Alto, CA
Sponsored by Women-In-Transition

Jan. 15   Marin UU Fellowship, Marin, CA
Sponsored by Women-In-Transition

Jan. 18   Monterey Peninsula College, Monterey, CA
Sponsored by Women-In-Transition, MPC
Community Services

Jan. 20   Margaret Fuller Day proclaimed by Mayor Diane
Feinstein
First Unitarian Church, San Francisco, CA
Sponsored by Women-In-Transition

Jan. 21   UU Berkeley Fellowship, Berkeley, CA,
Sponsored by Women-In-Transition

Jan. 25   Santa Barbara UU Society, Santa Barbara, CA
Sponsored by Women-In-Transition

Jan. 26   Palos Verdes-Pacific UU Church, Palos Verdes, CA
Sponsored by Women-In-Transition

Jan. 27   First Unitarian Church of Los Angeles, CA
Sponsored by Women-In-Transition

Jan. 29   First Unitarian Church, San Diego, CA, Part I
Proceeds to help ratify E.R.A.
Sponsored by Women-In-Transition, Church Social
Responsibility-Service Committee, UU Women's
Federation

Feb. 15 Unitarian Church, Arlington, Virginia
Partially funded by VEATCH

Feb. 16 Lockwood Mathews Museum, Norwalk, CT

March 9 Winchester Unitarian Society, Winchester, MA
Partially funded by VEATCH

March 23 The Channing Series, "I Call That Mind Free,"
Agassiz Theater, Radcliffe Yard, presented
by the Cambridge Forum in cooperation with the
William Ellery Channing Bicentennial Celebra-
tion Committee of the Unitarian Universalist
Association and the Institute of Politics;Video
Taping at Channel 56, Cambridge, MA,
co-sponsored by the First Parish in Cambridge, the
Lowell Institute, the M.I.T. Chaplains, the
United Ministry at Harvard and Radcliffe

March 29 Meetinghouse, Unitarian Universalist Society,
Manchester, CT
Partially funded by VEATCH

April 13 Metro District UU Meeting, Paramus, NJ

April 25 Long Island Area Council UU Dinner Meeting,
Flushing UU Church, Flushing, NY

May 2 First Unitarian Church, Des Moines, IA
Partially funded by VEATCH

May 3 Unitarian Church, Lincoln, NE
Partially funded by VEATCH

May 4 A.M. First Raymond B. Bragg Symposium
All Souls Unitarian Church, Kansas City, MO
Partially funded by VEATCH

May 4 P.M. First Unitarian Church, Omaha, NE
Co-sponsored by Second Unitarian Church of
Omaha, individual sponsors, and partially funded
by VEATCH

May 18   First Parish, Lexington, MA
              Sponsored by Women's Alliance and the Barbara
              Garland Drama Fund

May 20   Unitarian Universalist Fellowship, Midland, MI
              Partially funded by VEATCH

May 22   First Unitarian Church, Pittsburgh, PA
              Partially funded by VEATCH

June 10   Instituto Mexicano Norteamericano de Relaciones
              Culturales, Mexico City, Mexico

July 3-4   Boston Jubilee 350, Boston Center for the Arts,
              Boston, MA
              Sponsored by City of Boston and Margaret Fuller
              Foundation (to coincide with the opening of
              Judy Chicago's exhibit, *The Dinner Party*)

July 6   Center for Music, Drama and Art, Lake Placid, NY

Aug. 26   City Theater, Biddeford, ME
              Sponsored by Margaret Fuller Foundation with a
              grant from Maine Council for the Humanities and
              Public Policy; Margaret Fuller Day, proclaimed
              by Mayor John J. O'Leary, Jr.

Aug. 29   Wieden Auditorium, University of Maine at
              Presque Isle, ME
              Sponsored by Margaret Fuller Foundation with a
              grant from Maine Council for the Humanities and
              Public Policy

Aug. 31   Hancock Auditorium, Ellsworth, ME
              Sponsored by Margaret Fuller Foundation with a
              grant from Maine Council for the Humanites and
              Public Policy

Sept. 19   Edward Muskie Auditorium, Rumford High
              School, Rumford, ME
              Sponsored by Margaret Fuller Foundation with a
              grant from Maine Council for the Humanities and
              Public Policy

Sept. 21   Kresge Theater, Bowdoin College, Brunswick, ME
              Sponsored by Margaret Fuller Foundation with a
              grant from Maine Council for the Humanities and
              Public Policy

Sept. 26   Homecoming Weekend, Murray Grove, NJ

Oct. 3   Muhlenberg College, Allentown, PA
              Sponsored by College Convocations Committee
              with the help of the Lehigh Valley Association
              for Academic Women

Oct. 18   Mass Bay District Fall Conference, First Parish,
              Cambridge, MA

Nov. 2   Port Washington Public Library - Part II   –
              Port Washington, NY
              Sponsored by Nassau County Library System and
              Wantagh CAP, with a grant from New York
              Council on the Humanities

Nov. 3   Henry Waldinger Memorial Library, Valley Stream, NY
              Sponsored by Nassau County Library System and
              Wantagh CAP, with a grant from New York
              Council on the Humanities

Nov. 6   Wantagh Public Library, Wantagh, NY - Part II
              Sponsored by Nassau County Library System and
              Wantagh CAP, with a grant from New York
              Council on the Humanities

Nov. 7   Nineteenth Century Women Writers Interna-
              tional Conference, Student Center, Hofstra Uni-
              versity, Hempstead, NY – Part II
              Sponsored by Hofstra College of Liberal Arts and
              Sciences and Nassau County Office of Cultural
              Development

Nov. 8   North Shore Unitarian Universalist Society, Inc.,
              Caberet Theater, Plandome, NY

Nov. 13   Uniondale Public Library

Sponsored by Nassau County Library System and Wantagh CAP, with a grant from New York Council for the Humanities

Nov. 18   Seaford Public Library, Seaford, NY
Sponsored by Nassau County Library System and Wantagh CAP, with a grant from New York Council for the Humanities

Nov. 20   Hewlett-Woodmere Library, Hewlett, NY
Sponsored by Nassau County Library System and Wantagh CAP, with a grant from New York Council for the Humanities

Nov. 23   Manhasset Public Library, Manhasset, NY
Sponsored by Nassau County Library System and Wantagh CAP, with a grant from New York Council for the Humanities

Dec. 1   Baldwin Public Library, Baldwin, NY - Part II
Sponsored by Nassau County Library System and Wantagh CAP, with a grant from New York Council for the Humanities

Dec. 2   Oceanside Free Library, Oceanside, NY
Sponsored by Nassau County Library System and Wantagh CAP, with a grant from New York Council for the Humanities

Dec. 4   Shelter Rock Public Library, Shelter Rock, NY
Sponsored by Nassau County Library System and Wantagh CAP, with a grant from New York Council for the Humanities

Dec. 6   New Hyde Park Public Library, New Hyde Park, NY
Sponsored by Nassau County Library System and Wantagh CAP, with a grant from New York Council for the Humanities

Dec. 7   Stenson Memorial Library, Sea Cliff, NY
Sponsored by Nassau County Library System and Wantagh CAP, with a grant from New York Council for the Humanities

Dec. 22   Staged Reading, Theater Off-Park, New York, NY

1981 Jan. 12   Huntington NOW Benefit, New Community
                      Cinema, Huntington, NY

Jan. 24   Center for Music, Drama and Art, Part I
                      Lake Placid, NY

Jan. 25   Center for Music, Drama and Art, Part II
                      Lake Placid, NY

Feb. 25   Dickinson College, Carlisle, PA
                      Sponsored by Margaret Fuller Foundation with a
                      grant from The Public Committee for the Humanities
                      in Pennsylvania

Feb. 17   Franklin & Marshal College, Lancaster, PA
                      Sponsored by Margaret Fuller Foundation with a grant
                      from The Public Committee for the Humanities
                      in Pennsylvania

Feb. 19   Lock Haven State College, Lock Haven, PA
                      Sponsored by Margaret Fuller Foundation with a
                      grant from The Public Committee for the Humanities
                      in Pennsylvania

Feb. 23   Cambria County Library, Johnstown, PA
                      Sponsored by Margaret Fuller Foundation with a
                      grant from The Public Committee for the Humanities
                      in Pennsylvania

Feb. 26   Penn State University, Capital Campus,
                      Harrisburg, PA
                      Sponsored by Margaret Fuller Foundation with a
                      grant from The Public Committee for the Humanities
                      in Pennsylvania

March 1   Goddard Chapel, Tufts University, Medford, MA
                      Sponsored by Chapel Arts Series

March 2   Albright College, Reading, PA
                      Sponsored by Margaret Fuller Foundation with a

grant from The Public Committee for the Humanities in Pennsylvania

March 17   Kutzton State College, Allentown, PA
            Sponsored by Margaret Fuller Foundation with a grant from Pennsylvania Humanities Council

April 2   Lycoming College, Williamsport, PA
            Sponsored by Margaret Fuller Foundation with a grant from The Public Committee for the Humanities in Pennsylvania

April 7   Citizens Library, Washington, PA
            Sponsored by Margaret Fuller Foundation with a grant from The Public Committee for the Humanities in Pennsylvania

April 11   The Unitarian Society, New Haven, CT, Part I
            Sponsored by the Unitarian Women's Association

April 14   Lockwood-Mathews Museum, Norwalk, CT Part II

April 24   Accent on Women Conference, Community Arts Theater, University of Wisconsin, Madison, WI
            Co-Sponsored by UW-Parkside-UW-Extension Gateway Technical Institute's Women's Bureau, partially supported by a grant from UW-Parkside's Lecture and Fine Arts Committee

April 29   Quincy Public Library, Quincy, MA
            Sponsored by Cambridge Multicultural Art Center with a grant from Massachusetts Foundation for the Humanties and Public Policy

April 30   Cambridge Public Library, Cambridge, MA
            Sponsored by Cambridge Multicultural Arts Center with a grant from Massachusetts Foundation for the Humanities and Public Policy

May 3   Free Library, Philadelphia, PA
            Sponsored by Margaret Fuller Foundation with

a grant from The Public Committee for the Humanities in Pennsylvania

May 10   Allentown Art Museum, Allentown, PA, Part II
Sponsored by Margaret Fuller Foundation with a grant from The Public Committee for the Humanities in Pennsylvania

May 13   Newton Art Center, Newton, MA
Sponsored by Cambridge Multi-Cultural Arts Center with a grant from Massachusetts Foundation for the Humanities and Public Policy

May 14   Milton Public Library, Milton, MA
Sponsored by Cambridge Multi-Cultural Arts Center with a grant from Massachusetts Foundation for the Humanities and Public Policy

May 15   Sommerville Library, Sommerville, MA
Sponsored by Cambridge Multi-Cultural Arts Center with a grant from Massachusetts Foundation for the Humanities and Public Policy

May 16   Hyde Park Library, Hyde Park, MA
Sponsored by Cambridge Multi-Cultural Arts Center with a grant from Massachusetts Foundation for the Humanities and Public Policy

May 19   Museum of Fine Arts, Lecture Hall, Boston, MA
Sponsored by Cambridge Multi-Cultural Arts Center by a grant from Massachusetts Foundation for the Humanities and Public Policy with additional funding from Massachusetts Council on the Arts and Humanities and the Cambridge Arts Council

May 20   Melrose Public Library, Melrose, MA
Sponsored by Cambridge Multi-Cultural Arts Center with a grant from Massachusetts Foundation for the Humanities and Public Policy

May 21   Central Square Library, Cambridge, MA, Part II
Margaret Fuller Day proclaimed by Mayor Frank

Duehay
Sponsored by Multi-Cultural Arts Center with a
grant from Massachusetts Foundation for the
Humanities and Public Policy, the Massachusetts
Council on the Arts and Humanities, and the
Cambridge Arts Council

May 26   East Cambridge Library-Heritage Center, Part II
Sponsored by Cambridge Multi-Cultural Art
Center with a grant from Massachusetts Founda-
tion for the Humanities and Public Policy, the
Massachusetts Council on the Arts and Humani-
ties, and the Cambridge Arts Council

May 27   Lincoln Public Library, Lincoln, MA
Sponsored by Cambridge Multi-Cultural Arts
Center with a grant from Massachusetts Founda-
tion for the Humanities and Public Policy

May 28   Lowell City Library, Lowell, MA
Sponsored by Cambridge Multi-Cultural Arts
Center with a grant from Massachusetts Founda-
tion for the Humanities and Public Policy

May 30   Womyn's Theater Festival-1981, Studio Red Top,
Boston, MA
Produced by Feminist Amerikan Theater

July 11   Mt. Battie and Camden Opera House, Camden, ME
Margaret Fuller/Edna St. Vincent Millay Day.
Ceremony on top of Mt. Battie with "Renascence" read
by Laurie James where Millay wrote the poem with
remarks from Buckminster Fuller, Ramona Barth,
followed by dramatic presentation at Opera House.
Sponsored by Margaret Fuller Foundation

Aug. 9   Margaret Fuller Day, Suffolk County
Fire Island Festival of Women in the Arts,
Ocean Beach Community Center, Fire
Island, NY
Co-sponsored by the Margaret Fuller Founda-
tion and an ad hoc committee of women.

Oct. 18   Margaret Fuller Ossoli Square Dedication
Congregational Church, Cambridge, MA
Sponsored by City of Cambridge, Multi-Cultural
Arts Center, Cambridge Historical Commission,
Cambridge Arts Council, Community Develop-
ment Department, Radcliffe College, Depart-
ment of Human Service Programs, and Margaret
Fuller Foundation

Oct. 23   New Hampshire-Vermont District Fall Conference, Concord Unitarian Church, Concord, NH
Partially funded by VEATCH

Oct. 24   Unitarian Universalist Church, Portsmouth, NH
Sponsored by members and friends of the UU
Church of Portsmouth
Partially funded by VEATCH

Oct. 25   First Parish Unitarian Universalist Church,
Arlington, MA
Partially funded by VEATCH

Oct. 27   The Unitarian Church, Peterborough, NH
Sponsored by Unitarian Churches of
Peterborough and Wilton Center.
Partially funded by VEATCH

Oct. 28   All Souls Church, Brattleborough, VT
Partially funded by VEATCH

Oct. 29   The First Universalist Society, Hartland Four
Corners, VT   Sponsored by the Twin State Area
Ministry in Ascutney and the North Universalist
Chapel Society in Woodstock, VT
Partially funded by VEATCH

Nov. 2   Roseman Auditorium, University of Wisconsin,
Whitewater, WI
Sponsored by Wisconsin Humanities Committee
and University of Wisconsin-Extension

Nov. 3   Civic Center Campus, University of Wisconsin,
Milwaukee, WI

Sponsored by Wisconsin Humanities Committee
and University of Wisconsin-Extension

Nov. 4   Riverview School, University of Wisconsin,
            Manitowoc, WI
            Sponsored by Wisconsin Humanities Committee
            and Unversity of Wisconsin-Extension

Nov. 5   UW Center, Theater, Marinette, University of
            Wisconsin, Marinette, WI
            Sponsored by Wisconsin Humanities Committee
            and University of Wisconsin-Extension

Nov. 6   University Fine Arts Theater, University of
            Wisconsin, Marshfield, WI
            Sponsored by Wisconsin Humanities Committee
            and University of Wisconsin-Extension

Nov. 7   UW, Kathryn Ohman Theater-McCaskill, Univer-
            sity of Wisconsin, Superior, WI
            Sponsored by Wisconsin Humanities Committee
            and University of Wisconsin-Extension

Nov. 8   Pump House, University of Wisconsin
            La Crosse, WI
            Sponsored by Wisconsin Humanities Committee
            and University of Wisconsin-Extension

Nov. 9   UW Copper Top Theater, University of Wisconsin
            Richland Center, WI
            Sponsored by Wisconsin Humanities Committee
            and University of Wisconsin-Extension

Nov. 10   McMillan Memorial Library Arts Theater
            University of Wisconsin, Wisconsin Rapids, WI
            Sponsored by Wisconsin Humanities Committee
            and University of Wisconsin-Extension

Nov. 15   UU Church, Swampscott, MA
            Partially funded by VEATCH

Dec. 2   Instituto Mexicano Norteamericano de Relaciones
            Culturales, Mexico City, Mexico

Dec. 4		Instituto Mexicano Norteamericano de Relaciones Culturales, Guadalajara, Mexico
Dec. 8		Instituto Mexicano Norteamericano de Relaciones Culturales, Monterey, Mexico
Dec. 10 & 12		Instituto Mexicano Norteamericano de Relaciones Culturales, Mexico City, Mexico
1982	Jan. 10	First Unitarian Church, Brooklyn Heights, NY, Part II
	Jan. 16	Herrschaft Cultural Series, First Unitarian Church of Miami, FL
	Feb. 7	The First Parish in Weston, MA Presented by the Denominational Affairs Committee
	Feb. 12	First Unitarian Church of Monmouth County, Lincroft, NJ
	March 14	The Unitarian Church, Westport, CT, Parts I & II Sponsored by Women's Alliance
	March 25	Hasty Pudding Theater, Parts I & II Sponsored by Focus WIRE, Junior League of Boston, Cambridge, MA
	March 27	ERA Fund Raiser, Parts I & II, North Shore Unitarian Universalist Society, Inc., Plandome, NY Sponsored by Women's Group
	April 16	Unitarian Church of Fresno, CA Also sponsored by American Civil Liberties Union, Central Valley Pro-Choice Coalition, Coalition of Labor Union Women, Fresco Co. Democratic Women's Club, National Organization of Women, Planned Parenthood of Fresno, Women's Interantional League for Peace and Freedom
	April 24	First Unitarian Church, San Diego, CA, Part II

June 9   "O Excellent Friend!"
                Drama about Fuller and Emerson
                The Unitarian Universalist Church of Central
                Nassau, Garden City, NY

June 11   "O Excellent Friend!"
                UU Fellowship of Muttontown, NY

June 18   "O Excellent Friend!"   North Shore Unitarian
                Universalist Society, Inc., Plandome, NY

June 22   "O Excellent Friend!"
                UU General Assembly, Kresge Auditorium
                Bowdoin College, Brunswick, ME
                Sponsored by MSUU (Ministerial Sisterhood),
                The Emerson Committee, UU Historical Society,
                UUWF, Women in Religion, Denominational
                Affairs   Comm.,   North   Shore   Unitarian
                Universalist Society, Inc., Plandome, NY

Oct. 31   Edgecomb Town Hall, Midcoast Unitarian
                Universalist Fellowship, Edgecomb, ME

Nov. 7   All Souls Unitarian Church, Augusta, ME
                Sponsored by Margaret Fuller Forum

1983   March 5   Women's History Week,
                Unitarian Universalist Society, Stamford, CT
                Sponsored by UU Women of Stamford
                Partially funded by VEATCH

March 8   Bingham Humanities Building
                Women's History Week
                University of Louisville, Louisville, KY
                Sponsored by Women's Studies Committee and
                the Arts and Sciences Student Council

March 13   First Unitarian Church, Brooklyn Heights, NY, Part I
                Sponsored by Women's Alliance

April 4   "The One Woman Show Series"
                Muhlenberg Branch Library, New York, NY

Sponsored by Women In Theater, Network Inc.
and New York Public Library

Aug. 26   Network NCO Club, Celebration of Women's
Equality Day, Fort Gordon, Augusta, GA
Sponsored by USASC Federal Women's Program
and the Garden City of Federally Employed
Women

Aug. 29   Unitarian Church, Augusta, GA

Oct 9-10   City Theater, Hong Kong
Sponsored by Hong Kong Urban Cultural
Presentations

Oct. 12   Hong Kong Baptist College, Kowloon, Hong
Kong

Nov. 13   Channing Memorial Church, Newport, RI
Sponsored by Narragansett Cluster of Unitarian-
Universalist Churches
Partially funded by VEATCH
Publicized by NOW, the Business and Profes-
sional Women's Association, and Shirley Schiff
and Helen Steeves of Second Technical Day

Dec. 1   Armstrong Hall, Cornell College, Mt. Vernon, IA

1984   Feb. 21   Lecture, University of California at Berkeley,
Women's Center, Berkeley, CA

March 13   Women's Week '84, Ruby Diamond Auditorium,
Florida State University, Tallahassee, FL
Sponsored by The FSU Women's Eductional &
Cultural Center and School of Theater, Women's
Studies, English Department

March 14   Little Theater, Smithtown High Schhool East,
American Association of University Women,
Smithtown, NY

April 23-24 Community College of Rhode Island
Lincoln Campus, Providence, RI
Sponsored by Flanagan Campus Student Senate
and CCRI Theater

June 1-2-3 The Berkshire Conference of Women Historians
Smith College, Northampton, MA

June 24-28 National Women's Studies Conference
Rutgers University, NJ

Oct. 25 NY Institute of Technology, Old Westbury, NY
A public service program co-sponsored by NYIT's
Office of Student Services and Nassau County
Office of Cultural Development

Dec. 31 The Quaigh Theater Dramathon, New York, NY

1985 March 8 Women's Week, Shoreham-Wading River Public
Library, Shoreham-Wading River, NY

March 10 Bellport Unitarian Fellowship, Bellport, NY

March 12-13 Women's History Month, Russell Sage College,
Troy, NY

March 28 Gamma Lounge, Suffolk Community College,
Brentwood, NY

April 2 Bowdoin College, Brunswick, ME

April 13 North Bellmore Public Library, Bellmore, NY

May 10-11 Performance and lecture, Alderwood Hall and
Lucy Stern Hall Western Association of Women
Historians Conference, Mills College, Oakland, CA

August 19 "Life On A Star" Conference
Star Island, Isle of Shoals, NH

Oct. 2   "Community as Classroom" Lecture series-performance, in honor of 350th anniversary of the founding of Concord, sponsored by Concord-Carlisle Adult and Community Education, Concord-Carlisle Human Rights Council, the Concord Museum, Orchard House, and the Thoreau Lyceum, Concord Adult Education, Concord Academy, Concord, MA

1986   April 26   County Line Fair, North Shore Unitarian Universalist Society, Inc., Plandome, NY

Oct. 18   "Daughters of the Revolution"
Unitarian Universalist Fall Renewal Conference
Murray Grove, NJ

Nov. 3   D'n'A Reading Series, Actor's Outlet, New York, NY

1987   Oct. 14   Unitarian Universalist Association Headquarters, Chapel, Boston, MA

Oct. 20   Dedication of the Margaret Fuller Room at the Marriott Hotel, Kenmore Square
Cambridge, MA

Oct. 21   Dedication of the Margaret Fuller plaque
Cambridge City Hall, Cambridge, MA
Sponsored by City of Cambridge, Cambridge Historical Commission and The Margaret Fuller Network

1988   Feb. 2   Talk, Community Church, New York, NY

March 4-6-11-13-18-20-25-27
The Thirteenth Street Theater, New York, NY

March 9   Talk, Hunter College, Women's Center, New York, NY

March 13   Flushing Unitarian-Universalist Church, Flushing, NY

March 16   YMCA, 53rd Street, Sponsored by Women-in-Theater
            New York, NY

March 22   Talk, Suffolk Community College, Selden, NY

March 24   Talk, Molloy College, Rockville Center, NY

March 26   Talk, Brooklyn Unitarian Church, Brooklyn, NY

March 27   Talk, AAUW, Pen & Brush, New York, NY

March 30   Sagamore Hill National Historic Site
            Oyster Bay, NY
            Sponsored by United States Department of the
            Interior

April 6-7-8-10-13-17-20-27
            The Thirteenth Street Repertory Theater
            New York, NY

April 24   Keene Unitarian Universalist Church, Keene, NH

May 1   Muttontown Unitarian Universalist Fellowship,
            E. Norwich, NY

May 4   Brescia Hall
            The Elvira M. Dowell '36 Memorial Program,
            College of New Rochelle, New Rochelle, NY,
            a gift from George M. Dowell

May 7   Women's Vote Rally, Huntington NOW
            Huntington, NY

May 14   Keynote, Delta Kappa Gama Keynote Speech,
            New York State Convention President's
            Banquet, Mariott Hotel, Uniondale, NY

May 24   Saint Agnes Branch, New York Public
            Library, New York, NY

May 15-22-29
            The Thirteenth Street Repertory Theater, NY, NY

June 5-12   The Thirteenth Street Repertory Theater, NY, NY

July 3-10-17-24-31
             The Thirteenth Street Repertory Theater, NY, NY

Aug. 14-Sept. 2   The Edinburgh Fringe Festival, Royal Scots
             Club, Edinburgh, Scotland (Nine performances)

Aug. 19   Talk, "Margaret Fuller's Experiences in Edinburgh"
             Musselburgh Library, Edinburgh, Scotland

Sept. 11-18-25
             The Thirteenth Street Repertory Theater, NY, NY

Oct. 2-9-16-23-30
             The Thirteenth Street Repertory Theater, NY, NY

Oct. 6   Shelter Rock Public Library, Albertson, NY

Oct. 7   Women In Performance, NY University, NY, NY

Nov. 2   Special Performance, Women's History Group
             The Thirteenth Street Repertory Theater, NY, NY

Nov. 13-20-27
             The Thirteenth Street Repertory Theater, NY, NY

Dec. 4-11-18
             The Thirteenth Street Repertory Theater, NY, NY

1989   January 1-8-15-22-29
             The Thirteenth Street Repertory Theater, NY, NY
            February 5-12-19-26
             The Thirteenth Street Repertory Theater, NY, NY

           March 5-12-19-26
             The Thirteenth Street Repertory Theater, NY, NY

           March 13   Molloy College, Rockville Center, NY

March 19   Unitarian Universalist Ocean County Congrega-
            tion, Murray Grove, Lanoka Harbor, NJ

March 22   Suffolk Community College, Selden, NY

March 26   County Line Unitarian Universalist Fellowship,
            Amityville, NY

March 31   Manhattan Plaza, New York, NY

April 2-9-16-23-30
            The Thirteenth Street Repertory Theater, NY, NY

April 18   Fortnightly Club, Masonic Temple
            Rockville Center, NY

May 7-21-28
            The Thirteenth Street Repertory Theater, NY, NY

May 13   First Parish, Norwell Center, Norwell, MA

June 4-11-18-25
            The Thirteenth Street Repertory Theater, NY, NY

July 2-9-14-15-16-21-22-23-28-29-30
            The Thirteenth Street Repertory Theater, NY, NY

Aug. 6-13   The Thirteenth Street Repertory Theater, NY, NY

Sept. 3-10-17-24
            The Thirteenth Street Repertory Theater, NY, NY

Sept. 19   Keen College, Union City, NJ

Oct. 1-8-15-22-19
            The Thirteenth Street Repertory Theater, NY, NY

Nov. 5-12-19-26
            The Thirteenth Street Repertory Theater, NY, NY

Dec. 3-10-17-31
            The Thirteenth Street Repertory Theater, NY, NY

1990   Jan. 7-14-21-28

          The Thirteenth Street Repertory Theater, NY, NY

        Feb. 4-11-18-25

          The Thirteenth Street Repertory Theater, NY, NY

        March 4-11-18-25

          The Thirteenth Street Repertory Theater, NY, NY

        March 9-10-11

          Staged Readings, "O Excellent Friend!"
          Medicine Show Theater Ensemble, NY, NY

        March 27   SB Union Auditorium, SUNY, Stony Brook, NY

        April 1-8-15-22-29

          The Thirteenth Street Repertory Theater, NY, NY

        May 6-13-20-27

          The Thirteenth Street Repertory Theater, NY, NY

        June 3-10-17-24

          The Thirteenth Street Repertory Theater, NY, NY

        July 1-8-15-22-29

          The Thirteenth Street Repertory Theater, NY, NY

        Dec. 1   Women's Int'l. League for Peace and Freedom,
                Nassau Branch, 75th Anniversary of WILPF,
                Community United Methodist Church, Massapequa,
                NY, Co-sponsored with CUMC Outreach Com-
                mission, Committee on Role & Status of Women

1991   Jan. 13   West Hempstead Public Library
                West Hempstead, NY

        March 8   Small Press Center, New York, NY

        April 5-6   "Legends Alive!" series, Old South Meeting House,
                Boston, MA, Funded by the Lowell Institute

        April 17   "Night of 1000 Stars" series, Hillcrest Branch,
                Queens Borough Public Library, Hillcrest, NY

April 19   "O Excellent Friend!", Wantagh Library
              Wantagh, NY

April 25   Garden City Public Library, Garden City, NY
              Sponsored by Friends of the Garden City Public
              Library and The Garden City Exchange

April 30   Reading, WNYE radio station
              Small Press Center, New York, NY

May 20   Bellrose Library, Bellrose, NY

June 4-Aug.13   The Great Plains Chautauqua Society, Inc.
              10 city tour, OK, KS, NE, SD, ND

1992 Jan. 21   The Little Theater, Kean College, Union, NJ

March 7   Author's Reading, "LitEruption"
              Powell's Bookstore, Portland, OR

March 9   Talk, Lewis & Clark College, Portland, OR

March 12   Long Beach City College, Long Beach, CA

March 15-22-29
              The Burbage Theater, Los Angeles, CA

April 5-12-19-26
              The Burbage Theater, Los Angeles, CA

May 3-10-24-31
              The Burbage Theater, Los Angeles, CA

June 10-Aug.19   The Great Plains Chautauqua Society, Inc.
              10 city tour OK, KS, NE, SD, ND

Oct. 1   Lecture, "Margaret Fuller's Italian Letters"
              Oneonta Italian-American Club and the Columbus
              500 Committee, Morris Hall, State University College
              at Oneonta, NY

Oct. 21   Newton High School, Newton, MA

Nov. 1   Huntington UU Fellowship, Huntington, NY

1993 Jan. 5   The Community Club of Garden City
                 Garden City, NY

Jan. 22   ACE, Huntington, NY

March 26   The First Unitarian Universalist Church
              Yarmouth, ME

March 28   Midcoast Unitarian-Universalist Fellowship
              Edgecomb, ME

April 23   Copaigue Library, Copaigue, NY

June 3-Aug 10
              The Great Plains Chautauqua Society, Inc.
              10 city tour, OK, KS, NE, SD, ND

July 3-5   The Margaret Fuller Festival, Oregon, IL
              Sponsored by the Rock River Women

Oct. 16   Rogue Community College, Rogue River, OR
              Sponsored by Rogue Community College
              Humanities Department

Oct. 19   Lane Community College, Eugene, OR

Nov. 4   Upland Library, "Democracy in America" series
              Riverside, CA
              A public program of the Inland Empire Educa-
              tional Foundation Humanities Division, made
              possible in part by a grant from the California
              Council for the Humanities, a state affiliate of the
              National Endowment for the Humanities

Nov. 5-11 A.M San Bernardino Valley College Auditorium, CA
              "Democracy in America" series
              A public program of the Inland Empire Educational
              Foundation Humanities Division, made possible in

part by a grant from the California Council for the Humanities, a state Affiliate of the National Endowment for the Humanities

7:30 P.M. Chaffey College Cafeteria, Rancho Cucamonga, CA, Host, Wignall Museum-Gallery, Chaffey College, "Democracy in America" series
A public program of the Inland Empire Educational Foundation Humanities Division, made possible in part by a grant from the California Council for the Humanities, a state affiliate of the National Endowment for the Humanities

Nov. 6 2:30 A.M. Noble Creek Community Center, Beaumont Library District, CA
"Democracy in America" series
A public program of the Inland Empire Educational Foundation Humanities Division, made possible in part by a grant from the California Council for the Humanities, a state affiliate of the National Endowment for the Humanities

7:30 P.M. Watkins Hall, University of CA, Riverside
"Democracy in America" series
UCR Women's Resource Center, A public program of the Inland Empire Educational Foundation Humanities Division, made possible in part by a grant from the California Council for the Humanities, a state affiliate of the National Endowment for the Humanities

1994 March 25 Long Island Federation of Women's Clubs, Inc.
The Woman's Club of Great Neck, Inc.
Great Neck, Long Island, NY

July 2 Teacher's Institute, SUNY University
Albany, NY
Sponsored by New York Council for the Humanities

1995   March 7   Women's Resource Center
                        University of Wisconsin, Oshkosh, WI

           March 11   Benefit for Old Folks Home at Lokod,
                        Transylvania, sponsored by the International Associa-
                        tion of Religious Women Unitarian Universalist Congre-
                        gation at Shelter Rock, NY, Women's Group and
                        Denominational Affairs

           March 21   Long Street Theater
                        University of South Carolina, Columbia, SC
                        Sponsored by Department of English

           April 19-20 Lecture and slide presentation
                        Swedenborg Library, Boston, MA

           August 13   First Unitarian Church, Portland, OR

1996   March 10   Benefit, Twelfth Night Club, Inc., New York, NY

           April 4   SUNY, Geneseo, NY
                        Sponsored by Women's Center

           Nov. 8-9-10 Merchant's House Museum, New York, NY

1997   Jan. 26   Lecture, "Swedenborg, Transcendentalism, &
                        The Margaret Fuller Factor,"
                        The New Church, Swedenborgian, New York, NY

           March 19   Talk and discussion, "The Grassroots Experience: Off
                        and On Stage with Margaret Fuller." Presented by The
                        Hofstra Cultural Center and the Hofstra Department of
                        Drama and Dance, Hofstra University, New York, NY
                        Sponsored by Wantagh CAP and made possible, in
                        part, with public funds from the New York State
                        Council on the Arts Decentralization Program admin-
                        istered by the Long Island Arts Council

March 22   Talk, "The Incredible Story of How Margaret Fuller
              and I Got to Harvard." Bellmore Library, NY
              Sponsored by Wantagh CAP and made possible, in
              part, with public funds from the New York State
              Council on the Arts Decentralization Program admin-
              istered by the Long Island Arts Council

April 13   Talk, "How Margaret Fuller and I Got To Harvard."
              Wantagh Library, NY Sponsored by Wantagh CAP
              and made possible, in part, with public funds from the
              New York State Council on the Arts Decentralization
              Program administered by the Long Island Arts
              Council

April 18   Talk, "Failure Is Impossible, If You Keep Up Chutspah,"
              Wantagh Senior Center, NY
              Sponsored by Wantagh CAP and made possible, in
              part, with public funds from the New York State
              Council on the Arts Decentralization Program
              administered by the Long Island Arts Council

April 27   Community Church of New York, NY; Benefit for
              Women and Religion

RAMONA X's
EXERCISE IN EXORCISM

Note: Ramona X. gives permission to copy, adapt, or use this "Exorcism" in any way.

Why burn? The answer is simple. Read your Bible — your Bibles of the world, and then ask, how else raise theological consciousness.

My Man-of-God mate has had a closing refrain to our marriage battles of four decades: "A man is the product of his culture." Amen.

Just as the devil zapped the litttle girl of "The Exorcist" movie so she had no freedom, so has a patriarchal culture zapped both man and woman.

Male bonding from caveman to Confucius to Chamber-of-Commerce man excludes, except for "servicing," wo-man and thereby any truly hu-man man-woman relationship.

A feminist exercise in exorcism in which women and men take part is long overdue.

Harvard University theologian Harvey Cox defines exorcism as "that process by which the stubborn deposits of town and tribal pasts are scraped" from the social consciousness of man. No stimulents or dental floss can scrape out our patriarchal past. Only fire can smoke out the sexists.

We burn to break the cultural clutch of 115 generations. It is a "worship" service. We pay worth to what is worthy. We spew out what is not. Good theater? Of course. But also good theology.

For exorcism is a prayer that God will expel certain demonic qualities.

So also the demons of feminist rage. Ours is a primal scream of fury at being zapped. We realize with Eric Ericson that we have "allowed" ourselves to be "infantalized" and "victimized." And to add today's rightful rhetoric, "down-graded," "stunted," "dehumanized," "humiliated," "mutilated."

No more! We give Tertullian or Confucius a symbolic karate kick in the groin to undo momentarily the rape of the centuries. We set a fire under the patriarchy to rekindle our quest for personhood. We burn to inflame our crusading fervor, comparable to St. Paul's himself and make misogynous society more nervous.

Elemental fire can both inflame and purge. William Lloyd Garrison burned the Constitution. Pacifists burned their draft cards. Feminists in the same spirit burn the raw, sadistic, sexist words of history's saints.

We no longer light a candle to the Blessed Virgin. We do in our burnings "light up" the road to liberation as we see it.

The phallic imperialism of the past must be highlighted for what it is. For today's patriarchal put-downs come from the machos of yesterday.

The gut issues of women's liberation cannot be legislated away.

In our short second wave of feminism we have made some impact on the substance but litttle on the spirit of sexism.

St. Angela is still with us. Said saint drank the water with which she had washed the leper, lapped up his vomit and filled her mouth with his excrement.

Jesus rewarded her after three hours with her rosary. Modern Mary Magdalens are still, in spirit, washing Jesus' feet. Modern Mary's are still picking up and washing their men-folk's socks, if not their feet, and putting the toilet seats down after them. The suffering saint—the masochist, the martyr — the "endurer" lives on. For most women are still most "comfortable" in the Judeo-Christian tradition and the patriarchal power structure it has begat. Our worship service is to create in women the "divine discontent" lauded by Emerson.

Hail Mary to Dr. Mary Daly who gives us a philosophical and theological basis for the women's movement — and religious hope.

She has shown us that the "eternal woman" of the Bible is the other side of the coin on which appears "The Girl" of Hugh Hefner and James Bond. One is on a pedestal; the other is used as a footstool. One is superhuman; one is subhuman. Both are "abysmally, hopelessly non-human." Hefner's sex-object centerfold is not a role model. But neither is the faceless fauning pie-in-the-sky mentality religious woman eulogized from St. Paul to the Pope.

"No way" is said in many ways — to create a dialogue and proclaim the feminist credo.

Germaine Greer describes the way of an eminent academician "sister" in England who took delight as she sat with the dons at table in farting and belching. "Such extreme slatternliness," Greer notes is "a deliberate reaction against feminine murmuring and pussyfooting." And so likewise to burn sexist bible quotes at church altars is to make a feminist statement against the obsequious genuflect.

Today's men and women already are painfully polarized. There is nowhere to go but up. The farting female is no more obscene than the young macho priest at a Riverside church alter in 1974.

Rev. Ms. Carter, one of the 11 women "irregularly" ordained to the Episcopal priesthood, was serving the priest communion. Said holy man sipped the wine, drew his fingernails across her hand on the chalice, drawing blood. "I hope you burn in hell," he told her.

The primitive savage who feared woman's menstrual blood emerges again from his ecclesiastically gilded cave. Scratch the back of his man-of-God and out comes a Neanderthal species.

The young priest's hate and fears, to the point of drawing blood, may or may not be an omen of bloodshed ahead as the Women's Revolution becomes the nation's second Revolution. That depends — on how many men — and women — like him come kicking and screaming into the 20th Century.

Apocalyptically yours,
Sister-in-Christ of a lifetime,

Ms. Ramona Barth

Sample for yourselves the wisdom (?) of the ages — typical biblical, philosophical and theological quotes.*

The Confucian Marriage Manual (551-479 B.C.)

The five worst infirmities that afflict the female are indocility, discontent, slander, jealousy and silliness... Such is the supidity of women's character, that it is incumbent upon her, in every particular, to distrust herself and to obey her husband.

Aristotle (384-322 B.C.), De Generatione Animalium

The female is a female by virtue of a certain lack of qualities — a natural defectiveness.

The Hindu Code of Manu V (Circa A.D. 100)

In childhood a woman must be subject to her father; in youth to her husband; when her husband is dead, to her sons. A woman must never be free of subjugation.

The Koran (Circa A.D. 650)

Men are superior to women.

Church Father St. Clement of Alexandria (96 A.D.)

Let us set our womenfold on the road to goodness by teaching them to display real sincerity in their submissiveness, to observe silence. Every woman should be overwhelmed with shame at the thought that she is a woman.

Tertullian (A.D. 220)

Woman is a temple built over a sewer, the gateway of the devil. Woman, you are the devil's doorway. You should always go in mourning and in rags.

---

*Some of the quotes are paraphrased from the original text.

St. John Chrysostom (345-407 A.D.)

Among all savage beasts none is found so harmful as woman.

St. Ambrose (354-430 A.D.)

Adam was led to sin by Eve and Eve by Adam. It is just and right that woman accept as lord and master him whom she led to sin.

St. Augustine (354-430 A.D.)

Any woman who acts in such a way that she cannot give birth to as many children as she is capable of makes herself guilty of that many murders just as with the woman who tries to injure herself after conception.

Daily Prayer of the Orthodox Jewish Male

Barush Atah Adonai, Elohayne Melek Ha-Olan, Sheloh Assani Yishah... Blessed art thou, O Lord our God and King of the Universe, that thou didst not create me a woman.

Old Testament, Book of Deuteronomy

If the tokens of virginity be not found for the damsel, then they shall bring out the damsel to the door of her father's house and the men of the city shall stone her with stones that she die.

Exodus 20:17 and 22:16-17

You shall not covet your neighbor's house, or his wife or his manservant, or his maidservant, or his ox, or his ass. If a man seduces a virgin who is not betrothed, and he's with her, he shall give the marriage present for her and make her his wife. If her father utterly refuses to give her to him, he shall pay money equivalent to the marriage present for virgins.

Job 25:4

How can he be clean that is born of woman?

Leviticus (XV, 19)

And the Lord spake unto Moses saying: speak unto the children of Israel, saying: if a woman be delivered, and bear a manchild then she shall be unclean seven days...but if she bear a maid-child, then she shall be unclean two weeks.

Genesis 3:16

God said to woman Eve, I will greatly multiply thy sorrow and your pain in childbearing. In pain thou shalt bring forth children...and thy desire shall be to thy husband and he shall rule over thee.

Ecclesiastes 7:26-28

I find a woman more bitter than death; she is a snare, her heart a net, her arms are chains. No wickedness comes anywhere near the wickedness of a woman. May a sinner's lot be hers.

From the Letters of St. Paul, Timothy and Ephesians

Man is the image of God and the mirror of his glory, whereas woman reflects the glory of man. For man did not originally spring from woman, but woman was made out of man; and man was not created for woman's sake, but woman for the sake of man.

It is shameful for a woman to speak in church. Wives should regard their husbands as they regard the Lord.

Wives, submit yourselves unto your own husbands...for the husband is the head of the house.

As in all the churches of the saints, the women should keep silence in the churches. For they are not permittted to speak but should be subordinate even as the law says. If there is anything they desire to know, let them ask their husbands at home.

St. Paul from the Phillips Bible

You must lean and adapt yourselves to your husbands. The husband is the head of the wife.

Thomas Aquinas (1225-1279) Summa Theologica

Woman is defective and misbegotten. She is by nature of lower capacity and quality than man.

Martin Luther (1483-1546)

If a woman grows weary and, at last, dies from childbearing, it matters not. Let her die from bearing; she is there to do it.

John Knox (1505-1572)

Woman in her greatest perfection was made to serve and obey man, not to rule and command him.

Samuel Butler (1612-1680)

The souls of women are so small that some believe they've none at all.

Soren Kierkegaard (1813-1855)

What a misfortune to be a woman! And yet the worst misfortune is not to understand what a misfortune it is.

Karl Barth (1886-1968)

Woman is ontologically subordinate to man.

Pope Pius XII (1876-1958)

The pains that, since original sin, a mother has to suffer to give birth to her child only draw tighter the bonds that bind them; she loves it the more, the more pain it has cost her.

Pope Pius XII (1945)

A woman's function, a woman's way, a woman's natural bent, is motherhood. Every woman is called to be a mother, mother in the physical sense, or mother in the sense more spiritual, more exalted, yet real nevertheless.

Deuteronomy 22:20-21

But if the thing is true, that the tokens of virginity were not found in the young woman, then they shall bring out the young woman to the door of her father's house, and the men of her city shall stone her to death with stones, because she has wrought folly in Israel by playing the harlot in her father's house; so you shall purge the evil from the midst of you.

Exodus 22:16-17

If a man seduces a virgin who is not betrothed, and lies with her, he shall give the marriage present for her, and make her his wife. If her father utterly refuses to give her to him, he shall pay money equivalent to the marriage present for virgins.

Job 25:4

How can he who is born of woman be clean?

Leviticus 12:1-2, 5

The Lord said to Moses, "Say to the people of Israel, if a woman conceives, and bears a male child, then she shall be unclean seven days; as at the time of her menstruation she shall be unclean. But if she bears a female child, then she shall be unclean two weeks...."

Genesis 3:16

To the woman he said, "I will greatly multiply your pain in childbearing; in pain you shall bring forth children, yet your desire shall be for your husband, and he shall rule over you."

Ecclesiastes 7:26-28

And I found more bitter than death the woman whose heart it snares and nets, and whose hands are fetters; he who pleases God escapes her, but the sinner is taken by her.

1 Timothy 2:9-12,15

Also that women should adorn themselves modestly and sensibly in seemly apparel, not with braided hair or gold or pearls or costly attire, but by good deeds, as befits women who profess religion. Let a woman learn in silence with all submissiveness. I permit no woman to teach or to have authority over men; she is to keep silent.

Yet woman will be saved through bearing children if she continues in faith and love and holiness, with modesty.

Ephesians 5:22-24

Wives, be subject to your husbands, as to the Lord. For the husband is the head of the wife as Christ is the head of the church, his body, and is himself its Savior. As the church is subject to Christ, so let wives also be subject in everything to their husbands.

BIBLIOGRAPHY

Allen, Margaret Vanderhaar, *The Achievement of Margaret Fuller*. University Park and London, The Pennsylvania State University Press,1979.

Barth, Ramona Sawyer, "Unitarian Women of the 19th Century." *Journal of Liberal Religion,* Volume 7, no. 3, 1946, pp. 133-148.

Blanchard, Paula, *Margaret Fuller from Trancendentalism to Revolution*, New York, Delacorte Press/Seymour Lawrence, 1978.

The Chautauqua Readers, the North Dakota Humanities Council, Bismarck, North Dakota.

Chevigny, Bell Gale, *The Woman and the Myth*, New York: The Feminist Press, 1976.

Chicago, Judy, "The Dinner Party: A Symbol of Our Heritage," Anchor/ Doubleday, 1979, a complete documentation of the creation of *The Dinner Party*, contains color photographs of the plates, black and white illustrations and historical information about the women represented.

Davall, Irene, An Open Letter to Ramona Barth, Feminist Party Chaplain, Alna, Maine, *Feminist Party News,* Fall 1973.

James, Laurie, *Men, Women and Margaret Fuller*. New York: Golden Heritage Press, Inc., 1990.

James, Laurie, *Outrageous Quesions, Legacy of Bronson Alcott and America's One-Room Schools,* Golden Heritage Press, Inc., 1994.

James, Laurie, *Why Margaret Fuller Is Forgotten*. New York: Golden Heritage Press, Inc., 1988.

James, Laurie, *The Wit and Wisdom of Margaret Fuller Ossoli*. New York: Golden Heritage Press, Inc., 1988.

Little, Stuart W. *Off-Broadway: The Prophetic Theatre*. New York: Coward, McCann & Geoghegan, Inc., 1972.

MacLaren, Gay,. *Morally We Roll Along*. Boston: Little, Brown and Company, 1938.

Ossoli, Margaret Fuller. *Woman in the Nineteenth Century*. New York: Greeley & McElrath, 1845.

Ossoli, Margaret Fuller, *Summer on the Lakes*. Boston: Charles C. Little & James Brown, 1843; New York: Charles C. Francis, 1844.

Urbanski, Marie Mitchell Olesen, *Margaret Fuller's Woman in the Nineteenth Century*. Westport, CT: Greenwood Press, 1980.

INDEX

ALSO AVAILABLE
from
GOLDEN HERITAGE PRESS, INC.

Vol. I — *The Wit and Wisdom of Margaret Fuller Ossoli*, edited by Laurie James

❖ An intriguing sampler of Fuller's diaries, journals, letters, articles and books, arrranged by subject for easy reference.

❖ Zero in on the substance of Fuller's brilliant mind and expression — words as relevant today as over a century ago. Quotable passages.

❖ A book to treasure forever for thought and inspiration.

96 pages, in quality paperback, references, footnotes, bibliography.

Vol. II — *Why Margaret Fuller Is Forgotten*, by Laurie James

❖ Why is a world celebrity in the 1840s forgotten?

❖ A singular story — typical of how famous women have been buried in history.

Fuller's book on equality — the first in America — sent shock waves throughout the USA and Europe. Author Laurie James traces how Fuller's achievement has been slighted as her first co-biographers, Ralph Waldo Emerson, Clarke and Channing mutilated her letters and papers and portrayed her to conform to the standard of womanhood of the day. The facts show how scholars today have followed this same pattern. 72 pages, in quality paperback, footnotes, bibliography.

Vol. III — *Men, Women, and Margaret Fuller*, by Laurie James

❖ A major biography bound to have impact.

❖ A "battle of the sexes" ... relevant today.

❖ Based on available research past biographers have undervalued.

The story emcompasses the Transcendental circle of friends, including Nathaniel Hawthorne, Henry David Thoreau, Bronson Alcott, Thomas Carlyle, Theodore Parker and many others. Revitalizes the noble spirit of the day — ideals of individualism, truth, beauty, harmony of nature, the divinity of humankind and faith in America. 500 pages, in quality paperback, featuring the full color Thomas Hicks portrait, with photos of the Transcendentalists, footnotes, page notes, bibliography, appendix, index.

Outrageous Questions, Legacy of Bronson Alcott and America's One-Room Schools, by Laurie James

❖ What was school like 150 years ago?

❖ What was "toeing the crack?"...The most popular punishment?

❖ Remember stories about trudging miles through snow to school?

❖ Who was Bronson Alcott? His outragoues questions?

The father of the author of *Little Women*, Bronson Alcott believed children could learn by answering questions. This books speaks to the nostalgia of the "good old days," constrasting traditional methods with Alcott's groundbreaking ideas.

Because Margaret Fuller, as teacher in his school, recorded his questions, his Conversation on Conscience is included, and readers can compare their answers with what students said in 1836. Appeals to both adults and children. 102 pages, in quality paper/hardcover. Creative suggestions for adults working with children, original drawings by John Hartnett, photos of one-room school houses, biographical information.

ORDER FORM

Please send the following books:

Qty.   Amount

_____ *The Wit and Wisdom of Margaret Fuller Ossoli*   _____
         paper @ $8.50 each; Volume I; ISBN 0-944382-00-2

_____ *Why Margaret Fuller Ossoli Is Forgotten*   _____
         paper @ $8.50 each; Volume II; ISBN 0-944382-01-0

_____ *Men, Women and Margaret Fuller*   _____
         paper @ $19.95 each; Volume III; ISBN 0-944382-02-9

_____ *How I Got To Harvard, Off and On Stage*   _____
         with Margaret Fuller – paper @ $14.95 each;
         Volume IV; ISBN 0-944382-033-7

_____ *Outrageous Questions, Legacy of Bronson Alcott*   _____
         and America's One-Room Schools
         paper @ $10.95 each; hardcover @ $16.95 each;
         ISBN 0-944382-05-3, paper; ISBN 0-944382-06-1, hardcover

                Total   _____

                New York State Sales Tax (residents only)   _____

                Postage and Handling: $3.50 first book;   _____
                $1.50 each additional book

                Amount Enclosed   _____

SHIP TO: (Please print clearly)

Name:_____

Address:_____

City, State, Zip_____

IF THIS IS A LIBRARY BOOK, KINDLY PHOTOCOPY THIS PAGE.

MAIL ORDERS TO:

GOLDEN HERITAGE PRESS, INC.
500 W. 43rd Street, Suite 26J
New York, N. Y. 10036-4336